Teaching Controversial Issues in the Classroom

0 6 MAY 2023

WITHDRAWN

Also available from Continuum

Education, Extremism and Terrorism, Dianne Gereluk
Philosophy of Education: An Introduction, Richard Bailey
Symbolic Clothing in Schools, Dianne Gereluk
Teaching Citizenship Education: A Radical Approach, Ralph Leighton
Teaching the Holocaust in School History, Lucy Russell
Teaching and Learning and the Curriculum, Emmanuel Mufti and
    Mark Peace

Teaching Controversial Issues in the Classroom

Key Issues and Debates

Edited by

**Paula Cowan and
Henry Maitles**

continuum

Continuum International Publishing Group

The Tower Building	80 Maiden Lane
11 York Road	Suite 704
London SE1 7NX	New York NY 10038

www.continuumbooks.com

British Library Cataloguing-in-Publication Data
A catalogue record for this book is available from the British Library.

ISBN: 978-1-4411-8244-9 hardcover
      978-1-4411-2484-5 paperback
      978-1-4411-3693-0 eBook (ePub)
      978-1-4411-3630-5 eBook (PDF)

Library of Congress Cataloging-in-Publication Data
A catalog record for this title is available from the Library of Congress.

Typeset by Newgen Imaging Systems Pvt Ltd, Chennai, India
Printed and bound in India

To Stephen, Elliot, Naomi and Gemma
Clare, Laura and Hannah

Contents

Acknowledgements

We wish to thank Lord Chief Rabbi Jonathan Sacks and Professor Yehuda Bauer for permission to include their quotations respectively at the beginning of Chapters 8 and 9, and to Trentham Books for permission to publish a quote by Archbishop Emeritus Desmond Mpilo Tutu at the beginning of Chapter 16. Particular mention to Dr Gillian Klein for her assistance at the initial stages and to Alison Baker and Rosie Pattinson at Continuum for their support.

List of Contributors

Paula Cowan is Senior Lecturer in the School of Education at the University of the West of Scotland, UK. She is the author of curricular teaching materials – *The Holocaust: A Teaching Pack for Primary Schools* (Learning and Teaching Scotland, 2000), *The Holocaust: A Teaching Pack for Secondary Schools* (Learning and Teaching Scotland, 2002) – and is a contributor to *The Chambers Dictionary of Beliefs and Religions* (Chambers Harrap, 2009). She is a member of the editorial board of the *Scottish Educational Review*, and a UK delegate on the Task Force for International Co-operation on Holocaust Education, Remembrance and Research.

Ian Davies is Professor of Education at the University of York, UK. He is the author of many books and articles about citizenship, including *The Sage International Handbook of Education for Citizenship and Democracy* (Sage, 2008) and *100 + Ideas for Teaching Citizenship* (Continuum, 2011). He edits the journal *Citizenship Teaching and Learning* and his many international projects include working for the Council of Europe and as a Fellow of the Japan Society for the Promotion of Science.

Ross Deuchar is Professor of Research in the School of Education at the University of the West of Scotland, UK. His recent work has focused on the sociology of gangs, marginalized young people, issues of territoriality and youth offending. His publications include *Citizenship: Enterprise and Learning* (Trentham, 2007) and *Gangs, Marginalised Youth and Social Capital* (Trentham, 2009). He is currently the President of the Scottish Educational Research Association.

Walter Humes is Visiting Professor of Education at the University of Stirling, UK. He has previously held professorships at the universities of Aberdeen, Strathclyde and the West of Scotland. In 2007 he received the John Aitkenhead Award for services to education from the Institute of Contemporary Scotland. Along with Professor T. G. K. Bryce of Strathclyde University, Scotland, he is co-editor of *Scottish Education, 3rd Edition: Beyond Devolution* (Edinburgh University Press, 2008).

Michele Kahn is Associate Professor in the Studies in Language and Culture Department at the University of Houston–Clear Lake, Texas, where she teaches courses in multicultural education and language. She serves on various boards, including the International Association of Intercultural Education (IAIE) and the Gay, Lesbian, Straight, Education Network (GLSEN), Houston, Texas. She is also an associate editor for the journal *Intercultural Education*.

Andy Lawrence is a history teacher at Hampton School, Middlesex, UK. He is a Fellow of the Imperial War Museum's Holocaust Education Programme and has published work in *Teaching History* (2010). He is also the volunteer education co-ordinator for the Survivors Fund, has written numerous resources covering the Rwandan genocide and has organized educational initiatives that have been featured in the *Guardian*, in *BBC History* magazine and on the BBC.

Henry Maitles is Professor of Learning and Teaching in the School of Education at the University of the West of Scotland, UK. He is the author of *Values in Education: We're Citizens Now*, (Dunedin Press, 2005; Discovery Publishing House, New Delhi, 2007) and the editor of *Exploring Cultural Perspectives in Education* (ICRN Press, 2008). He is on the editorial boards of *Educational Review, Genocide Studies and Prevention* and the *Journal for Critical Education Policy Studies*, and was joint editor for *Educational Review* in 2010.

Neil McLennan is National Development Officer for Enterprise in Education at Learning and Teaching Scotland, UK. He has advised universities on schools and community engagement projects and is the author of *Active Learning History* (Leckie & Leckie, 2010). He is the President of the Scottish Association of Teachers of History.

Martin Myers is a Research Consultant and writer specializing in work that looks at Gypsy families and their experiences of education in the United Kingdom. He is currently based at the Open University, where he is finishing his PhD dissertation, which looks at the wider relationships between Gypsies and their neighbours. He is co-author (with Kalwant Bhopal) of *Insiders, Outsiders and Others: Gypsies and Identity* (University of Hertfordshire Press, 2008).

Audrey Osler is Visiting Professor of Education at the University of Leeds, UK, where she was research professor and founding director of the Centre for Citizenship and Human Rights Education. She has also held visiting positions at the University of Washington, Seattle; Utah State University; Hong Kong Institute of Education; Buskerud University College, Norway; and Birkbeck, London. Her research is transdisciplinary and addresses questions of social justice, citizenship and human rights. Her many publications include *Students' Perspectives on Schooling* (Open University Press, 2010) and *Teachers and Human Rights Education* (Trentham, 2010, with Hugh Starkey).

Alistair Ross is Emeritus Professor of Education at London Metropolitan University, UK, and also holds a Jean Monnet *ad personam* professorship, awarded by the European Commission. He is the co-editor of *What's Fair? Young Europeans' Constructions of Equity, Altruism and Self-Interest* (with M. Dooly; Universitat Autonoma de Barcelona Press, 2010) and is the author of *A European Education: Citizenship, Identities and Young People* (Trentham, 2008). He is a member of the editorial board of Citizenship Teaching and Learning.

Jill Rutter is Research and Policy Officer at Daycare Trust, UK, the national early childhood education and childcare charity, and an Associate Fellow at the Institute for Public Policy Research. She was also a senior lecturer in Citizenship Education at London Metropolitan University, UK, and taught geography in secondary schools. She has published extensively on all aspects of migration in the United Kingdom and abroad. Her recent research has included studies of the Congolese and Nigerian communities in the United Kingdom, on refugee integration and on the impact of migration on public services in the United Kingdom. Her publications include *Refugee Children in the UK* (Open University Press, 2006) and *Refugees: We Left Because We Had To* (Refugee Council 1991, 1996, 2003).

Geoffrey Short is Reader Emeritus in Educational Research at the University of Hertfordshire, UK. He has published widely in the area of race, ethnicity and education, specializing over the past two decades in how the Holocaust is taught in British and Canadian schools. In the late 1990s, he acted as a consultant to the Council of Europe on its Holocaust education programme. He is co-author of *Race and the Primary School: Theory into Practice* (with Bruce Carrington; Routledge, 1998) and *Issues in Holocaust Education* (with Carole Ann Reed; Ashgate, 2004).

Stephen D. Smith, MBE, is Executive Director of the University of Southern California Shoah Foundation Institute for Visual History and Education. He is the co-founder of the UK Holocaust Centre and the Aegis Trust for Genocide Prevention. He has published widely in the areas of genocide and the Holocaust. His publications include *Making Memory: Creating Britain's First Holocaust Centre* (Quill Press, 1999) and *The Holocaust and the Christian World* (with Carol Rittner and Irena Steinfeldt; Continuum, 2000). He is a US delegate on the Task Force for International Co-operation on Holocaust Education, Remembrance and Research.

Geri Smyth is Reader in Education at the University of Strathclyde, UK. Her particular research interests relate to the education of bilingual pupils, the diversification of the teaching profession and refugee integration. She is currently Principal Investigator on the ESRC-funded seminar series Diverse Teachers for Diverse Learners and has edited a special issue of the *Journal of Refugee Studies* on the theme of refugee integration.

Frances Simpson is Lecturer in Education at the University of the West of Scotland, UK. Her research interests are science and social studies, and she has worked on an AstraZeneca project on Transition in Science. She is the co-author of curricular teaching materials, *5–14 Science, Middle Primary Pupil and Teacher Books* (with Nicholas Souter; Hodder Stoughton, 2004) and *Successful Placement Teaching in Scotland* (with Jane Medwell; Learning Matters, 2008).

Barry van Driel is International Director for Teacher Training and Curriculum Development at the Anne Frank House, Amsterdam, the Netherlands, and a senior education consultant to the Office for Democratic Institutions and Human Rights (ODIHR). He is the author of *Confronting Islamophobia in Educational Practice* (Trentham, 2005) and *Challenging Homophobia* (with Lutz van Dijk; Trentham, 2007). He is editor in chief of the journal *Intercultural Education* and was the Secretary General of the International Association for Intercultural Education from 2002 to 2009.

Preface and Framework

Paula Cowan and Henry Maitles

The central aim of this book is to try to answer what we believe are three key questions in today's school communities: What values should schools aim to help develop in young people? Why should controversial issues play a role in this? How can teachers and educators contribute? As these are such challenging questions and as there is currently little agreement about them, this book raises as many issues as it does answers, for teachers, educators and parents alike. It highlights the debate around specific controversial issues and suggests ways in which schools, teachers and educators can begin to meaningfully address them.

Events in the world – from mass movements that strive for democracy and human rights to everyday issues relating to racism, immigration and social injustice – impinge on our lives. In this era of media saturation and social networking, this has a particular – some may claim 'spectacular' – impact on the lives of young people. Whether it be children's rights in Europe, the ending of communist one-party rule in central and eastern Europe in the late 1980s, or mass movements outside Europe – such as the movement for democracy in China that included the demonstrations in Tiananmen Square in 1989, the overthrow of the racist apartheid regime in South Africa in 1990 or the 2011 mass demonstrations that demanded an end to dictatorship in the Middle East – these are defining moments. In particular, in the confrontations with the army, in essence there are two models of citizen here – the 20-year-olds *in* the tank and the 20-year-olds *in front of* the tank.

When is the right age to teach controversial issues?

It has been claimed (e.g., by Scruton et al., 1985) that controversial political and/or social issues are not suitable for young people under 16. Sir Cyril Norwood, headmaster of Harrow, claimed in 1943, a time when ex-Harrovians dominated the cabinet, that 'Nothing but harm can result from attempts to interest pupils prematurely in matters which imply the experiences of an adult' (Norwood, 1943, 8). Frazer (1999) maintained that this kind of attitude is alive and well and is nurtured by a worry by both the right and the left in politics that teachers will be biased in their teaching of controversial issues.

This view has been widely challenged (Advisory Group, 1998; Cheung and Leung, 1998; Cohen, 1981; Cowan and Maitles, 2002, 2007, 2010; LTS, 2002; Maitles and Deuchar, 2004; Ross, 1987), and in many countries it has been argued that elements of political and citizenship understanding should be introduced early in the primary school (from 5 years of age onwards). Yet in common with other contentious or difficult issues, the argument is often raised by teachers, parents and indeed some politicians, that students in school (particularly lower secondary and primary students, perhaps up to age 16) are too young to discuss complex, controversial issues which, it is argued, need a greater maturity. Yet young children, seeing these issues presented in the media and on the internet, are, as this book shows, keen to discuss and understand them. Indeed, as Holden (1998) points out, it is entirely possible that these types of issues can be better discussed by younger students in primary schools, as they have both the space in the curriculum and the disposition to discuss them. The main point may not be the ascertainment of the right age to teach and/or learn these types of issues but the methodology that is used. Supple (1991) claims that students may be especially receptive to antiracist initiatives at a young age, as their views are not yet fully formed.

In particular, around the topic of the Holocaust, there is much debate about 'curricular creep' – a fear of raising disturbing issues with ever younger pupils in the primary school. In responding to pedagogical issues such as Piaget's theories of children's intellectual and moral development, which suggest that young students are unable to abstract and satisfactorily understand these kinds of topic, Short (in Short and Reed, 2004) cites a number of Piaget's critics who have influenced teachers to raise their expectations of children's abilities. A contrasting viewpoint is conveyed by Totten (1999), on the grounds that the Holocaust is inappropriate and too complex for this age group to study, and by Kochan (1989), who objects to its teaching to the 'immature and unsophisticated', claiming that such teaching can have deleterious consequences for students. In this book, we present evidence that challenges such theoretical claims and supports the teaching of this and other controversial issues to primary students.

Interdisciplinary teaching

Practical reasons for teaching controversial issues to younger, indeed primary, students include the primary school offering more opportunities to adopt a cross-curricular, interdisciplinary approach than the secondary. This method is advocated by Supple (1993) in her study of teaching the Holocaust in secondary schools, which she argued required the coordination of Holocaust teaching between subject departments to be effective. It seems obvious that learning will be much deeper if students study the Holocaust as, for example, part of a history unit, through English literature (*The Diary of Anne Frank*, or a novel in the Holocaust context such as *Number the Stars*), through religious and moral education (Judaism or social justice) and citizenship education (human rights). Although primary teachers may allow their students to reflect on what they have learnt in a history lesson through, for example, the expressive arts, this integrative teaching strategy, is not common practice in secondary schools. Here teaching can be often disjointed and fragmented. Indeed the curriculum in Scotland is aiming for more interdisciplinary teaching across primary and secondary sectors (Scottish Executive, 2004). In 2010 the General Teaching Council (Scotland) commended one secondary school teacher for innovative practice in this area (Cowan, 2010). In her school, the Holocaust provided a context for learning activities in art, drama, maths, German, technology, history and English. While this type of teaching may soon be the norm in Scotland, there is no indication that this approach is gathering momentum elsewhere in the United Kingdom.

Furthermore, the primary school offers more continuity than the secondary. Primary teachers have the flexibility to seize the moment and respond to students' responses instantly or, if necessary, follow up their lesson the next day. Secondary students may not see the relevant teacher for a few days or more. Finally, it is possible that teaching controversial issues in the primary school can clarify points of information and provide opportunity for classroom or group discussion and that a primary grounding in this area may well contribute to students' understanding of more complex issues in later studies.

The British Government and the devolved governments across the United Kingdom have strongly endorsed the need for developing students' awareness of contemporary, controversial issues and for enabling the skills of decision making, reasoned argument and bringing critical approaches to evidence. By so doing, it is argued, students may emerge not only with a fuller understanding of democracy, but also with an ability to live democratically in adult life. Hahn (1998) found that where there was the opportunity to explore controversial public policy issues in an atmosphere where several sides of an argument can be aired and where points of view are encouraged even where they differ from the teacher's and other students', there is a greater likelihood of the development of the kinds of skills needed for democratic life. Hahn concludes that groups where this is encouraged showed comparatively higher levels of political efficacy, interest, trust and confidence than their peers without such experiences. Further, these students were more likely to develop attitudes that have the potential to foster positive attitudes towards civic participation. Thus, the full realization of developing informed student skills and attitudes towards the controversies involved in democratic life will require short-term and long-term strategies on behalf of all members of a school community.

This kind of political discussion, it might be argued, is best kept outside the classroom, perhaps in student forums. But even where there are functioning and well-organized pupil councils, there must be space in the classroom to discuss socially or politically sensitive issues, whether they be local issues relating to bullying, racism, homophobia and animal welfare, or such international events as the 2003 Iraq War, terrorism or globalization.

Difficulties in discussing controversial issues

We should be clear that this is not an easy strategy. There are many constraints on schools which mitigate against the discussion of controversial issues. First, there are teacher worries about their skills to handle open-ended discussions, which they might not be able to control or direct. The IEA study of political consciousness in 28 European countries (Torney-Purta et al., 2001) found that in many countries secondary teachers are afraid to tackle controversial issues because, almost by definition, the discussion becomes multidisciplinary and they are uncomfortable in that zone; secondly, there are structural constraints in schools, from the lack of tradition in discussion to the physical layout of classrooms, which might not be conducive to group work or active learning approaches; thirdly, there are external constraints, ranging from the assessment-driven agenda in schools and worries about what parents might think about controversial discussion, to the influence of the mass media and politicians and what might be perceived as influencing students in some way or other. Nowhere is this more problematic in Scotland, Northern Ireland and parts of England (e.g., Liverpool) than over an issue such as sectarianism and/or the peace process in Northern Ireland. Yet it is vital that this kind of issue is not avoided. Smith (2003) points out that it raises an absolutely crucial issue: can a concept of citizenship 'based on equal rights and a shared sense of belonging . . . moderate, transcend or displace identity politics and concepts of nationality'. And as if this is not problematic enough, there is the point of limitations to compromise and consensus. Learning in this area suggests to students that there is not always a compromise available, no matter what efforts are made, and it is this inability that leads to the kind of violent scenes we see on our TV screens and, sometimes, on our streets. This itself is a valuable lesson and can be extrapolated to other conflicts (such as Afghanistan) across the world. The role of the teacher in this becomes crucial. As Agostinone-Wilson (2005), Ashton and Watson (1998) and Stradling (1984) suggest, the teacher needs to be confident enough and have the honesty and confidence to suggest to students that they are not just independent observers but do have a point of view, which also can and should be challenged. While this is an area of some discussion in Britain, Wrigley (2003) points out that in Germany, teachers are encouraged to allow discussion around controversial issues, present a wide range of views and be open about their own standpoint while allowing for all views to be challenged. In the very slim curriculum guidelines in Denmark, teachers are encouraged not to overplan so that, in discussion with their students, issues deemed relevant for discussion can be included. However, in analysing how high school students understood the place of classroom discussion, Hahn (1998) found that students in the Netherlands did not try to persuade each other, even when discussing highly controversial issues that they felt strongly about, whereas in German and US state schools and English private schools there was strong argument and persuasion. Interestingly, she found that there was virtually no discussion on political issues in the state sector in England even in social science classes, where she gathered that the primary purpose was to prepare for external examinations. Indeed, it is crucial, according to Ashton and Watson (1998), that teachers understand their proactive role where necessary; otherwise backward ideas can dominate the discussion. Further, teachers have to gently point out that these issues being discussed have not yet been resolved and are open-ended in terms of outcome. Students have little problem with this and are not as dogmatic as adults when it comes to changing attitudes and political understanding.

We are still in the infancy of teaching controversial issues, although many of the ideas and practices described in this book flow from long-established practice in schools. While there is evidence of much good practice it is also true that the political-literacy part of citizenship education is boringly, routinely introduced so as to appease audit forms and inspectors. This is a shame, as its enthusiastic introduction can lead to better relationships, better behaviour, less bullying and better learning as students feel that the school and classroom are where they can meaningfully contribute and discuss issues that seem relevant to their understanding of the outside world.

Using a mixture of research evidence, methodological approaches and case studies and involving classroom teachers, university academics and non-governmental organization workers, the aims of this book are to

- promote an awareness of the importance of teaching controversial areas in the primary and secondary contexts;
- develop one's understanding of teaching and learning of specific controversial issues;
- show how specific controversial issues can be introduced and developed in schools.

This introductory chapter provides the context for teaching controversial issues. The rest of the book is divided into four sections. Part 1, **The Context**, raises issues around citizenship – both children's rights and identities and global issues, along with human rights, democracy and issues surrounding gang culture. Part 2, **War and Peace**, discusses issues around nuclear weapons, Western intervention and peace education. Part 3, **Genocide**, involves discussion around the peculiarities and universality of genocide, teaching about genocides, the Holocaust – including raising it in multicultural classes and visiting the Auschwitz-Birkenau Memorial and Museum – and Rwanda. Part 4, **Racism and Discrimination**, discusses Islamophobia, anti-Semitism, discrimination against the Roma, homophobia and xenophobia towards migrants. We conclude by drawing out some policy implications.

We appreciate that this book does not raise every controversial issue, and the nature of our world is such that new ones are always emerging. This book highlights both the importance of controversial issues and the need to bring these into our classrooms and suggests approaches to assist their teaching. Many teachers enter the teaching profession because they want to make a difference. Teaching controversial issues effectively is one way in which this can be achieved.

References

Agostinone-Wilson, F. (2005), 'Fair and Balanced to Death: Confronting the cult of neutrality in the teacher education classroom', *Journal for Critical Education Policy Studies*, 3 (1), www.jceps.com/?pageID=article&articleID=37.

Ashton, E., and Watson, B. (1998), 'Values Education: A fresh look at procedural neutrality', *Educational Studies*, 24 (2), 183–93.

Cheung, C., and Leung, M. (1998), 'From Civic Education to General Studies: The implementation of political education into the primary curriculum', *Compare* 28 (1), 47–56.

Cohen, L. (1981), 'Political Literacy and the Primary School: A Dutch experiment', *Teaching Politics*, 10 (3), 259–67.

Cowan, P. (2010), 'Holocaust Studies in Schools', *St. Andrews in Focus*, 43.

Cowan, P., and Maitles, H. (2002), 'Developing Positive Values: A case study of Holocaust Memorial Day in the primary schools of one local authority in Scotland', *Educational Review*, 54 (3), 219–30.

—(2007), 'Does Addressing Prejudice and Discrimination through Holocaust Education Produce Better Citizens?' *Educational Review*, 59 (2), 115–30.

—(2010). 'Policy and Practice of Holocaust Education in Scotland', *Prospects*, 40, 257–72.

Frazer, E. (1999), 'Introduction: The idea of political education', *Oxford Review of Education*, 25 (1–2), 5–22.

Hahn, C. (1998), *Becoming Political.* Albany: State University of New York Press.

Holden, C. (1998), 'Keen at 11, cynical at 18?', in C. Holden and N. Clough (eds), *Children as Citizens.* London: Jessica Kingsley, pp. 46–62.

Kochan, L. (1989), 'Life over Death', *Jewish Chronicle*, December 22, 22.

LTS (2002), *Education for Citizenship: A Paper for Discussion and Development.* Dundee: Learning and Teaching Scotland.

Maitles, H., and Deuchar, R. (2004), '"Why Are They Bombing Innocent Iraqis?": Political literacy among primary pupils', *Improving Schools*, 7 (1), 97–105.

Norwood, C. (1943), *Curriculum and Examination in Secondary Schools.* London: HMSO.

Ross, A. (1987), 'Political education in the primary school', in C. Harber (ed.), *Political Education in Britain.* London: Falmer Press, pp. 9–25.

Scruton, R., Ellis-Jones, A., and O'Keefe, D. (1985), *Education and Indoctrination.* Harrow: Education Research Centre.

Short, G., and Reed, C. (2004), *Issues in Holocaust Education.* Hampshire: Ashgate.

Smith, A. (2003), 'Citizenship Education in Northern Ireland: Beyond national identity', *Cambridge Journal of Education*, 33 (1), 15–31.

Stradling, R. (1984), 'The Teaching of Controversial Issues: An evaluation', *Educational Review*, 36 (2), 121–9.

Supple, C. (1991), *The Teaching of the Nazi Holocaust in North Tyneside, Newcastle and Northumberland Schools: A Report.* North Tyneside: MBA.

—(1993), *From Prejudice to Genocide: Learning about the Holocaust.* Stoke-on-Trent: Trentham.

Torney-Purta, J., Lehmann, R., Oswald, H., and Shulz, W. (2001), *Citizenship and Education in Twenty-Eight Countries*. Amsterdam: IEA.

Totten, S. (1999), 'Should There Be Holocaust Education for K-4 Students? The Answer Is No'. *Social Studies and the Young Learner*, 12, 36–9.

Wrigley, T. (2003), *Schools of Hope: A New Agenda for School Improvement*. Stoke-on-Trent: Trentham.

Part 1
The Context

Democracy, Trust and Respect

Walter Humes

2

Starting points

The teaching of controversial issues presupposes commitment to a set of fundamental values and principles essential to a democratic way of life. It also calls for a range of pedagogic skills to ensure that the risks associated with such teaching are, as far as possible, avoided. However, as will be shown, both of these requirements are potentially problematic, reflecting the contested nature of political systems and educational aims. For some people, this might suggest that controversial topics should be introduced into the curriculum only sparingly and with considerable caution. This chapter will argue that, on the contrary, the disputed nature of the territory makes it all the more essential to present challenging material in order to encourage young people to engage constructively with the complexities of the modern world.

Democracy

John Dewey's *Democracy and Education*, first published in 1916, remains one of the fullest statements of the links between the evolving character of democracy, the social and pedagogic implications for schooling and the importance of active engagement by learners with topics that connect with their experience outside school (Dewey, 1966). In the 1960s the Humanities Curriculum Project, led by Lawrence Stenhouse, sought to extend these connections: its aim was 'to develop an understanding of social situations and human acts and of the controversial value issues which they raise' (Stenhouse, 1975, 127). Towards this end the project focused on several key themes, including war, race relations and law and order. These themes, which have continuing relevance today, immediately opened up questions on which views were likely to be diverse. Can there ever be a just war? How is the identity of individuals and nations affected by immigration and ethnic diversity? In a democracy, how can the law strike a fair balance between freedom and authority? Given concreteness, and translated into contemporary terms, these questions could easily become the following. Is the involvement of Britain and the United States in Iraq and Afghanistan compatible with international law? To what extent have policies on equality and human rights helped to ensure fair opportunities in education and employment for minority ethnic groups? Have we moved too far in the direction of a 'surveillance society', or are curtailments on individual freedom a necessary price to pay in an era of global technology and international terrorism? To address these questions adequately would require accurate factual information, clearly defined concepts and sharp interrogation of a range of arguments – all deeply 'educational' requirements.

Stenhouse and his team considered the best way to approach such controversial subjects. One requirement was the provision of a large bank of material, representing different views, from which teachers and students could choose; the material would be added to as each project developed. To ensure that different perspectives were represented and heard, the teacher's role would be one of 'procedural neutrality'. This approach did not mean that the process was value-free. Certain values underpinned the whole exercise; they included rationality, sensitivity and a readiness to listen to the views of others. Promoting deeper understanding of complex issues was a central aim and this involved not only access to reliable evidence, but also direct experience (where this was possible), imaginative experience (through drama and literature, e.g.), critical analysis and independent judgement. The importance of extended discussion, in which different 'voices' were heard, meant that there was a significant shift in the traditional role of the teacher, from an 'expert' who could pronounce authoritatively on matters of fact and on ethical issues to a facilitator of understanding based on student engagement with challenging material and deep thinking about disputed issues.

For this to be achieved successfully, the culture of the classroom has to be fair and open-minded. Building trust – creating an ethos in which students feel confident enough to contribute to discussion without fear of judgemental teacher intervention – is an essential part of the process (Humes, 2010). Although schools are now generally much more enlightened places than they used to be, they are not, and cannot be, fully democratic institutions. Teachers are subject to various legal and contractual requirements which hold them responsible for the care and safety of students in their charge: this sets limits to the degree of freedom that is permissible. Further constraints derive from the compulsory nature of schooling (until the age of 16 in the United Kingdom): the option of educating children at home is possible for only a small minority of parents. These are important qualifications but the effective teaching of controversial issues requires a greater degree of democracy than some 'traditional' schools have been inclined to allow. Thus the implications extend beyond the work carried out by individual teachers within their classrooms to affect the disciplinary regime of the school as a whole and the managerial style adopted by senior staff. Encouraging young people to think for themselves inevitably presents challenges to established practices and calls for reasoned responses, negotiation and compromise. This, in itself, is a profoundly educational experience for all concerned.

Trust and respect

It can be seen from the example of Stenhouse that interest in teaching controversial issues is not new. What is perhaps new, however, is the social and political climate in which such teaching now takes place, a climate marked by a lack of trust and a decline in respect for many forms of authority. This is a recurring theme in recent philosophical and sociological literature and poses particular challenges for teachers. The 2002 Reith Lectures, entitled 'A Question of Trust', sought to explore the cultural significance of the heavy emphasis on the audit and accountability of public institutions, and concluded that it signalled a lack of trust in traditional professional groups (O'Neill, 2002). Again, Richard Sennett refers to 'Robust empirical evidence [that] backs up the cliché that people today have lost trust in politics and in politicians' (Sennett, 2006, 173). The same writer has observed, 'Modern society lacks positive expressions of respect and recognition for others' (Sennett, 2004, xiii).

The importance of trust and respect in learning has been emphasized by several writers. The philosopher Bernard Williams, writing about truth, has stated, 'A necessary condition of co-operative activity is trust, where this involves the willingness of one party to rely on another to act in certain ways' (Williams, 2002, 88). The establishment of such patterns of mutual cooperation takes time to develop, 'slowly rooting into the cracks and crevices of institutions' (Sennett, 1998, 24). Tom Bentley makes the point more forcefully: 'the bedrock of an effective learning relationship is trust. Trust, the willingness that people will act in good faith and honour their commitments, is what underpins the development of fair, cohesive communities' (Bentley, 1998, 166). And, in relation to respect, he says, 'Relationships based on mutual respect support motivation in ways that frameworks based on control are unable to do. They also fit more closely with the values held by younger people' (ibid., 53).

Traditionally, a great deal of trust has been invested in teachers – in their knowledge and expertise, in their concern for accuracy and truth, in their ability to establish standards of achievement and to set good examples. If they are judged to fall down on one or more of these expectations, their professional role is weakened and their potential contribution to society undermined. Fortunately, public trust in and respect for teachers remains fairly high. In a 2009 study conducted by the market research organization Ipsos Mori, teachers came second only to doctors in a poll designed to assess public perceptions of various occupations. By contrast, politicians and journalists were rated the least trustworthy. This result has considerable implications for the teaching of controversial issues. The written and spoken statements of politicians and journalists represent major sources of information and opinion on matters of public debate. There has, however, been a great deal of concern in recent years about the effects of 'spin', lobbying, public relations and 'reputation management' on access to accurate information about the way government and other institutions operate. Insofar as this distorts understanding, the quality of public discourse suffers: if the reliability of significant public figures is called into question, then the teacher's task is made that much more difficult. Moreover, the ramifications extend beyond the availability and accuracy of information on particular subjects. If young people come to hold the view that anything a politician might say or a journalist might write is suspect, then the basis of democracy is undermined.

This is a problem not just for the United Kingdom but for countries across Europe. Evidence from the European Social Survey from 2001 onwards, based on a series of studies on topics such as citizen involvement in democratic processes and perceptions of economic morality, suggests that low trust of politicians is a cross-national trend (European Social Survey, n.d.). Furthermore, the assumption that the situation might be worse in countries from the former Soviet bloc was not borne out. Allegations of political corruption are just as likely to surface in France or Italy as in Bulgaria or Slovenia. In such a climate of mistrust, the role of teachers in trying to uphold allegiance to democratic principles becomes even more challenging.

It is important to trace how this general concern manifests itself in the day-to-day demands of teaching. An example which makes the connection between the school curriculum and its wider political context will serve to illustrate the point. In 2004, Scotland began the process of developing a new curriculum for 3- to 18-year-olds (Scottish Executive, 2004). The general principles underlying it received widespread approval, though its journey to implementation in 2010 was marked by a degree of uncertainty and some teacher resistance (Priestley and Humes, 2010). All youngsters are expected to develop four 'capacities' aimed to promote the qualities of successful learners, confident individuals, effective contributors and responsible citizens. The present writer posed the question 'Are Members of Parliament (MPs) a good example of the four capacities?' (Humes, 2009). Most MPs would certainly qualify as 'confident individuals' as it takes a fair measure of self-assurance to enter the political arena and pronounce on the issues of the day. The expenses scandal which rocked the UK Parliament in 2009 might cast doubt on whether MPs qualified as 'successful learners' since they clearly had difficulty in understanding the rules and, in some cases, in simple arithmetical calculation. Likewise, if the biblical adage that it is more blessed to give than to receive is taken as a standard, MPs would fail as 'effective contributors'. Overall, therefore, politicians would seem to have difficulty in qualifying as 'responsible citizens'. This should not be viewed simply as the personal aberrations of a few greedy men and women and an opportunity for satirical comment. It undermines trust in our political system and weakens the basis of democracy, which partly depends on respect for those who are elected to positions of power. This message breeds cynicism among the young and may lead to disengagement from the political process. It also makes the task of teachers trying to promote positive messages about citizenship far from easy.

At the same time, skilfully handled, such episodes can provide an opening for a thoughtful exploration of important questions. What is it reasonable for the public to expect from their elected representatives? What constitutes fair financial reward for the role politicians are expected to fulfil (and how should it compare with the salaries of other public officials, such as senior civil servants)? What forms of accountability are appropriate? Does there come a point where too much transparency might be regarded as personally intrusive? This line of questioning might be applied to another group that has recently been subject to much public disapprobation – senior staff in the financial services sector. Public trust in bankers, city traders and financial advisers is at an all-time low following the economic crisis of 2008 and its aftermath. There is much scope for senior students to explore the reasons for this. Interpretations vary. Some take the view that what happened was a result of global trends which were beyond the control of any one individual or institution. Others view the collapse of banks and the free fall in share values as the result of cynical manipulation by powerful international players without regard for the consequences for savings, pensions, employment and financial stability. Once again, important issues relating to trust and respect arise, both in relation to the values which a democracy should try to uphold and in relation to the sensitive way in which such issues need to be handled in the classroom.

The role of the teacher

The examples given so far are clearly more suitable for older rather than younger children. Many controversial topics do require a level of maturity for worthwhile discussion to take place but the essential groundwork, whereby children learn to assess the difference between fact and opinion, to appreciate the importance of gathering evidence from diverse sources and to listen to and respect views that may differ from their own, should begin early. A number of charitable organizations, such as Oxfam and the Citizenship Foundation, produce helpful resource materials designed for the full age range which can be easily accessed on the internet. Furthermore, many primary teachers encourage learners to talk about items in the news and use their professional judgement in deciding which items might provide good material for wider discussion in the classroom. Throughout the process, professional judgement is crucially important. For example, the use of some film footage of natural disasters, which may be readily available on the internet, may be judged too distressing for young children. The presence of both Jewish and Muslim children in the classroom will call for particularly delicate handling of developments in the Middle East. The teaching of environmental topics and topics relating to the use of military force needs to take account of the fact that the parents of some children may work in the oil industry or the armed forces. And the diversity of social and cultural mores to which children are now subject means that topics relating to family life, sexual behaviour and alcohol and drug consumption are especially hazardous. But schools exist partly to extend, not simply confirm, experience, and this involves exposing youngsters to alternative ways of life and values different from those encountered at home. This may sometimes be an uncomfortable learning experience which, in the short term, causes some confusion. However, the process of working through that confusion, within a supportive environment, can stimulate serious thinking and serve as the basis for deep learning. The notion that all learning can be smooth and unproblematic is one that misrepresents the nature of the process.

Engaging with challenging subjects can be disturbing, but it can also be intellectually liberating.

One of the pedagogical questions that arise from the teaching of controversial subjects is whether it is appropriate for teachers to declare their own position on contested topics. If such issues are considered important and worth teaching, it would be illogical to conclude that teachers should pretend to have no views on them. By including difficult subjects in the curriculum, the implicit message is that they merit careful reflection and the development of a considered position. But teachers do need to think very carefully about when and how they might reveal where they stand and whether, in some cases, they should only do so if asked directly. Their role as authority figures means that any views they might express are likely to carry particular weight, perhaps especially for students who lack confidence in their own capacities.

There is also the matter of fairness in the assessment of students' work. Here again trust comes into the picture. Students should feel able to trust teachers to assess their work fairly, even if they express views that may not accord with a teacher's own. This suggests that teachers should certainly not state their position 'up front' at the start of a lesson since doing so might short-circuit the learning process. Their principal role is to promote learning through engaging as many students as possible in serious thinking about the topics under discussion. Anything that might undermine that – such as a premature disclosure of a preferred stance – is to be avoided. But that is not the same as saying that the teacher should pretend to a degree of impartiality that is actually dishonest. Procedural neutrality is not to be confused with indifference to the substantive issues which the controversial topic raises. What is important, however, is that where teachers do reveal their own thinking, they should be careful to emphasize that students are not expected to follow suit and that new knowledge may require a revision of thinking. This is especially true in the case of rapidly advancing scientific fields (such as genetics and neuroscience) where the pace of change can alter perspectives quite quickly. All this reinforces the point made earlier: that mutual trust and respect in the teaching/learning relationship is not something that can simply be willed or commanded. It depends on daily acts of commitment that gradually create a climate in which teachers and students develop enhanced understanding of not only the complex issues they are exploring, but also of each other as human beings with different perspectives on the world.

Conclusion

Engaging with controversial issues in an open-minded way is an essential part of learning to appreciate the complex nature of current social and political events. It can be regarded as a key element in citizenship education, the scope of which was delineated in the Crick Report (QCA, 1998). For Crick, there was an urgent need to promote 'political literacy' to counter the disenchantment with politics evident in the decline in the number of young people who voted at elections. A healthy democracy requires citizen involvement and community activism; otherwise there is a risk that the political class becomes detached from the interests and concerns of ordinary people. This has implications not only for the form and content of the school curriculum, but also for the education of teachers. To present controversial issues effectively, teachers need to be well-informed about a wide range of social, economic, political and cultural affairs. This suggests that there is a case for requiring all intending teachers to take a course – perhaps with the title 'Understanding the Modern World' – which would give them insight into both the substantive topics which might feature in a school-based programme on controversial issues and the pedagogic approaches which might serve to stimulate pupil interest and motivation.

It has been argued above that the teaching of controversial issues is particularly challenging at the present time because there has been a decline in the trust and respect previously accorded to major institutions. Furthermore, sources of information and ideas are both more extensive and, in some cases, less reliable than they used to be; the principles which underlie the selection of material need, therefore, to be clearly articulated and convincingly justified. A serious cultural challenge to the kind of deep thinking and extended discursive exploration that effective learning requires also comes in the shape of the fashion for rapid and abbreviated forms of language (evident in the widespread use of texting and bullet points). The 'bullet point' mentality, clearly seen in the way in which politicians seek to convey their messages in short 'sound bites', is inimical to proper analysis and forecloses on the kind of thoughtful engagement with meaning and policy that is needed. Genuine political literacy requires sensitivity to language, to the importance of conceptual clarity, to cohesion and consistency in argument and to the need for qualification and the avoidance of loose generalizations and unsubstantiated assertions. The task facing teachers is thus both demanding and vitally important. Good teaching represents a powerful bulwark against the kind of shallow thinking that weakens the quality of public discourse and, by extension, the principles on which democracy depends.

Suggested questions

- If there is a lack of trust in, and respect for, public figures and major institutions, how does that affect the work of schools and teachers in trying to promote the ideals of democracy?
- What are the advantages and limitations of teachers adopting a position of 'procedural neutrality' in the teaching of controversial issues?
- Should all prospective teachers (primary and secondary) be required to take a course in understanding the modern world to equip them for addressing controversial issues in the classroom?

Further reading

- Claire, H., and Holden, C. (eds) (2007), *The Challenge of Teaching Controversial Issues*. Stoke-on-Trent: Trentham Books.
- Oxfam (2006), *Teaching Controversial Issues*. Oxford: Oxfam.

References

Bauman, Z. (2002), *Society Under Siege*. Cambridge, UK: Polity Press.

Bentley, T. (1998), *Learning Beyond the Classroom*. London: Routledge.

Dewey, J. (1966, first published 1916), *Democracy and Education*. London: Collier-Macmillan.

European Social Survey (no date), *Monitoring Attitude Change in Over 30 Countries*. www.europeansocialsurvey.org.

Field, J. (2003), *Social Capital*. London: Routledge.

Humes, W. (2009) 'Are MPs a good example of the four capacities?', *Times Educational Supplement Scotland*, 5 June.

Humes, W. (2010), 'Controversy as a stimulus to learning: A lesson from the past', in T. L. K. Wisely, I. M. Barr, A. Britton and B. King (eds), *Education in a Global Space: Emerging Research and Practice in Initial Teacher Education*. Edinburgh: IDEAS, pp. 175–9.

O'Neill, O. (2002), *A Question of Trust*. Cambridge: Cambridge University Press.

Priestley, M., and Humes, W. (2010), 'The Development of Scotland's Curriculum for Excellence: Amnesia and déjà vu', *Oxford Review of Education*, 36 (3), 345–61.

QCA (1998), *Education for Citizenship and the Teaching of Democracy in Schools* (Crick Report). London: Qualifications and Curriculum Authority.

Scottish Executive (2004), *A Curriculum for Excellence: The Curriculum Review Group*. Edinburgh: Scottish Executive.

Sennett, R. (1998), *The Corrosion of Character*. New York: Norton.

—(2004), *Respect*. London: Penguin.

—(2006), *The Culture of the New Capitalism*. New Haven, CT: Yale University Press.

Stenhouse, L. (1969), 'Handling Controversial Issues in the Classroom', *Education Canada*, 9 (2), 12–21.

—(1975), *An Introduction to Curriculum Research and Development*. London: Heinemann.

Williams, B. (2002), *Truth and Truthfulness*. Princeton, NJ: Princeton University Press.

3 Gangs and Territorialism

Ross Deuchar

In the early twenty-first century, there is a strong concern surrounding young people's behaviour both within the United Kingdom and outwith. Young people are often viewed as potential deviants and criminals, and the current preoccupation with gang culture is one symptom of this wider public paranoia (Deuchar, 2009a). But the word 'gang' is often used loosely within the contemporary context of insecurity and concern about youth disorder, and often misused by the mass media and by law and order politicians (McNeill, 2009).

In this chapter, I draw upon an operational definition of the word 'gang' based upon accumulated insights gathered from my own previous work and those accrued from earlier studies (Thrasher, 1927; Patrick, 1973; Deuchar, 2009a). Thus, a gang,' is conceptualized as a group of young people who engage in 'conflict' associated with 'attachment to local territories' or cultures and characterized by violence (Deuchar, 2009a, 56). Of course, not all young people who hang around on the streets are involved in these activities but the public mistrust of youth means that they are often assumed to be so.

Cultures of fear, social disadvantage and gang violence

Public space, and particularly the street, has always been regarded as an important source of youth leisure (Muncie, 2004). Young people in deprived urban communities may lack both the financial resources and personal agency to be able to use sports clubs or leisure centres or even to visit the cinema. Therefore, the street takes on particular significance, presenting young people with opportunities to hang around with their friends, free of adult supervision. But while the majority of youngsters may enjoy spending time on the streets doing nothing, external observers often misinterpret 'doing nothing' as 'loitering with intent' (Muncie, 2004, 231).

As a result of the increasing paranoia about young people's behaviour in urban communities, zero tolerance policing has been combined with high levels of surveillance via CCTV cameras across the United Kingdom (Muncie, 2004). These strategies have been based on the 'broken windows' rationale, which assumes that there is a causal link between minor disorder and crime and that, if left unattended, activity such as loitering will lead to more major criminal incidents (Wilson and Kelling, 1982). The impact of these measures often appears to be an increase in public fear, institutional mistrust of youth and the alienation and frustration of young people (Deuchar, 2009a).

For the minority of young people who do engage in violence, it is often as a result of a perceived divergence between cultural goals and aspirations and social and structural disadvantage (Durkheim, 1895; Merton, 1938). For young people living in deprived urban communities, the search for a sense of status and identity may be frustrated by a lack of opportunities to access conventional forms of social capital (Deuchar, 2009a). Young men, in particular, may turn to the only resources available to them – physical strength and aggression – as a means of defending local geographical territories and, in so doing, gaining a sense of status and reputation (Barry, 2006). They may become susceptible to peer pressure and recruited to participate in gangs (as I have defined them) by older men in local housing schemes (Barker, 2005). Although it has often been claimed that gangs are male-dominated and that females tend to play only a subordinate role, some research suggests that females do form their own gangs and that many take pride in fighting and compete with males on their own terms (Campbell, 1991). Research suggests that gang membership may provide young people with a sense of social identity and bonding (Patrick, 1973; Deuchar, 2009a), but it can also lead to social confinement through the emphasis on the fear and intimidation associated with territorial violence (Deuchar, 2009a).

Prevention and intervention to address gang culture

Traditional means of responding to gang problems throughout the world have been based largely on suppression and enforcement techniques such as gang sweeps, anti-loitering statutes and the use of temporal and spatial restrictions such as Anti-Social Behaviour Orders (ASBOs), curfews and short-term custodial sentences (Deuchar, 2010; Howell, 2010). However, an exclusive focus on enforcement cannot be expected to eradicate gang problems since gang violence emerges as a result of social exclusion and incapacitation (Howell, 2010).

A focus on *prevention* and *intervention* needs to lie at the heart of addressing issues of gang culture. Vigil (2010) argues that prevention strategies need to begin in the early childhood years, before age 8 or 9. Introducing young people to creative and physical activities that can then 'compete with the allure of the streets and gang activities' will be essential (ibid., 165). For older children, intervention should focus on those young people who are 'peripherally but not yet deeply connected' to gang culture and should focus on social and emotional aspects of their development (ibid).

Accordingly, positive and engaging forms of primary and secondary education may play an important role in enabling teenagers to reflect upon the risks and dangers associated with gang violence and territorial behaviour (Deuchar, 2010). By exploring issues of self-identity, the perceived benefits and disadvantages of gang membership and alternative approaches to conflict resolution, young people will become empowered to make choices and will feel more supported and integrated into their communities (Feinstein and Kuumba, 2006).

The current educational policy framework within the United Kingdom provides rich opportunities for creating opportunities to intervene in and support the lives of vulnerable young people in this way. The Every Child Matters in England and Wales and the More Choices, More Chances and Getting It Right for Every Child (GIRFEC) agendas in Scotland are examples of national initiatives aimed at re-engaging hard to reach young people and ensuring that shared values and citizenship are very much to the fore. A focus on responsible citizenship, with an emphasis on active learning and the discussion of controversial social and moral issues, is at the centre of Scotland's Curriculum for Excellence. An important feature is the building of respectful, trusting relationships between teachers and students as a means of enabling young people to feel safe enough to discuss such contentious and challenging issues.

The discussion of gang culture and territorial issues in the classroom

Where young people feel they have positive and trusting relationships with teachers, the discussion of controversial issues associated with gang culture, territorialism and alternatives to violence can be addressed through secondary school subjects such as social studies, health and well-being and religious and moral education. The issues are best approached via the combined use of active learning techniques such as small-group brainstorming, games and case-study analysis. Examples of each of these approaches now follow. These examples adopt and modify practical ideas originally created by Feinstein and Kuumba (2006) and draw upon evidence of young people's voices and perspectives emerging from research into Glasgow gang culture as a further stimulus for discussion.

Example 1: Small-group brainstorming – gains and costs of gangs

The current media preoccupation with anti-social youth and gang culture in deprived communities can lead some young people to begin to identify with the stigmatizing labels attached to them. They come to believe that they are deviant and separated from their wider communities even if they are not. It is thus important for young people to recognize the differences between group and gang involvement and to explore the gains and costs of gang membership.

Teachers can begin by writing the question 'What is a gang?' in the middle of a piece of flip-chart paper and inviting participants to form small groups to discuss the thoughts that occur to them in response to this question. Teachers can then go through the same process with the question 'Why are young people in gangs?' Teachers can encourage students to recognize the difference between a friendship group and a gang. They can enable students to realize that some young people may be attracted to gangs as a means of gaining a sense of social bonding but that gang membership also brings about exposure to conflict and violence. Discussion can centre on facilitating students to recognize the root causes of this type of violence, which is often brought about by peer pressure and the desire to gain a sense of recognition and reputation among their friends. Young people can also discuss the impact of long-term engagement in gang violence, such as limited social mobility brought about by fear. Reference to the voices of young people from Glasgow (both male and female), captured in recent research data (Deuchar, 2009a, 2009b), helps to open up this discussion:

> I hang about wi' lassies so people think I'm a part o' a gang, but it's just lassies. – Amy, age 16

> You might go into a gang because you think that there'll be less chance of something else, another gang attacking you because you're in a gang. – Fatima, age 16

> At the time you're buzzin', man . . . there's guys come in and punch you . . . you're lyin' on the ground and you could go to hospital – maybe a coma. – Rossco, age 18

> I've got a hoose but they offered me the scheme right across fae us, and obviously I can't get a hoose there because then as soon as you get there you'll just get the door kicked in. So you stay in your own scheme because you know everybody. – Baz, age 16 (Deuchar, 2009a, 42, 54, 55, 58; 2009b, 13)

The classroom discussions that can emerge around the illustrations from young people's own experiences combined with the voices of young Scottish people from the above research study will facilitate a deeper analysis of the gains and costs of gang membership. They will enable young people to make informed decisions about gang membership and to focus on their future goals in relation to social and recreational activity. It has been argued that 'self-proclaimed gang and non-gang members' tend to differ most significantly in terms of self-classification (Feinstein and Kuumba, 2006, 12). Discussion and debate around the controversial issues of group and gang culture, social bonding, status, identity, violence and social mobility will enable young men and women to make informed choices about how they wish themselves and others to view them. Most of all, it will enable them to explore the impact of stigmatizing labels and to realize that not all young people who hang around together need identify themselves as gang members. By moving away from labelled reactions, young people can adopt a new sense of status and identity and even change their lifestyles and preferred socialization patterns in response to their new identities (Muncie, 2004).

Example 2: Game – 'Bombs and Shields'

Evidence suggests that the onset of youth violence and offending can be linked to deficits in pro-social capital (such as trust, reciprocity and social integration), traditionally channelled via the role models that emerge within supportive family environments (Barry, 2006). The presence of negative and destructive family influences and/or delinquent peer networks in a young person's life can increase vulnerability towards beginning to engage with gangs (as we have defined them). In turn, participation in gang violence can become a catalyst for some young people to progress towards more serious and persistent offending. Vulnerable young people may simultaneously view older, more established gang members as both heroes and villains – to be admired and feared at the same time.

Teachers can initiate opportunities for young people to explore and reflect upon these conflicting influences in their lives. The use of an active, whole-class game can help to stimulate such discussion and reflection. Each young person is asked to choose one other person in the group but not to reveal his or her identity to anyone else – this person is to be the chooser's 'bomb', and the chooser must keep as far away from the bomb as possible. While moving actively around the room, the teacher asks the youngsters to each pick another person to act as a 'shield', the goal being for each youngster to keep the person chosen as the shield between himself or herself and the 'bomb'. Subsequent discussion will centre on the feelings that young people experience while avoiding their bombs and trying to stay close to their shields. Young people will be encouraged to think about the real 'bombs' and 'shields' in their lives and whether these labels can simultaneously be applied to the same person (e.g., a gang member that appears to protect them but then leads them into crime). Reference to research evidence (Deuchar, 2009a) will again deepen this discussion and complement the emerging views from the youth participants:

> My dad was a (gang) member . . . my ma' tried to keep me as far away as possible because my dad got shot because of the gangs. – Baz, age 16
>
> You jump about wi' your pals. That's how it starts – you back up your pal and because one person's fightin' wi' your pal, yoos all end up fightin. – Willie, age 18
>
> Obviously if one your pals is part of the gang and then all of a sudden you just end up talking to them and then you'll end up wi' them and then . . . you're fightin' and stuff like that. – Baz, age 16 (Deuchar, 2009a, 57, 154)

Example 3: Case study analysis – chain reactions

The conflict that can emerge within the context of gang culture can have consequences for young people's feelings of trust and safety within communities. For young people living in communities dominated by gang culture and territorialism, an important focus for the classroom is to explore the causes and consequences of conflict. As well as addressing young people's specific anecdotes of issues that emerge from gang culture and responding spontaneously to incidents that spill over into the school, it is also helpful to examine case studies of young people's experiences. Teachers can provide real-life examples of violence and encourage students to examine the causes, consequences and possible alternatives. The following example from recent research (Deuchar, 2009a), Eddie's story, provides ample opportunities for teachers to explore these issues with students:

> On a Saturday night about seven years ago, I was attacked by a gang of youths . . . I received a punctured lung and slashes on my face. This happened only about three to four streets from where I live. I was in hospital for over a week and had to get a tube inserted into my side to drain blood from my lung. I also had to get an awful lot of stitches in my face. I was in a lot of pain. When I left hospital I felt very low in confidence and ashamed that I had been attacked. I thought it would never happen to me, especially not so close to home. The night it happened I was out my face on drugs. I was also drinking heavily that day . . . I was heavily involved in gang fighting and have attacked people in the past and thought it was brilliant until I got attacked. (Deuchar, 2009a, 150)

In this case study, Eddie recounts his experiences as a victim of violence and the impact this had on his physical, social and mental health. He makes links between this violent incident and his own involvement in gang culture, while also reflecting on the impact of his alcohol and drug intake. In discussing and analysing his story, students can begin to explore the factors that intensified Eddie's experience of being a victim of crime while also considering the alternatives that he might have chosen. Teachers can facilitate discussion about the ways in which young people who are perpetrators of violence can also become the victims. Subsequent discussion with students can centre around the need for empathy, self-respect, respect for others and conflict resolution. Involvement in this type of risky, controversial discussion and case study analysis opens up opportunities for teachers to explore the root causes and impact of gang violence while guiding students on a journey to becoming peace-building citizens (Bickmore, 2007).

Concluding discussion

The current public concern about young people's behaviour in urban communities has led to the overuse of the word 'gang' and a perception that all young people should be regarded as potential deviants. In this chapter, I have drawn upon an operational definition of the word 'gang', characterized by violence and attachment to territories. I have argued that the involvement in such activity by a minority of young people is often driven by feelings of social exclusion and marginalization. Accordingly, an exclusive focus on suppression and enforcement techniques fails to address the underlying causes of gang involvement. There is an increasing recognition that educational interventions play an important role in the lives of young people who are peripherally but not yet deeply involved in gangs.

Across the United Kingdom, recent policy developments have emphasized the need for reaching out to marginalized youth, empowering them to make informed choices and building positive citizenship. Schools that are located in gang-affected neighbourhoods need to do this by engaging students in the discussion of the controversial issues surrounding territorialism, conflict and violence. The active learning approaches outlined in this chapter provide a stimulus for discussion where young people can consider the meaning and nature of gang involvement, issues of self-identity and the conflicting influences on their lives, the root causes and consequences of violence and alternative approaches to conflict resolution available to them.

In particular, the discussion that can emerge from examining case studies of young lives, such as Eddie's (above), will enable students to explore the causal sequence behind violent acts (Feinstein and Kuumba, 2006). Teachers can draw upon this controversial discussion as a means of introducing students to more creative and assertive, non-violent options for 'constructively and effectively resolving conflict' while also encouraging them to avoid the sources of conflict by engaging in diversionary initiatives (Bickmore, 2007, 139). Multi-agency partnerships between schools and external partners such as youth workers, social workers, health care professionals and local further education colleges are valuable here. Teachers can refer students to a wide range of alternative social, recreational and educational projects that divert their attention away from gang violence and help them to channel their aggression into more creative pursuits.

For youngsters on the margins of gang involvement, discussing the controversial issues underpinning gang involvement may provide an important platform for the building of empathy, self- and peer-respect and the accumulation of conflict-resolution strategies. Indeed, young people who live their lives in communities dominated by poverty and deprivation and who suffer from a lack of social mobility due to the territorial issues that dominate their housing estates may view the school curriculum as irrelevant if it ignores the dominant social issues that they experience and struggle with on a daily basis (Bickmore, 2007).

Encouraging students to engage in open discussion about the sources, triggers, truths and misconceptions surrounding gang membership, conflict and violence while also engaging in a range of diversionary initiatives can help to stimulate the building of self-confidence and self-efficacy. Youngsters will find the courage and the wherewithal to stand up against the impact of negative peer pressure and engage in alternative pursuits while also encouraging others to do likewise. Thus, they will begin to look at the issues affecting them in a new way and develop a new sense of agency in being able to work towards social and cultural change.

Suggested questions

- How do *you* define the concept of a gang and what are the possible reasons that young people in your school's community might become attracted to gang culture?
- What conflicting influences might family and peer networks be having on the students in your school?
- To what extent and in what ways does territorial violence impact upon your students' lives and what are the possible causes and consequences?

Further reading

- Deuchar, R. (2009a), *Gangs, Marginalised Youth and Social Capital*. Stoke-on-Trent: Trentham Books.
- Patrick, J. (1973), *A Glasgow Gang Observed*. London: Eyre Methuen.
- Thrasher, F. M. (1927), *The Gang: A Study of 1313 Gangs in Chicago*. Chicago: University of Chicago Press.

References

Barker, G. T. (2005), *Dying to be Men: Youth, Masculinity and Social Exclusion*. Oxon: Routledge.

Barry, M. (2006), *Youth Offending in Transition: The Search for Social Recognition*. London: Routledge.

Bickmore, K. (2007), 'Taking risks, building peace: Teaching conflict strategies and skills to students aged 6 to 16+', in H. Claire and C. Holden (eds), *The Challenges of Teaching Controversial Issues*. Stoke on Trent: Trentham, pp. 131–46.

Campbell, A. (1991), *The Girls in the Gang*. Oxford: Basil Blackwell.

Deuchar, R. (2009a), *Gangs, Marginalised Youth and Social Capital*. Stoke-on-Trent: Trentham Books.

—(2009b), 'Urban Youth Cultures and the Re-building of Social Capital: Illustrations from a pilot study in Glasgow', *A Journal of Youth Work*, 1, 7–22.

—(2010), 'Prevention through formal and informal education', in M. Herzog-Evans (ed.), *Transnational Criminology Manual: Volume 3*. Netherlands: Wolf Legal Publishers, pp. 169–91.

Durkheim, E. (1895 [reprinted 1964])), *The Rules of Sociological Method*. New York: Free Press.

Feinstein, J., and Kuumba, I. (2006), *Working with Gangs and Young People: A Toolkit for Resolving Group Conflict*. London: Jessica Kingsley.

Howell, J. C. (2010), 'Lessons learned from gang program evaluations', in R. J. Chaskin (ed.), *Youth Gangs and Community Intervention*. New York: Columbia University Press, pp. 51–66.

McNeill, F. (2009), 'Supervising young offenders: What works and what's right?', in M. Barry and F. McNeill (eds), *Youth Offending and Youth Justice*. London: Jessica Kingsley, pp. 132–53.

Merton, R. (1938), 'Social Structures and Anomie', *American Sociological Review*, 3, 672–82.

Muncie, J. (2004) *Youth and Crime*. London: Sage.

Oulton, C., Day, V., Dillon, J., and Grace, M. (2004), 'Controversial Issues: Teachers' attitudes and practices in the context of citizenship education', *Oxford Review of Education*, 30 (4), 489–507.

Patrick, J. (1973), *A Glasgow Gang Observed*. London: Eyre Methuen.

Thrasher, F. M. (1927), *The Gang: A Study of 1313 Gangs in Chicago*. Chicago: University of Chicago Press.

Vigil, J. D. (2010), 'Multiple marginality and human development: Applying research insights for gang prevention and intervention', in R. J. Chaskin (ed.), *Youth Gangs and Community Intervention*. New York: Columbia University Press, pp. 155–71.

Wilson, J. Q., and Kelling, G. (1982), 'Broken windows', *Atlantic Monthly*, March, 29–38.

The Citizenship Agenda

Alistair Ross

4

Citizenship education is, and should be, a controversial area, and educators need to work to ensure that it is approached in a way that encourages discussion, argument and debate. It would be very easy for citizenship education to be incorporated as a mechanism of state control and to become part of the way in which the state generally promoted a form of national homogeneity. Citizenship education could very easily be used in any political system to promote conformity, in which the minimal obligation of occasional voting and of some voluntary contribution to the community became the maximum expected level of activity. It could be used to convince students in the United Kingdom, for example, that, following the Whig tradition of history, the present political system represents the best of all possible system of civic rights in the best of all possible worlds (as Dr. Pangloss would have put it in *Candide*).

Herbert Marcuse set out the concept of repressive tolerance in an essay of that title in 1969:

> the background limitations of tolerance are normally prior to the explicit and judicial limitations as defined by the courts, custom, governments,

etc. . . . Within the framework of such a social structure, tolerance can be safely practiced and proclaimed.

The tolerance which enlarged the range and content of freedom was always partisan – intolerant toward the protagonists of the repressive status quo. The issue was only the degree and extent of intolerance. In the firmly established liberal society of England and the United States, freedom of speech and assembly was granted even to the radical enemies of society, provided they did not make the transition from word to deed, from speech to action. (Marcuse, 1969, 101–2)

Citizenship education could thus be seen as having the function of creating homogeneity, supporting a monolithic culture and identity. For example, the United Kingdom asks prospective citizens to take a test on life in Britain. This is explained as part of

[t]he journey to citizenship: Being a British citizen or getting indefinite leave to remain doesn't mean you have to lose your own identity. There will, however, be things about life in the UK that you should know about before making a long-term commitment to the country. (UK Home Office, 2010)

Posing a question such as 'In which year did a married women get the right to divorce her husband? (1837, 1857, 1875, 1882)' (Official Practice Citizenship Test) might be seen as entailing an unrelenting degree of standardization, to say the least. Citizenship education could also be seen as celebratory, supporting the existing system of representative democracy as the pinnacle of development. Texts such as the Magna Carta, the Statute of Westminster, and the Bill of Rights (Hayek, 1960) suggest the uniqueness of the Western development of a political system. And thirdly, citizenship education could very easily promote minimal activism. The curriculum subject could very easily be interpreted to promote political quietism, generating just sufficient political activity to provide legitimacy in the face of the apparent 'democratic deficit' (Brynner et al., 1994; Ross, 2008a).

Against these three potential misuses of citizenship education, I here propose three principles that would make this area both controversial and relevant to the lives of young people.

Citizenship education to promote various and multiple identities

Identity has been used in various ways in different disciplines within the social sciences. How an individual understands herself or himself as a distinct and detached being has different meanings and is analysed in different ways in psychology and in sociology. Here I focus more on how individuals construct or negotiate their identity in social settings, describing or projecting themselves as members of particular groups or as having particular social roles. This conceptualization of identity has particular significance for citizenship, as one of the categories around which an identity can be constructed.

Citizenship is about identity. Identity is not singular; an individual in modern society has a multitude of identities – linguistic, gendered, social class, political allegiance, religious identities (none of which have territorial connotations) – and also identities linked to a sense of place: the city, the region, the nation, and perhaps larger entities. This group of identities can be seen as nested, one within the other, and membership of one group does not preclude simultaneously being a member of another. Identities that were perhaps once in history simple and unchanging ascriptions now become multiple, complex and overlapping. 'The concept of *diaspora* disrupts and unsettles our hitherto settled conceptions of culture, place and identity' (Hall, 1996, 207). Identification with a group is contingent: who we say we are depends on who asks us – where, when, and in what context – and on who else there is in the equation.

Traditionally, citizenship has very much been identified as a form of participation that is inherently located in an attachment to a place. But this is not necessarily so; a community need not have spatial characteristics. Citizenship and civil identity can be constructed in terms that do not necessarily relate to national identity. The social constructivist view of ethnicity and of national identity sees these as subjective terms, used to create a distinctive but contingent category. Concepts of boundary construction and maintenance helps explain how social organization, order and group membership is maintained. Similar explanations can be used to account for national identities, where the construction of bonds based on a presumption of shared group ideas, cultural artefacts and emotions is possible even where members do not know each other personally. This was particularly advocated by Anderson (1983, rev. 1991), who described national identities as 'imagined communities' and argued that nation state communities create group identities that are larger than the personal and direct: an imagined political community.

The growing effects of globalization are transforming social and cultural experiences, and thus changing concepts of identities, and making it possible for the individual to hold and express multiple identities. The movement of individuals, capital, consumer goods and technology – much of which has been accentuated by the European Union – has given rise to new configurations of identity in an almost kaleidoscopic manner. Globalization has been matched by localization and an increased regionalism.

Amartya Sen has attacked 'the fallacy of singular identity'; he argues that 'forcing people into boxes of singular identity try[s] . . . to understand human beings not as persons with diverse identities but predominantly as members of one particular social group or community' (Sen, 2006, 176), whereas we might wish to identify ourselves with a whole variety of possible identity descriptors. In his own case, he suggests he has identities as a feminist, an Asian, an Indian citizen of Bengali origin, a British resident, a man, a non-believer, and a defender of gay and lesbian rights (ibid., 19).

Globalization – particularly the globalization of youth culture – has brought new potential identities to young people around particular styles of music, fashion, leisure pursuits and social networking. For many young people in Europe, identities are likely to include a national identity, but one that is rather less pronounced than the national identity of their parents or grandparents and one that is shared with identity attachments to other 'places', including a town, a region or a part of Europe – or sometimes with humanity as a whole. In one sense, these identities compete with each other, in that particular circumstances will lead to the selection of one particular identity to contrast with 'the others', but current research is showing that many young Europeans are content to elide between different locational identities or to fuse together particular combinations (Ross, 2008b). The willingness to identify with a single location as a marker of identity appears to be considerably weakened, Lutz et al. (2006) draw on extensive Eurobarometer detail to suggest that a growing proportion of young people in the European Community are acknowledging an at least partial sense of European identity, alongside their national identity; the degree to which this is accepted varies by nationality, gender and social class, as well as by age.

This has important implications for the idea of citizenship, particularly in its 'classical' form. Those who continue 'to share a space' may continue to 'share an identity', but for many people in Europe, and particularly for younger people, an individual will share more than one space. Is citizenship then also shared? And if so, is any particular specific civic identity diluted or weakened?

Citizenship education to extend human rights

Citizenship education has a core that focuses on the rights and obligations that are entailed in membership of our various civic communities. This can become a very simple exposition of conventional and long-held political rights: I argue that a more radical approach – and one more likely to resonate with young people – is to focus on the development and extension of rights and on where rights are denied.

The UN Convention on the Rights of the Child (1989) sets out young people's minimum entitlements and freedoms, founded on respect for the dignity and worth of each individual regardless of race, colour, gender, language, religion, opinions, origins, wealth, birth status or ability. It is the first legally binding international instrument to incorporate the full range of human rights – civil, cultural, economic, political and social. Article 42 requires that we 'make the principles and provisions of the Convention widely known, by appropriate and active means, to adults and children alike'. So citizenship teachers should, through their curriculum, teach all children and young people that they, and all children, have these unconditional rights. They should develop a sense of being connected with other children globally, and thus see themselves as 'global citizens'. They should also understand they must respect the rights of others – that they have responsibilities. This contributes to developing a positive, socially responsible identity. And finally, they should realize that they have a responsibility to themselves to use their rights. These points are identified in UNICEF's Case for 'Rights-Respecting Schools' (2008), based on the UN Convention.

How teachers teach these ideas will transmit overwhelming powerful messages about the standing, status and power of the student. Teaching practices vary enormously, but repeated studies show how much teaching is authoritarian, based on a transmission model, and full of discourses that disempower the learner. Many researchers have shown how most classroom interactions, although set as questions, were either forms of social control, or were seeking to test student capacity or success in absorbing knowledge. It is rare for a teacher's questions in the classroom to genuinely seek the views, opinions or experiences of the learner in a way designed to elicit information that the teacher does not already have. Most questions – other than the 'are you paying attention?' control questions – are framed to see if the student can guess what's in the teacher's mind. 'What is the capital city of Sweden?' is a very different sort of question to 'What do you think of Sweden's record on human rights?'

How should the citizenship teacher promote human rights and equity? The UNESCO proposal suggests nine broad approaches:

1. Teachers and teaching assistants themselves should model rights-respecting behaviour; for example, listening to students' views and showing respect for their opinions, avoiding put-downs and sarcasm and avoiding the use of 'blanket' sanctions on the whole class when only individual students have misbehaved. Teachers should also show respect for teaching assistants and any adults in the school.
2. Young people should have regular opportunities to give teachers feedback on what helps them learn and what they enjoy most about their lessons, and to comment on what might hinder their learning or not prove helpful to learning.
3. Practice in schools and classrooms should emphasize mutual support and collaboration between members of the classroom and school communities.
4. Teachers need to make sure that students have as many opportunities as possible to make choices about their learning, so that they are empowered and learn responsibility.
5. As far as possible, students should be involved in the assessment of their own learning and the evaluation of their own work. This practice could be coupled with supportive evaluation of each other's work.

6. Teachers can use a wide variety of teaching strategies and routes to learning, recognizing that students may differ in their preferences for how they learn.

7. Teachers should work actively to ensure that students respect and value each other's similarities and differences and support each other. It is possible for schools to have low incidences of negative behaviour, such as name-calling and racist and sexist comments.

8. Teachers should make good use of the language and vocabulary provided by the Convention on the Rights of the Child, which provides schools with a language and vocabulary that can be regularly and consistently applied to a wide range of moral issues. This extends from behaviour issues in the classroom and playground to all aspects of the curriculum for global citizenship, such as on fair trade, sustainability and equalities issues.

9. For the successful controversial citizenship class, the Convention gives a framework for asking questions about moral issues and issues of justice. This helps to extend and consolidate students' understanding of human rights and wider moral and political issues. It is a basis for asking questions about rights, needs, responsibilities – and the possible disrespect and denial of rights.

Students should learn they have rights now, even though they are *young* people. That is, rights are not earned or awarded at a certain age. This is of much greater interest to them than being prepared for what they may acquire later in life. They are citizens *now* and not pre-citizens.

It is critical to recognize that the practices described here – concerning what is taught and how and when – are political decisions and that the ability to make these decisions should be part of the repertoire of all teachers. These decisions are critical to the success of learning and to the kind of society that we need to develop. Teaching is full of decisions, every moment, and the decisions made are not mechanical, technical or value-free.

Citizenship education to promote active engagement

A considerable literature has developed on 'the democratic deficit' (Moravsci, 2004). In many democratic states the level of participation in elections appears to be falling from election to election, and it is claimed that the percentage of young people voting also tends to be lower than that of older people. On the other hand, many in the citizenship education movement, and others, also aspire to educational processes that empower active citizens – individuals who will critically engage with, and seek to affect the course of, social events. Active citizenship is, very broadly, about doing things, while passive citizenship is generally seen as related simply to status, to the act of being. The distinction between active and passive citizenship has been particularly debated over the past five years (Ireland et al., 2006; Nelson et al., 2006), and though there is no consensus, the model suggested by Kennedy (2006) may be helpful.

Kennedy's model distinguishes four forms, or levels, of activity in citizenship. Conventional political activity – the level at which those concerned with the democratic deficit would have us act – is engaging in voting, in belonging to a political party, and in standing for office. The first of these, though an activity, may be regarded by many as minimalist action, but these kinds of traditional conformity are nevertheless participation, and participation with a view to changing civic society.

The second form lies in social movements, in being involved with voluntary activities – either working as a volunteer with agencies or collecting money on their behalf. This form of participation in civil society (as opposed to the former civic action) is essentially conformist and ameliorative in nature; it is action to repair rather than to address causes or even to acknowledge possible causes. These first two forms constitute what is sometimes derided as the 'voting and volunteering' approach to citizenship education.

The third form consists of action for social change; the individual becomes involved in activities that aim to change political and social policies. These activities range from letter writing and signing petitions to working with pressure groups and participating in demonstrations, pressure groups and other groups trying to influence decision making. This form also includes illegal variants, such as taking part in occupations and writing graffiti, and participating in other forms of civil disobedience. Common to both legal and non-legal forms of activity is a conflictual model of civic and civil change.

The fourth active form involves enterprise citizenship, an essentially individualist model of citizenship action, in which the individual engages in such self-regulating activities as achieving financial independence, becoming a self-directed learner, being a problem solver and developing entrepreneurial ideas. This is very much an economic model of citizenship activity and is individualistic in its range.

These four forms in no sense make up a hierarchy or sequential form of development – the individual does not need to progress through one form to achieve the next. Any curriculum should see these as concurrent activities to be encouraged at any age or stage of development.

Kennedy also distinguished two forms of passive citizenship. The first of these is concerned with national identity, where the individual does no more than understand and value the nation's symbolic and iconic forms – its institutions, flag, anthem and political offices. This kind of passive citizenship is commonly taught through transmission models of education, through civic education and the hidden curriculum of unspoken mores, structures and assumptions.

A second and variant form of passive citizenship is seen in patriotic fervour, a more extreme national identity that includes military service and unconditional support for one's country against any claims of other countries. This form of passive citizenship would inculcate values of loyalty and unswerving obedience and stress the value of social stability and hard work.

But these distinctions are not necessarily clear-cut, and Nelson and Kerr's analysis (2006) demonstrates that there are strong cultural variations in what might be considered as appropriate forms of active citizenship. In some countries it is clearly considered that many of the attributes characterized above as forms of passive attributes concerned with accepting status are elements of active citizenship that are to be encouraged and developed. This may depend on the particular historical development and configuration of the state; in some countries (perhaps particularly in Europe) there is a greater perception that citizenship and national identity may now be seen as social constructs and that active citizenship may embrace a diverse range of relevant political scenarios in which to be a 'politically active citizen'. The idea of multiple citizenship has been discussed earlier, and ideas about multiple citizenship have been developed by the European Union (1992, 1993) and the Council of Europe (2002).

These variant forms of citizenship all imply a much greater sense of activity than passive citizenship, or even of conventional active political behaviour. Thus aspects of the global citizenship education programme might usefully be incorporated into citizenship education, as separation appears to constrain both movements. Active citizenship, it is now being suggested, moves necessarily beyond the confines of the nation state.

Differentiating citizenship education as active and passive is controversial. The development of citizenship as a simple passive identity has led to some issues as individuals are formally incorporated as citizens in France, for example, while others identify parallel issues of identity and civic belonging among young people from non-German heritages in Germany. Active citizenship – particularly the third form identified above – implies action for change, in a variety of ways, that might challenge and overturn the status quo. This might be through participation in campaigning activities on environmental change, global poverty, inequalities or other aspects of government policy.

Conclusions

These three strands are linked, and together they change citizenship education into a movement that challenges the establishment and empowers the individual, that creates solidarities between individuals and that promotes social equity and the extension of rights. Recognizing and valuing both our pluralities and our commonalities, and the ability to use our identities contingently is critical for survival in contemporary societies, and this transforms our conception of 'national' civic identity. Teasing out the issue of how rights are established and won turns the understanding of these rights from a passive acceptance of historical change to engagement and aspiration for change – and, coincidentally, is a much more interesting subject for young people. And focusing on activity and citizenship empowers young people, equipping them with the potential for agency in the development of their futures.

Suggested questions

- What identities do you currently project? In which contexts to particular identities come to the fore? How have your senses of identities changed over time?
- Consider your own practices in promoting young people's understanding of human rights. What might you do that would realize a rights-respecting classroom or institution?

- What issues motivate young people that you are responsible for? How might you use these to promote active citizenship, in particular, action for social change?

Further reading

- Anderson, B. (1983, rev.1991), *Imagined Communities: Reflections on the Origin and Spread of Nationalism*. London: Verso.
- Arthur, J., Davies, I., and Hahn, C. (eds) (2008), *SAGE Handbook of Education for Citizenship and Democracy*. London: Sage.
- Ross, A. (2008b), *A European Education: Citizenship, Identities and Young People*. Stoke-on-Trent: Trentham.
- Sen, A. (2006), *Identity and Violence: The Illusion of Destiny*. London: Allen Lane.
- UNICEF (2008), *The case for 'Rights-Respecting Schools'*, http://rrsa.unicef.org.uk/?nodeid=rrsa&section=6.

References

Anderson, B. (1983, rev. 1991), *Imagined Communities: Reflections on the Origin and Spread of Nationalism*. London: Verso.

Bynner, J., and Ashford, S. (1994), 'Politics and Participation: Some antecedents of young people's attitudes to the political system and political activity', *European Journal of Social Psychology*, 24 (2), 223–36.

Council of Europe (2002), *What Is Education for Democratic Citizenship – Concepts and Practice*. www.coe.int.

European Union (1992), 'Treaty on European Union, Maastricht', *Official Journal C 191*, 29 July.

—(1993), 'Green Paper on the European Dimension in Education', 29 September, COM (93) 457 final.

Hall, S. (1996), 'Introduction: Who needs identity?', in D. Hall and Paul du Gay (eds), *Questions of Cultural Identity*. London: Sage.

Hayek, F. A. (1960), *The Constitution of Liberty*. Chicago: University of Chicago Press.

Kennedy, K. J. (2006), '*Towards a Conceptual Framework for Understanding Active and Passive Citizenship*'. Unpublished report in Nelson, J. and Kerr, D., www.inca.org.uk/pdf/Active_Citizenship_Report.pdf

Kerr, D., and Ireland, E. (2004), 'Making Citizenship Education Real', *Education Journal*, 78, 25–7.

Lutz, W., Kritzinger, S., and Skirbekk, V. (2006), 'The Demography of Growing European Identity', *Science*, 314 (5798), 425.

Marcuse, H. (1969), 'Repressive tolerance', in R. P. Wolff, B. Moore and H. Marcuse (eds), *A Critique of Pure Tolerance*. Boston: Beacon Press, pp. 95–137.

Moravsci, K. A. (2004), 'Is There a Democratic Deficit in World Politics? A framework for analysis', *Government and Opposition*, 39 (2), 336–63.

Nelson, J., and Kerr, D. (2006), *Active Citizenship in INCA Countries: Definitions, Policies, Practices and Outcomes: Final Report*. London: Qualification and Curriculum Authority.

Ross, A. (2008a), 'Organising a curriculum for active citizenship education', in J. Arthur, I. Davies and C. Hahn (eds), *SAGE Handbook of Education for Citizenship and Democracy*. London: Sage, pp. 492–505.

—(2008b), *A European Education: Citizenship, Identities and Young People*. Stoke-on-Trent: Trentham.

Sen, A. (2006), *Identity and Violence: The Illusion of Destiny*. London: Allen Lane.

UK Home Office (2010), *Life in the UK*. UK Border Agency, www.lifeintheuktest.gov.uk/htmlsite/test_intro_40.html (accessed 4 September 2010).

UNICEF (2008), The case for 'Rights-Respecting Schools', http://rrsa.unicef.uk/?nodeid=rrsa&section=6.

United Nations (1989), *The UN Convention on the Rights of the Child*. New York: United Nations.

Global Citizenship 5

Frances Simpson

Chapter Outline

Origin of the species: Where has Global Citizenship Education come from?

Teachers in the United Kingdom face ever-increasing demands from both the formal and informal curricula and pressure from external groups seeking to have their cause prioritized. Choices have to be made; often he who shouts loudest (particularly to the press or the government) wins the day, and a new focus appears in the curriculum documents. However, unless new material appears relevant and easy to integrate, teachers are unlikely to engage with it. Global Citizenship Education appears to have followed this route. It has remained on the sidelines despite apparent governmental backing and pressure from concerned parties and from teachers who have maintained a focus on curriculum development and new pedagogies and conscientiously included Global Citizenship Education in their teaching.

The controversial issue here is not something within the subject but the subject itself. Within this chapter I will explore how the lack of an agreed definition or place for Global Citizenship Education has led to its marginalization within education and to the lack of engagement of teachers, and I will seek a way forward.

Despite a huge push by NGOs (non-governmental organizations), academic supporters and inclusion in some curriculum documents, Global Citizenship Education seems to be fading from view, and there would appear to be a degree of tokenism about the government response. For example, in the early version of the Scottish Government education website, Learning and Teaching Scotland (LTScotland.org.uk), Global Citizenship appeared as a major heading on the home page, yet at the time of writing (2011) it is buried within 'Learning across the Curriculum' under 'Themes'.

In England and Wales, Global Citizenship had appeared as one of eight dimensions to be explored across the curriculum in 'The Global Dimension in Action', produced by Qualifications and Curriculum Authority (QCA) (2007c), but this has now been withdrawn in a recent streamlining, and it now only appears within Citizenship at two levels.

To try to understand the position, nature and challenge of Global Citizenship Education, it is useful to consider the meaning and origin of the term. Various authors (Marshall, 2005; Davies, 2006) have explored the concept of Global Citizenship Education and tried to identify a common meaning of the term. It tends to be viewed as a natural development combining two subjects – Global Education and Citizenship Education. Davies (2006) discusses this in some detail by posing the question, Is Global Citizenship not just 'more informed' local citizenship education? From her subsequent discussion, it becomes obvious that it is far more complex than this simple definition. The difficulty of pinning down the term is highlighted by Rapoport (2009), who identifies a number of views, from the general position of developing citizens who are aware of and care about contemporary affairs in the world, to much more specific values- and rights-based concerns.

Humes (2008) agrees that the difficulty of defining 'Global Citizenship' is compounded by the difficulty of defining the term's two words.

Both are subject to a variety of interpretations. 'Global' could be interpreted as having an economic, political, cultural, technological or environmental focus.

'Citizenship' can be viewed

- as building social capital where terms such as 'trust', 'respect', 'networks' and 'community' feature;
- as a way of countering the perceived breakdown of society or of protecting groups perceived to be disadvantaged and providing remedy for this;
- as carrying a personal impact – one's sense of identity and role in the community;
- as a way of sustaining a (democratic) system of government.

Humes (2008) suggests the diversity is wider still and uses the example of employees in a large multinational business who pride themselves on being leaders in Global Citizenship. They are motivated, not by altruistic ideals, but by commercial concerns – concerns focused on doing good business. This view of the term sits uneasily with that of the NGOs – charitable organizations committed to eliminating, among other things, world poverty and social injustice. One such NGO, Oxfam, an organization considered to be a driving force in promoting Global Citizenship Education in schools, provides a definition that is widely used in education: the global citizen is someone who

- is aware of the wider world and has a sense of his or her role as a world citizen;
- respects and values diversity;
- has an understanding of how the world works economically, politically, socially, culturally, technologically and environmentally;
- is outraged by social injustice;
- participates in and contributes to the community at a range of levels from the local to the global;
- is willing to act to make the world a more equitable and sustainable place;
- takes responsibility for his or her actions. (Oxfam, 2006)

This wide definition, which demands extensive knowledge of global issues, is intimidating in exhorting the reader and would-be global citizen to take action. The use of the word 'outrage' indicates strong emotion, motivating people to act to bring about a change. This is a tall order and is likely to be well outside the comfort zone of most teachers. The danger of presenting the concept in this way is that it can deter those new to the area and those who lack confidence. It is not easy to identify how we could act towards making the world 'a more equitable and sustainable place'. We are well aware of how little our feelings and opinions seem to count in the decisions made by those in power in our own country, let alone on the world stage. Yet for many in the field, the crux of Global Citizenship Education is being active, and without this element, they consider there is a danger that it will become nothing more than 'international do-goodery' (Wringe, 1999, in Davies, 2006, 7).

Oxfam defines knowledge and understanding within Global Citizenship to include social justice and equity, diversity, globalization and interdependence, sustainable development, peace and conflict and, in addition, identifies skills, values and attitudes that it considers essential elements. The inclusion of these aspects within the umbrella term 'Global Citizenship' is not consistently reflected elsewhere.

The Scottish curriculum identifies Global Citizenship as a theme which includes education for citizenship, international education and sustainable development across all curricular areas – thus including citizenship education within global citizenship (LTS website). The national curriculum in England and Wales (QCA, 2010) only mentions aspects of Global Citizenship within citizenship education in key stages 3 and 4 (QCA, 2007a; 2007b) as extensions of and contexts for citizenship and currently appears to have no reference to sustainable development and other aspects. The Irish curriculum avoids using the term but has a strand of citizenship education running through a number of subjects including geography and personal social health education (PSHE), some of which refer to the wider world (NCCA website). Other authors identify sustainable development as including Global Citizenship (Inman and Rogers, 2006). The confusion of whether it includes or is included within sustainable development or citizenship is yet another difficulty. None of the curricular documents appears to offer it a significant role. It would appear that as Marshall (2005) points out, while there is a growing awareness of the importance of Global Citizenship Education, space has not been provided within the curriculum.

The lack of an agreed definition and location for Global Citizenship adds to the difficulty in establishing its identity. The conflicting ideals of

NGOs who would prefer it – whatever they identify 'it' to be – as a cross-curricular theme and the reality of finding space, time and teacher commitment in a packed curriculum are highlighted by Marshall (2005). The preferred notion that it is not a subject in its own right but should be an integral part of all curricular areas leaves it without a champion. One of the dangers of this approach is that because it is the responsibility of everyone, it becomes, de facto, the responsibility of no one.

Existence of the species – the need for Global Citizenship Education

The international dimension in education has never been more important. Our young people are becoming global citizens and the job market in which they will compete is an international one.

(DFES, 2004)

Acknowledgement, such as that above, of the international nature of our lives might be seen as a driver for Global Citizenship Education. Quite rightly, governments are concerned that the education system should deliver young people who are well equipped for working in the world into which they will emerge as adults.

Teachers, it would appear, see the need for global awareness – a poll of teachers (IPSOS MORI, 2009) suggested that while the vast majority of teachers (94%) in England see global learning (including Global Citizenship) as an important aspect of teaching in schools, the proportion of teachers who actually consider that they are preparing children to deal with the fast changing and globalized world is just over half (58%). This link between global education and preparing children for the future is a common theme.

We are in an era of globalization. One only has to look at the goods on supermarket shelves to be aware of a growing reliance on goods from around the world to maintain current lifestyles. Young adults in the United Kingdom now compete with those from EU countries and the wider world for jobs at all levels. Increasingly workplaces are filled with an international assortment of employees.

Across the world, sophisticated technology is becoming embedded in daily lives. Young people in particular are already global citizens linking to the internet for information, amusement and communication from the time they awake until they fall asleep at night. Electronic social networking does not recognize many boundaries; they chat to each other as easily across continents as across the road. Businesses across the world have developed electronic presence to develop world markets where before they would be confined to their small factory or village. It is now almost as easy to buy goods direct from the far side of the world as to buy them from the shop down the road. Elsewhere in the world, the difficulties of providing landlines for communication over desert and savannah have been completely overtaken by mobile technology. People in remote areas can now communicate easily with the rest of the world, and mobile phones and computers are to be found in some of the poorest and remotest areas. A Masai warrior out on the plains and a Buddhist monk in remote Tibet will most likely have a mobile phone tucked in their cloaks.

Events that happen almost anywhere in the world are brought to our attention with astonishing speed via TV, the internet, computers and pocket devices. But as we view what is happening elsewhere, the reverse is now also true: the rest of the world now sees us – our society and culture; our lifestyles, decision making, politics, love of celebrity and fame and lack of integrity in our dealings with them – all revealed in colour on screens across the globe.

One result of the global communication revolution is that the lives of people around the world have become integrated and interdependent. On a trip to Kenya in 2010, I was challenged by a local guide about the volcanic eruption in Iceland that had disrupted air traffic. He wanted to know how we in the United Kingdom were going to make sure that future eruptions were not going to disrupt flights. The story enfolded that the local flower producers who employed most of the local population (and polluted the local lake) exported most of their produce to the United Kingdom. Their business had been severely disrupted by the cancellation of flights, and some workers had been laid off. In such a poor area of Kenya where most homes are very basic, I discovered that local people were very aware of the wider world and felt closely linked.

This is undoubtedly a time of change, and our species (and many others) is under threat from global warming and overpopulation. For centuries there have been warnings of apocalypse and destruction of man.

From medieval times to the 1960s, with the Cold War in full flight, destruction of humanity has been a pressing issue. Preparing young people for the unknown future is a problem that has echoed down the generations.

The challenges of the future are likely to be met and overcome, as they were in the past, by human ingenuity, adaptability and desire for survival, but the shape of the societies that will meet these challenges will be determined by the values and moral judgements of the people in them. Within individual countries, populations are becoming multicultural, and people are learning how to live and work together. These diverse populations increase the ties between countries.

However, the current problems faced by the world are not going to be solved by the actions of a collection of Western powers; they will require the joint efforts of people across the globe. Already, it seems that as globalization increases, fewer decisions are made within one country or by a collection of Western powers; they are being made jointly by larger groups of countries and by the UN and other global organizations.

Young people need, now more than ever, to have a sound basic understanding of prejudice; they need personal values that include a sense of equity, justice and an appreciation of their own responsibility in the wider global arena. While global education is needed to help young people understand the geography and cultures they engage with, the need for them to develop values and integrity, to understand rights and responsibilities, becomes more pressing.

Survival of the species – how do we make sure that Global Citizenship finds its place in the classroom?

In accepting that there is a need for Global Citizenship Education as a tool for giving the next generation the values and qualities to thrive in their future, the challenge is how to bring it into the curriculum. Endless argument about definition and structure, the desire for it to be the province of everyone rather than firmly located in a suitable subject area, appears to have reduced Global Citizenship Education within the curriculum. Many teachers are not engaging with it – and who can blame them? Leighton (2004) reports on some research carried out in a small number of schools into the perceptions of citizenship education (which, as the study was carried out in England, could be taken to include Global Citizenship). He paints a picture of unquestioning adherence to curriculum guidelines, a lack of importance related to the lack of formal assessment but a general acceptance by staff that this was a good thing.

Yet it would appear that students are very interested in global issues. A small-scale study by Davies et al. (2004) in which school students identified their needs suggested that students' had a 'sophisticated concept of global citizenship' which included an understanding of 'evaluation of everyone, co-operation or unity, interconnectedness and being involved by helping the environment or by being willing to protest.' Pupils need to know about and understand significant contemporary global issues and events, particularly war and conflict, and also the political background to issues of HIV/AIDS, poverty, pollution and human rights.' The curriculum and assessment were seen as constraining and led to a lack of depth of study. The same research identified issues for teachers: they were lacking confidence and felt unable to tackle controversial issues for a number of reasons, including ethnic tensions in the class, anxiety that would be caused by discussion of war and the inappropriateness of expressing their own views.

While progress has undoubtedly been made in the intervening time, there is little sign that teachers are signing up to Global Citizenship Education in any numbers. Research in Canada (Larsen and Faden, 2008) identified five main factors restricting engagement of a group of primary school teachers:

- They felt limited by their own lack of knowledge or engagement with the Global Citizenship Education agenda;
- Absence of good support materials to use;
- Lack of professional development;
- Lack of support from the curriculum;
- A feeling that these issues were too political, and they were uncomfortable dealing with them.

In conclusion, there are a number of barriers to be overcome before teachers will feel confident and be competent to deliver effective Global

Citizenship Education. For effective teaching to become embedded across all levels of education, Global Citizenship Education must be presented in a way that makes it accessible and practical.

The first barrier has to be the difficulties in defining the term, difficulties caused by so many different agendas being in play. If we want this to be part of our children's education – and it would appear that many people agree that it should be (e.g., Davies, 2004; Larsen and Faden, 2008; Leighton, 2004) – then we need to come to a new, straightforward agreement of what we mean and even come up with a new name for it.

The second barrier is the curriculum itself. Perhaps Global Citizenship Education needs to be firmly rooted in discrete areas of the curriculum such as PSHE and social studies, where teachers already have a level of expertise and can confidently engage with the sometimes challenging nature of the content. From here it might then grow and spread out to other subject areas as part of cross-curricular activity and on to whole-school engagement, but from the start it would have a definite location and identity. As teachers' continued professional development becomes less 'expert led' and 'top down' and more collegiate, with teachers working with their colleagues to develop themes and issues, perhaps partnerships will develop to support teachers who lack confidence.

Another barrier comes from the lack of commitment of governments. While they use appropriate terms, they are often more focused on the economic aspects of the global agenda than those of citizenship. New active-learning and pupil-led pedagogy, such as that encouraged by the Scottish curriculum, may lead the way forward. The latest document from Learning and Teaching Scotland provides some excellent examples of classes and schools taking forward the Global Citizenship agenda (LTS, 2011). The curriculum highlights the need for a pupil-led approach, and if, as research shows, pupils are keen to know and understand the world they live in, they themselves could be the drivers of future development. Perhaps we need to further investigate their opinions and views and be more responsive.

Suggested questions

- What does Global Citizenship Education mean to you? Is it an inclusive, overarching term or part of a collection of concepts?

- Should we continue to use such a contested term as 'Global Citizenship Education', or do we need some new terminology that has a specific content?
- How can we help young people to become knowledgeable about world issues and redefine for themselves the term 'global citizens'?

Further reading

Peters, M., Britton, A., and Blee, H. (2008) *Global Citizenship Education: Philosophy, Theory and Pedagogy*. Rotterdam: Sense Publishers.

References

Davies, L. (2006), 'Global Citizenship: Abstraction of framework for action?' *Educational Review*, 58 (1), 5–25.

Davies, L., Harber, C., and Yamashita, H. (2004), *Key Findings from the DFID Project Global Citizenship: The Needs of Teachers and Learners*. Birmingham: Centre for International Education and Research (CIER).

DEA, Ipsos MORI (2009), *An Ipsos MORI Research Study on behalf of DEA Our Global Future: How Can Schools Meet the Challenge of Change?* http://clients.squareeye.com/uploads/dea/documents/dea_teachers_MORI_mar_09.pdf (accessed 21 November 2010).

DFES (2004), *Putting the World into World Class – An International Strategy for Education, Skills and Children's Services*, www.education.gov.uk/publications/eOrderingDownload/1077-2004GIF-EN-01.pdf (accessed August 2011).

Humes, W. M. (2008), 'The discourse of global citizenship', in M. Peters, A. Britton and H. Blee (eds), *Global Citizenship Education: Philosophy, Theory and Pedagogy*. Rotterdam: Sense Publishers, pp. 41–52.

Inman, S., and Rogers, M. (eds) (2006), *Building a Sustainable Future: Challenges for Initial Teacher Training*. Godalming, Surrey: WWF-UK. www.ltscotland.org.uk/Images/DevelopingGlobalCitizens_tcm4-628187.pdf.

Larsen, M., and Faden, L. (2008), *Supporting the Growth of Global Citizenship Educators*. Brock Education 17, Learning and Teaching Scotland, www.ltscotland.org.uk.

Leighton, R. (2004), 'The Nature of Citizenship Education Provision: An initial study', *Curriculum Journal*, 15 (2), 167–81.

LTS (2011), *Developing Global Citizens Within Curriculum for Excellence*. Edinburgh: Scottish Government. www.ltscotland.org.uk/Images/DevelopingGlobalCitizens_tcm4-628187.pdf (accessed 21 November 2010).

Marshall, H. (2005), 'Developing the Global Gaze in Citizenship Education: Exploring the perspectives of global education NGO workers in England', *International Journal of Citizenship and Teacher Education*, 1 (2), pp. 76–92.

NCCA, National Curriculum for Eire, www.curriculumonline.ie/en/ (accessed 21 November 2010).

Oxfam (2006), *Education for Global Citizenship – A Guide for Schools*. Oxford: Oxfam Development Education Programme. www.oxfam.org.uk/education/gc/files/education_for_global_citizenship_a_guide_for_schools.pdf.

QCA (2007a), *Citizenship – Programme of Study for Key Stage 3 and Attainment Targets (an Extract from the National Curriculum 2007)*, http://curriculum.qcda.gov.uk/uploads/QCA-07-3329-pCitizenship3_tcm8-396.pdf (accessed 21 November 2010).

—(2007b), *Citizenship – Programme of Study for Key Stage 4 and Attainment Targets (an Extract from the National Curriculum 2007)*, http://curriculum.qcda.gov.uk/uploads/QCA-07-3330-pCitizenship4_tcm8-397.pdf (accessed 21 November 2010).

—(2007c), *The Global Dimension in Action – A Curriculum Planning Guide for Schools*. www.globaldimension.org.uk/uploadedFiles/AboutUs/qcda_global_dimension_in_action.pdf (accessed 21 November 2010).

—(2010), National Curriculum for England and Wales, http://curriculum.qcda.gov.uk/ (accessed 21 November 2010).

Rapoport, A. (2009), 'A Forgotten Concept: Global citizenship education and state social studies standards', *Journal of Social Studies Research* 33 (1), 91–112.

Part 2
War and Peace

Discussing War in the Classroom   6

Henry Maitles

Chapter Outline

Since the end of the Cold War in 1989 there have been more than 120 wars. It had been assumed that there would be a reduction in conflict as the USA and USSR were no longer in direct military competition, yet the number of armed conflicts and civilian casualties has increased, particularly following the 9/11 attack on America and the consequent War on Terror. While there is widespread teaching about the two world wars in schools, there is far less about current armed conflicts. The discussion in history classes around these wars tends to develop ideas around futility and waste in the former and 'the just war' in the latter. Paradoxically (and indeed similarly with the wars in Iraq and Afghanistan) rarely is World War II put in the context of imperial tensions and rivalries. The Iraq and Afghanistan conflicts are more problematic, primarily because they are both active and governments and the media avoid discussions around the morality of war, preferring a 'support our boys' type approach. Nonetheless, the deaths of civilians (seemingly unquantifiable) and troops make discussion challenging, though essential. This chapter will discuss issues relating to discussing the Iraq War with school students and examine a case study of where this was done.

In the case of the outbreak of war in Iraq in 2003, there were a number of possible responses in schools. There had been mass campaigns in the run-up to this war, which had involved literally millions of people – many of them school students – marching and protesting against the war. Some schools (primary and secondary) created space to discuss the issues while others shied away from it. In common with other contentious or difficult issues, the argument was heard that primary students are too young to discuss an issue such as the Iraq War, which, it was argued, needs a greater maturity. Yet, the media images in a global age means that students of all ages are exposed to these issues and, as the evidence below shows, are keen to discuss and try to understand them. Indeed, as Holden (1998, 46) points out, it is entirely possible that these issues can be better discussed by younger students as young children tend to have 'a strong sense of social justice and they want to be active in working for change'; by the time they finish secondary school 'these same pupils may be sceptical, possibly even cynical, admitting that they are unlikely to participate in democratic processes'. Bruner's viewpoint, which is supported by Ross (1984), Holden (1998) and White (1999), that 'young people can be taught anything in an intellectually honest way at any age,' (1960; cited in Short, Supple and Klinger, 1998, 62) implies that the main issue may not be the ascertainment of the right age to teach or learn these types of issues but the methodology that is used. When there were discussions, there seems to be evidence that teachers conducted them with professionalism and integrity, seeing topical issues not just as current affairs topics but as ways to get their students to develop citizenship skills of inquiry, evaluating and critical thinking.

Discussion and debate as a teaching approach around the Iraq War seems to have been best introduced where there was already a space for discussion around topical issues. In one of the primary schools examined by Birkett (2003), the delivery every morning of the free paper led to 'Metro time', where her primary students picked issues that interested them to discuss; a similar approach was taken by the teacher in the case study below. This meant that when the attack on Iraq took place, students saw discussion around it as natural, as it was the key issue in the media. Hofkins suggests that the threat and reality of terrorist attacks in London required a response by local schools, because 'it is impossible for the lunacy and strife dominating the outside world not to impinge'

(Hofkins, 2004, 23). The strategy in some schools was to give students the space to expound their views and then, without necessarily questioning the views, develop stronger understanding of possible contradictions in their thinking. Birkett interviewed primary and secondary students who wanted to discuss the Iraq War and showed that teachers introduced discussion in relevant ways. The importance was summed up by one of the interviewees in year 9 (aged 12 years) who felt that there was a need for 'the class, the whole class talking about the war so people can learn the facts about it . . . if we had the chance to talk to the teacher and ask questions it would help. I want the facts. Then I can make up my own mind'. One primary teacher interviewed by Maitles and Deuchar (2004) summed it up:

> I don't think you can ever completely hide your own views and I didn't, but I think you can allow the discussion to flow by using phrases like 'well, that's your opinions and I possibly agree with you' and then you move on.. . . To be fair, they probably were aware that I held similar views to them about Bush, but I never overtly said anything to them. But I think children can get a feel from you. But I think you can be objective if you let them have the run of things. It was very much their discussion.

Primary school case study

In this large non-denominational primary school[1] located within a reasonably prosperous section of a West of Scotland town, Primary 7 students (aged 11–12) are encouraged to bring in news stories that are of interest to them as part of their weekly 'International News Day' session. The discussions provide a forum for students to express aspects of their political interest and demonstrate their strong engagement in world affairs, often at a very mature level. The main philosophical view underpinning the class teacher's approach appears to be the need for openness and for creating an ethos of encouragement for students to express their opinions, often in relation to quite controversial issues. Of the many issues of interest to students noted by the class teacher in recent years, she highlights teenage pregnancy, the use and misuse of drugs, animal rights and the debate about the teaching of religion in schools as being the most common. From early 2003, the class teacher noticed a strong interest developing among students about issues surrounding terrorism and the Iraq War.

The media appeared to play a large part in stimulating these particular students' interest and curiosity about the Iraq War, and the use of interactive sessions on international news issues provided a useful setting for them to share their curiosity, interest and personal opinions and also for the teacher to address some particular misunderstandings. Although she clearly encouraged students to express their opinions and saw the importance of demonstrating the value of these opinions to children, this teacher also took up the stance advocated by Ashton and Watson (1998) of 'critical affirmation' in allowing students to develop their arguments. The relationship, trust and respect between the students and the teacher is central in such an approach. Although proven to be highly successful, the class teacher felt that this approach was not as common among teachers as it should be. Through her own experience, she has observed the reluctance of some teachers to value students' opinions due to their fear of 'losing control' of classroom discipline. Her view was that teachers who have the confidence and courage to allow student participation and to value its worth can, in fact, minimize indiscipline because children will be less frustrated at school. This ties in with other research highlighting how a participatory, open approach can lead to a positive ethos in the class, even with students who are disruptive in other parts of the school and/or come to school with significant issues from home (Flutter and Rudduck, 2004; MacBeath and Moos, 2004; McIntyre and Pedder, 2005; Smith and Flecknoe, 2003; Maitles and Gilchrist, 2006).

The lessons and discussions around the Iraq War were observed and the class teacher was interviewed and group discussions carried out with a sample of nine of these Primary 7 students, who were all white. The study started several days before the outbreak of the war in March 2003 and continued until May 2003 (six weeks after the 'end' of the war). During their discussions about the Iraq War (Maitles and Deuchar, 2004), these students displayed a rich knowledge of topical and contemporary issues at international levels, as well as an awareness of the nature of democracy through their views about the future of Iraq and how it could and should be decided. Their views on humanitarian issues related to the war reflected a growing understanding of the nature of diversity and social conflict and a concern for the common good. In addition, their reflections on the underlying causes of the war illustrated their ability to engage in a critical approach to the evidence presented via the mass media. Students displayed a strong concern for human dignity and equality and the need to resolve conflict diplomatically, and were increasingly able to recognize forms of manipulation that may be used by political leaders in their attempts to justify the need for war. They appeared to have a growing understanding of human cultures, political structures, human rights and the underlying sources of conflict between communities. They also appeared to be developing a capacity to imagine alternative realities and futures for the people of Iraq through their discussion. Their ability to empathize with other communities and create reasoned argument in favour of democracy and against war clearly provided the foundations for active citizenship as outlined by the Advisory Group on Citizenship (1998) and Learning and Teaching Scotland (LTS) (2002), permeated by a sense of social and moral responsibility. These students reflected aspects of all three strands of Westheimer and Kahne's (2004) understanding of citizenship – personal moral responsibility, political understanding and social justice.

Observations in the classroom suggested that there were a number of benefits to these young students of their discussions around the war, such as:

- increasingly independent, reflective views about Iraq;
- a growing ability to draw personal conclusions about media evidence;
- the development of more mature views about political affairs and a determination to develop a deeper understanding of world affairs;
- increasingly strong emotional responses to war and humanitarian issues;
- increasing support for peace protests and means of social activism;
- a growing concern for the future of the world.

It was evident observing the class lessons that this particular class teacher involved here firmly believes that these children's interests in single-issue, environmental and Third World issues is not untypical of the wider primary-aged student population. However, it was also clear in discussion with her that she realized that her intense valuing of student opinions was not typical among professional peers. The evidence of her positive results with students helps to confirm the view that, when a respectful, trusting relationship can be developed between the teaching and support staff and the students and when the teacher encourages the students to develop their opinions, even the most controversial issues can be sensitively discussed in primary classrooms. The type of social empathy and tolerance that may emerge from such discussion combined with the ability to engage critically in the consideration of conflict reso- lution strategies may also assist students in dealing with more local con- troversial issues and incidents as they occur within their own lives in the school, on the playground and at home.

Secondary schools

There were some similarities in terms of the issues raised in secondary schools, although this was further complicated by 'walk outs' by high school students to join protests (discussed below). In one study designed to ascertain what students aged between 13 and 14 years thought about enterprising individuals and traits, the issue of the Iraq War (Saddam Hussein had just been captured) came up in discussion (Deuchar, 2006). The methodology was to use both observations and focus groups with structured but flexible questions. This school had sophisticated discus- sions around Iraq in the classroom, again based on newspaper stories. The students displayed a mature understanding of events. While they saw enterprising qualities in Tony Blair and George Bush, on the issue of the war, they considered these leaders to be at their weakest and least enterprising. The following student quotes show that while students were pleased that Saddam Hussein had been caught, they were under no illusions that this would end al-Qaeda activities:

> Student A: Saddam had put people in Iraq through some bad stuff . . . like killing people.
>
> Student B: I feel safer because you didn't know where he was – he could have been anywhere.
>
> Student C: I thought that maybe if they caught Saddam, it would get better.

Students had believed that the reason for the war was Iraq's stock of chemical weapons and were disillusioned that nothing had been found:

> Student D: George Bush came up with the idea that they had WMDs. And they go over to Iraq and they find nothing.
>
> Student B They didn't find anything . . . They said that there were bombs there but they've not found anything.

There was no doubt that all the students in the focus groups felt that they had been duped by the British Government and that, whatever the merits and justification of other war aims, this had led to a disillusion about the motives of both the British and US governments. In this, the students reflected general opinion about the war.

The interviewees knew that some school students had walked out to join anti-war protests and asked their views on this:

> Student B: It was a good idea because younger people in Scotland should get their say, instead of people thinking 'oh you're not mature enough you've not got the right brains to think about this'. But young people should have a choice.
>
> Student C: Maybe if enough do it, someone will notice it.
>
> Student E: Sort of aye and sort of no. . . . Aye because they're speaking their word and I think they've got a point, but no because no one's bothered to listen to them.

The outcry over the involvement of young people, particularly school students, in the Iraq War protests of 2003 were instructive of adult attitudes towards school students' involvement in activity. Most schools and local authorities discouraged involvement, exacerbating the situation by calling participation truancy, threatening to stop bursaries and, on occasion, suspending students (Birkett, 2003). The Secondary Heads Association's advice was 'treat it as normal truancy and take appropriate action' (SHA, 2003). Yet, there is also a sense in which the young people involved were telling us that the war was not solely an adult war, that some 40 per cent of the Iraqi population is under 14, that many of the victims of the war were their age and that they did not like what was being done in their name. Shouldn't they be congratulated for making adults think more deeply about the issues? Further, some educational psychologists suggest that it can be healthy for children to rebel occasionally: '. . . we have applauded schoolchildren demonstrations in other countries. Why not our kids?' (Maines, 2003, 21).

Some teachers might find this approach difficult, particularly as in the United States there have been a number of high-profile cases where teachers were disciplined for raising the very issue of events in Iraq (Garrison, 2006) and there is some practical advice from organizations such as the Centre for Research on Learning and Teaching (2005) and the National Association of School Psychologists (2002) on how to sensitively raise issues around war.

Conclusion

Discussing the Iraq War in schools raised key issues for teachers and support staff in schools. In a time of heightened public discourse and government priorities of education for citizenship, it would be reasonable to expect that school students should be able to discuss the issue within the safe and open structure of a classroom, where the teacher can ensure that all views are respected. The key lesson from the research into the experiences of discussing the Iraq War is to establish the discussion within an overall class ethos of openness and a climate of debate. General discussion on 'news' (generated if possible by the students through what they have read or watched on TV) at least once a week in primary and secondary schools means that discussions on issues around war are not parachuted in but are seen as part of a discussion and process that all students feel comfortable about. Where this is done, the discussions can be mature and raise understanding. Indeed, the knowledge, skills and values that are generated by the immediacy of the events can enhance the citizenship of the students in a way that abstract lessons sometimes cannot.

Suggested questions

- How would you justify discussing areas such as the Iraq War in a crowded curriculum?
- What are your thoughts on having discussion on contemporary 'difficult' issues in the class?
- How would you deal in class with students' deeply held conflicting views on war?

Further reading

- Centre for Research on Learning and Teaching (2005), *Guidelines for Instructors Concerning Discussions About the War in Iraq*. www.crlt.umich.edu/publinks/wariniraqdiscussion.php.
- Deuchar, R. (2006), 'Not Only This, but Also That! Translating the social and political motivations underpinning enterprise and citizenship education into Scottish schools', *Cambridge Journal of Education*, 36 (4), 533–47.
- Maitles, H., and Deuchar, R. (2004), '"Why Are They Bombing Innocent Iraqis?": Political literacy among primary pupils', *Improving Schools*, 7 (1), 97–105.

References

Advisory Group on Citizenship (1998), *Education for Citizenship and the Teaching of Democracy in Schools*. London: DfEE.

Ashton, E., and Watson, B. (1998), 'Values Education: A fresh look at procedural neutrality', *Educational Studies*, 24 (2), 183–93.

Birkett, D. (2003), 'It's their war too', *Guardian Education*, 25 March, 2.

Bruner, J. (1960), *The Process of Education*. New York: Harvard University Press.

Centre for Research on Learning and Teaching (2005), *Guidance for Instructors Concerning Class Discussions About The War in Iraq*. www.crlt.umich.edu/publinks/wariniraqdiscussion.php (accessed 10 March 2011).

Deuchar, R. (2006), 'Not Only This, but Also That!: Translating the social and political motivations underpinning enterprise and citizenship education into Scottish schools', *Cambridge Journal of Education*, 36 (4), 533–47.

Flutter, J., and Rudduck, J. (2004), *Consulting Pupils: What's in It for Schools?* London: Routledge Falmer.

Garrison, J. (2006), 'Retaliation alleged for teaching on Iraq War', *Los Angeles Times*, 26 August, 4.

Hofkins, D. (2004), 'Pupils' peace talks', *Times Educational Supplement*, 26 March, 24.

Holden, C. (1998), 'Keen at 11, cynical at 18?', in C. Holden and N. Clough (eds), *Children as Citizens*. London: Jessica Kingsley, pp. 46–62.

LTS (2002), *Education for Citizenship: A Paper for Discussion and Development*. Dundee: Learning and Teaching Scotland.

MacBeath, J., and Moos, L. (eds) (2004), *Democratic Learning: The Challenge to School Effectiveness*. London: Routledge Falmer.

MacIntyre, D., and Pedder, D. (2005), 'The impact of pupil consultation on classroom practice', in M. Arnot, D. MacIntyre, D. Pedder and D. Reay (eds), *Consultation in the Classroom*, Cambridge: Pearson, pp. 15–38.

Maines, B. (2003), in Birkett, D., 'It's their war too', *Guardian Education*, 25 March, 2.

Maitles, H., and Deuchar, R. (2004), '"Why Are They Bombing Innocent Iraqis?": Political literacy among primary pupils', *Improving Schools*, 7 (1), 97–105.

Maitles, H., and Gilchrist, I. (2006), 'Never Too Young to Learn Democracy!: A case study of a democratic approach to learning in a Religious and Moral Education secondary class in the West of Scotland', *Educational Review*, 58 (1), 67–85.

National Association of School Psychologists (2002), 'War in Iraq: Resources to help young people understand', www.teachersandfamilies.com/open/warteens.cfm (accessed 10 January 2011).

Ross, A. (1984), 'Developing Political Concepts and Skills in the Primary School', *Educational Review*, 36 (2), 131–9.

SHA (2003), in Birkett, D. 'It's their war too', *Guardian Education*, 25 March, 2.

Short, G., Supple, C., and Klinger, K. (1998), *The Holocaust in the School Curriculum: A European Perspective*. Strasbourg, Germany: Council of Europe Publishing.

Smith, P., and Flecknoe, M. (2003), 'Can Changing Teacher Behaviour Promote Greater Cooperation and Participation from All Members of a Difficult Class?', *Improving Schools*, 6 (2), 20–8.

Westheimer, J., and Kahne, J. (2004), 'Educating the "Good" Citizen: Political choices and pedagogical goals, PSOnline, www.apsanet.org (accessed 7 October 2010).

White, P. (1999), 'Political Education in the Early Years: The place of civic virtue', *Oxford Review of Education*, 25 (1–2), 59–70.

Note

1 In Scotland in the state sector there are denominational schools (for children of Catholic parents) and non-denominational schools.

Teaching for Inclusive Citizenship, Peace and Human Rights

Audrey Osler

Chapter Outline

Human rights belong to all human beings regardless of nationality or national citizenship. They cannot be taken away from us; they are inalienable. As the preamble to the Universal Declaration of Human Rights (UDHR) states,

> Recognition of the inherent dignity and of the equal and inalienable rights of all members of the human family is the foundation of freedom, justice and peace in the world. (United Nations, 1948)

The declaration marks a key step in the development of human rights in asserting that rights are not the gifts of governments but derive from our very humanity. The human rights project is cosmopolitan, expressing global human solidarity. Yet in nations across the globe, education systems reinforce a sense of national identity and national citizenship (Reid et al., 2010), which is, at best, inadequate preparation for living in an interdependent world and which, at worst, may actually foster a sense of superiority, indifference to the rights of other people in distant places and even hostility, war and violence.

This chapter examines the universal right to education for human rights and peace, as recognized by the member states of the United Nations. It reflects on human rights as principles for living together, on the relationship between human rights and peace and on ways in which human rights principles can be used to address politically sensitive or otherwise controversial issues. It reflects on the dissonance between declared commitments to human rights, on justice and peace and on some of the everyday practices in schools related to learning to live together, beginning with a discussion of education for citizenship.

Cosmopolitanism and citizenship

The human rights project is cosmopolitan, since it requires us to acknowledge and, where appropriate, to defend the dignity and rights of our fellow human beings across the globe, who are characterized as members of the same human family. This cosmopolitan vision, which can be expressed diagrammatically (Osler and Starkey, 2010), enables us to see, within the UDHR, the relationship between the goal of justice and peace in the world and key human rights concepts. From Figure 1

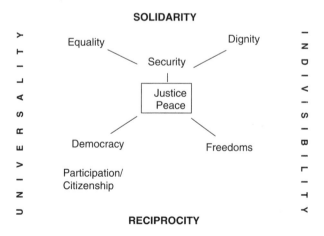

Figure 1 Key concepts in the Universal Declaration of Human Rights, 1948 (Osler and Starkey, 2010)

we can see that not only is the realization of justice and peace at the heart of the human rights project, but it is also closely linked to issues of security, both personal and global. Violence in its many different forms – whether interpersonal violence between students in school, expressed in bullying or racist or homophobic insults, or within or between nations, such as interethnic conflict, aggression and war – effectively serves to undermine the human rights project of peace and justice in the world.

Human rights and peace can only be fully realized when individuals have an opportunity to participate in decision making, and this implies democratic practices at *all* levels. At an award ceremony for teachers in Taiwan, designed to celebrate achievements in human rights education and hosted by the Deng Liberty Foundation, the *Taipei Times* reported board member Ronald Tsao as saying that when people are aware of human rights issues, 'they will know what to do when a democratically elected government goes astray'. Another board member, Lee Min-yung, observed, 'A lot of controversial political issues occur in Taiwan because people do not learn enough about protection of human rights at school' (Loa, 2010). Both board members recognize that knowledge about human rights is essential. A democratic governmental system does not automatically guarantee the realization of human rights, but it does make possible a process of accountability. This accountability depends on a citizenry which is educated in human rights. Authoritarian regimes, by contrast, do not expect to be held accountable by citizens. But it is insufficient for young people merely to be educated about human rights and democracy. They also need the opportunity to *practise* democratic participation skills. Both human rights and democracy are strengthened in school contexts where young people have access to knowledge about human rights and child rights and where students feel they have genuine opportunities to participate and to advocate for justice and equity (Carter and Osler, 2000; Osler, 2010).

The concept of universality is central to human rights; rights belong to all members of the human family, regardless of their citizenship or other aspects of identity. Universality of rights implies the absence of discrimination, with steps taken both to remove barriers to rights and to put in place legal frameworks to protect vulnerable groups.

Rights are indivisible. They come as a package, they are not offered as a menu, from which individuals or governments can select. This is not to deny that there may often be tensions between competing rights, such as freedom of opinion and expression, on the one hand, and the right to a fair and public hearing by an independent tribunal, in the case of a criminal charge, on the other. This means the freedom of the press is not limitless, and newspapers do not have the right, for example, to publish material which might prejudice a fair trial.

Rights demand human solidarity, something which is at the heart of cosmopolitanism. We need to be willing to recognize and defend the rights of strangers, including people with different cultures and belief systems from our own. Solidarity needs to extend beyond the borders of the nation state; yet it also applies to the nation state itself, which needs to demonstrate solidarity with other UN member states. Of the 192 members of the UN, two-thirds are classified as developing nations, likely to need the support of others in their efforts to guarantee the rights of inhabitants, notably their socio-economic rights. Finally, there is the key concept of reciprocity. An individual's rights cannot be secured unless others are prepared to defend those rights. This means inherent in the concept of human rights is the notion of responsibility. We all have a responsibility to protect the rights of others.

In our globalized world, our lives are interconnected with those of strangers in distant places. Our actions and behaviours and the decisions of the government we elect will have an impact not only on our own lives but also on others'. Our local communities are increasingly diverse, and we live alongside people with many different belief systems. Cosmopolitanism requires us to engage with difference, rather than create the illusion that it is possible to live parallel lives. Appiah (2006, 71) characterizes this day-to-day process of living together with people holding different values and beliefs as a pragmatic process: 'We can live together without agreeing on what the values are that make it good to live together, we can agree about what to do in most cases, without agreeing about why it is right'. Human rights provide us with some broad principles within which we can work and engage with each other and which we can apply in our efforts to resolve problems when we cannot easily agree what to do.

Citizenship education is most commonly perceived in terms of preparing young people for the rights and responsibilities of adult citizenship of the nation state. There are a number of difficulties with this, not least that it fails to fully recognize young people as rights holders and as citizens in the present, rather than as citizens in waiting (Verhellen, 2000). The UN Convention on the Rights of the Child confirms the status of the child as citizen, with children and young people accorded participation rights as well as rights relating to provision and protection. A second difficulty lies in the fact that in this age of globalization, with complex migration patterns and naturalization processes, not all learners will be nationals of the nation state in which they are schooled or necessarily aspire to national citizenship. To teach exclusively for national citizenship, focusing on the rights and duties of nationals, may be counterproductive if the intention is to promote cohesive communities, for such students will quickly feel excluded. Thirdly, much of what is promoted as education for national citizenship encourages learners to identify, first and foremost and often uncritically, with the nation state. It assumes that the democratic project is complete, rather than acknowledging the formal and informal barriers to full participation on the basis of gender, ethnicity or other aspects of identity. Education for national citizenship which demands blind allegiance or love of country can also be counterproductive. It demands a blind commitment to the nation state, rather than critical patriotism, which would involve efforts to achieve a more just society and inclusive democracy.

It is important to reflect on the meaning of patriotism, given the concerns of many political leaders to emphasize the role of education in developing a sense of belonging at the level of the nation state. Parekh defines patriotism within a pluralist society as a *commitment to a political community*:

> It does not involve sharing common substantive goals, . . . nor a common view of history which they may read differently, nor a particular economic or social system. . . . [C]ommitment to the political community involves commitment to its continuing existence and well-being . . . and *implies that one cares enough for it not to harm its interests and undermine its integrity.* (Parekh, 2000, 341–2; my emphasis)

This political commitment, according to Parekh, will be felt differently by different individuals and may range from 'quiet concern' to 'intense love'. The role of schools in fostering such political commitment is complex, since any attempt to foster emotional attachment in learners is not a one-sided process in which the student (and the teacher) is passively accepting a feeling of concern or love for the nation. Each individual is negotiating and interpreting the curriculum. As Parekh points out, political loyalty and criticism – of prevailing forms of government, institutions, policies, values and so on – are compatible so long as individuals do not undermine the integrity of the political entity and remain open to dialogue. Even young, primary-aged students are able to understand the notion of critical patriotism, whereby an individual cares enough about the country to criticize what is wrong (Osler, 2010).

Education for cosmopolitan citizenship (Osler and Vincent, 2002; Osler and Starkey, 2003, 2005) is based on shared human rights and permits learners to reflect on and practise citizenship at local and community scales, as well as at the national, regional and global scales. It is inclusive, rather than exclusive, since while not all learners may be national citizens, all are holders of human rights. So, for example, across Europe, all individuals living within each nation state can seek redress under the European Convention on Human Rights if they believe their rights have been infringed, whether or not they are citizens of the country in which they are living. Although governments have a responsibility for protecting human rights, human rights are not dependent in this respect on national citizenship rights.

Living within a plural society, we are making assessments of other cultures and beliefs all the time, whether we acknowledge this or not. Human rights provide us with some broad principles which allow us to examine cultural practices and values, including our own. They help us develop skills of intercultural evaluation (Hall, 2000; Parekh, 2000) and to avoid cultural relativism, a position where anything goes or anything can be accepted, simply because it is 'part of someone's culture'. All cultures are in a process of change. Cultures are not separate but interrelated, borrowing from each other. Educators need to help their students develop skills of intercultural evaluation based on human rights principles. This process involves self-evaluation and self-reflection. As Figueroa (2000) argues: 'Pluralism does not mean a radical relativism. That would be self-defeating. One must stand somewhere. It is not possible to stand nowhere. But neither is an attempt to stand everywhere tenable'. Programmes of education for democratic citizenship in multicultural societies require teachers and students to face some of the contradictions and tensions of citizenship (Osler, 2005). While citizenship can be conceived as inclusive, it is also used to exclude. The inclusive side of citizenship refers to universal human rights. All are included in this definition of a community of citizens. The challenge is to develop citizenship education programmes which build upon this inclusive and cosmopolitan vision of citizenship.

Human rights, peace and learning to live together

The UDHR is a moral commitment by the world's governments to uphold and promote human rights and peace. This commitment to human rights and peace has been reaffirmed and reinforced through many subsequent agreements, including the UN Conference on Environment and Development (Earth Summit, Rio de Janeiro, 1992), the World Summit for Social Development (Copenhagen, 1995) and the Habitat II conference (Istanbul, 1996). Effectively, the international community recognizes the interrelationship between human rights, peace and development in deliberating on a range of issues relating to social and economic development and the environment.

Human rights, which can be understood as principles for living together, are effective in establishing minimum standards for living together within a range of communities, including the community of the school. Article 29 of the UN Convention on the Rights of the Child confirms the right to education for human rights and peace. In particular, it sets out the aims of education for all children and refers to the obligation by the nation state to promote education for peaceful coexistence with others – in the community, the nation, and the wider world. Minimally, Article 29 implies that both teachers and young people are familiar with human rights. It also implies that all young people in multicultural nation states have some level of engagement and integration with children and young people from backgrounds different from their own, as well as an education which builds on and respects the child's home culture and her own identities. Additionally, Article 30 – which refers to the rights of children from ethnic, religious or linguistic minorities or of indigenous origin to enjoy their culture, practice their religion, and their language – has direct implications for schools.

Grover (2007, 60) argues that education for tolerance, in keeping with the provisions of Article 29, cannot be fostered where there is complete educational segregation. She concludes that it should 'be acknowledged that educating for peace will require states to mandate some level of educational integration of schoolchildren from diverse ethnic, religious, cultural and language groups'. Northern Ireland, which maintains a school system largely segregated by religious denomination, can be seen clearly to fall short of this standard. Yet in many other parts of the United Kingdom, particularly in cities, where market forces and a focus on 'parental choice' often divides children according to social class, ethnicity and religious affiliation, educational provision can equally be judged to fall short in relation to education for peace and justice.

Human rights principles also offer procedural and substantive standards in debates about contentious political and ethical issues. Based on equal dignity and recognition for all, human rights demand mutual respect for all persons in the discussion, regardless of their identities. Freedom of speech is an important principle, but it is set in tension with others' rights to human dignity and to feel secure and not threatened. Freedom of speech is not a limitless freedom to insult or abuse another.

Applying human rights: An illustrative example

The potential of human rights principles as procedural and ethical standards for debate were tested in a graduate class in education at Utah State University (USU) during autumn 2010. A fiercely debated topic on campus was the rights of lesbian, gay, bisexual and transgender (LGBT) citizens. In class, one student raised the question of vandalism against an LDS (Latter-day Saints/Mormon) church in Los Angeles, following the church's funding of Proposition 8, a ballot passed in the 2008 state elections which provided that 'only marriage between a man and a woman is valid or recognized in California' (Adams, 2010). In 2010 a district judge ruled that the ban on gay and lesbian marriage imposed by

Proposition 8 violated the right to equal protection under the US Constitution. The issue will probably be settled by the U.S. Supreme Court. This case allowed us to examine the rights of various parties through a human rights lens, using the Universal Declaration of Human Rights. It also allowed students to compare the US context with that of the UK, where since 2005 both same-sex and heterosexual couples enjoy equal legal entitlements, the former through civil partnership, the latter through marriage.[1]

USU began by considering the Mormon church and the rights of its members. The UDHR Article 1 states:

> All human beings are born free and equal in dignity and rights.

This applies, of course, to all parties in the case, regardless of religious beliefs or sexual orientation, as does Article 2, which asserts the principle of non-discrimination. Article 18 states:

> Everyone has the right to freedom of thought, conscience and religion.

This right includes freedom to change one's religion or belief, and freedom – either alone or in community with others, in public or private – to manifest one's religion or belief in teaching, practice, worship and observance. Importantly, Article 19 adds:

> Everyone has the right to freedom of opinion and expression.

So an act of vandalism on the Los Angeles church amounts to an attack on the freedom of worshippers to practice their religion. By extension, it may undermine worshippers' physical security (in contravention of Article 3) and effectively serve to limit the freedom of religion and public worship of other members of the faith elsewhere.

There is, however, nothing in the UDHR which equates freedom of thought, conscience and religion with an entitlement to impose one's moral standards deriving from religious belief on a wider public. The church leadership's support for Proposition 8 cannot be justified as a right. The leaders are entitled to believe that same-sex relationships are wrong, but cannot impose this moral stance on others.

Are Mormon leaders justified in speaking out against same-sex relationships? Article 18 suggests these leaders have a right to manifest their beliefs in teaching. However, this right must be tempered by a consideration of the impact of this teaching. If the direct or indirect outcome of their proclaimed beliefs undermines the 'right to life, liberty and security' (Article 3) of gays (and there is a documented history of homophobic murders and of the increased risk of bullying, self-harm and suicide among gay teens), then there is no right to place their security at serious risk. Freedom of belief and religion cannot be privileged so as to undermine the rights of others. As Article 30 confirms:

> Nothing in this Declaration may be interpreted as implying for any State, group or person any right to engage in any activity or to perform any act aimed at the destruction of any of the rights and freedoms set forth herein.

Does Proposition 8 undermine the rights of gay and lesbian citizens in banning same-sex marriage? We have noted the principles of equal dignity, equality of rights and non-discrimination. Article 6 asserts, 'Everyone has the right to recognition everywhere as a person before the law', and Article 7, 'All are equal before the law and are entitled without any discrimination to equal protection of the law'. Marriage is a legal contract which brings many privileges, including shared health care benefits, inheritance and other next-of-kin rights, pension entitlements and tax benefits. Article 16 neither anticipated nor ruled out same-sex marriage in the formula 'Men and women of full age, without any limitation due to race, nationality or religion, have the right to marry and to found a family'. The UDHR aimed to be inclusive of different family arrangements cross-culturally. The principles of equal recognition before the law and equal protection of the law apply regardless of sexual orientation. So all couples wishing to form a marriage contract, opposite-sex or same-sex, should be accorded this equal protection and recognition, according to the standards of the UDHR.

In debating these questions in class, and how human rights principles might be interpreted within a plural society, we needed to ensure that we essentialized neither Mormons nor members of LGBT communities. Not all Mormons nor all LGBT persons share the same beliefs or political opinions. Spokespersons for either community cannot be taken to represent the opinions of all; neither grouping is homogeneous. Some Mormons are gay (either openly or not), and some gays are Mormon. Not all gays want same-sex marriage, and not all Mormons are against it. Equally, the experiences of being Mormon in Utah and in other locations where the LDS church is not the dominant religion are likely to be very different.

Human rights as a utopian vision and a policy tool

The UDHR and subsequent human rights instruments can be read both as inspirational or utopian rhetoric and as realistic principles for challenging oppressive laws or state practices. Indeed, the UDHR was conceived following the horrors of World War II, and it is possible to interpret various articles of the Universal Declaration as a direct response to Nazi anti-Jewish decrees in the period 1933–43 (Osler and Starkey, 2010). This chapter has focused on the potential of human rights as principles for promoting justice and peace in the world through the processes of schooling. The UDHR presents both a utopian vision and an agenda for action. Teachers, equipped with knowledge and understanding of human rights, have the potential to transform citizenship curricula. Significantly, such teachers are also well positioned to take steps towards realizing a broader utopian vision of justice and peace in the world.

Suggested questions

- Can teachers develop respect for rights in an authoritarian school setting?
- To what extent is there a contradiction between a respect for global human rights and a national citizenship identity?
- How do we deal with controversial situations where there are competing rights?
- If young people are citizens (as opposed to citizens in waiting) what are the implications for our schools?

Further reading

Hall, S. (2000), 'Multicultural citizens: Monocultural citizenship', in N. Pearce and J. Hallgarten (eds), *Tomorrow's Citizens: Critical Debates in Citizenship and Education*. London: Institute for Public Policy Research, pp. 43–51.

Osler, A., and Starkey, H. (2003), 'Learning for Cosmopolitan Citizenship: Theoretical debates and young people's experiences', *Educational Review*, 55 (3), 243–54.

—(2010), *Teachers and Human Rights Education*. Stoke: Trentham.

Reid, A., Gill, J., and Sears, A. (eds) (2009), *Globalisation, the Nation-State and the Citizen: Dilemmas and Directions for Civics and Citizenship Education*. London: Routledge.

References

Adams, R. (2010), 'California's Proposition 8 gay marriage ban thrown out by court', *Guardian*, 4 August, www.guardian.co.uk/world/richard-adams-blog/2010/aug/04/proposition-8-gay-marriage-california.

Appiah, K. A. (2006), *Cosmopolitanism: Ethics in a World of Strangers*. New York: Norton.

Carter, C., and Osler, A. (2000), 'Human Rights, Identities and Conflict Management: A study of school culture as experienced through classroom relationships', *Cambridge Journal of Education*, 30 (3), 335–56.

Figueroa, P. (2000), 'Citizenship education for a plural society', in A. Osler (ed.), *Citizenship and Democracy in Schools: Diversity, Identity, Equality*. Stoke: Trentham, pp. 47–62.

Grover, S. (2007), 'Children's Right to be Educated for Tolerance: Minority rights and inclusion', *Law and Education* 19 (1), 59–70.

Hall, S. (2000), 'Multicultural citizens: Monocultural citizenship', in N. Pearce and J. Hallgarten (eds), *Tomorrow's Citizens: Critical Debates in Citizenship and Education*. London: Institute for Public Policy Research, pp. 43–51.

Loa, L-S. (2010), 'Teachers create human rights lessons for contest', *Taipei Times*, 13 September, www.taipeitimes.com/News/taiwan/archives/2010/09/13/2003482761/1 (accessed 20 December 2010).

Osler, A. (2005), *Teachers, Human Rights and Diversity: Educating Citizens in a Multicultural Society*. Stoke-on-Trent: Trentham.

—(2010), *Students' Perspectives on Schooling*. Maidenhead, UK: Open University Press.

Osler, A., and Starkey, H. (2003), 'Learning for Cosmopolitan Citizenship: Theoretical debates and young people's experiences', *Educational Review*, 55 (3), 243–54.

—(2005), *Changing Citizenship: Democracy and Inclusion in Education*. Maidenhead: Open University Press.

—(2010), *Teachers and Human Rights Education*. Stoke-on-Trent: Trentham.

Osler, A., and Vincent, K. (2002), *Citizenship and the Challenge of Global Education*. Stoke-on-Trent: Trentham.

Parekh, B. (2000), *Rethinking Multiculturalism: Cultural Diversity and Political Theory.* London: Macmillan.

Reid, A., Gill, J., and Sears, A. (eds) (2009), *Globalisation, the Nation-State and the Citizen: Dilemmas and Directions for Civics and Citizenship Education.* London: Routledge.

United Nations (1948), Universal Declaration of Human Rights, www.un.org/en/documents/udhr/index.shtml.

Verhellen, E. (2000), 'Children's rights and education', in A. Osler (ed.), *Citizenship and Democracy in Schools: Diversity, Identity, Equality.* Stoke: Trentham, pp. 33–43.

Note

1 At the time of writing, this UK compromise is being challenged by a case brought before the European Court of Human Rights. The case is being made that both marriage and civil partnership should be open to any couple, regardless of sexual orientation.

8 Nuclear War Education

Neil McLennan

Armies win wars, but it takes education to make peace. Because though war needs physical courage, peace needs moral courage to break with the past and turn enemies into friends.

Chief Rabbi Lord Jonathan Sacks, 1999

As we enter the twenty-first century, the educational issues surrounding nuclear war are changing fast. In the twenty-first century, missiles, not armies, may win wars. Just as military doctrine has changed, so too have old educational beliefs. Both issues are constantly evolving. Albert Einstein's statement 'Knowledge is wonderful but imagination is even better' could not be more applicable to current pedagogy and practice.

What is nuclear war education?

As long as there is a nuclear threat, there will remain a requirement for nuclear war education. However, what do we mean by 'nuclear war education'? The answer is multifaceted. In essence it is based on a balance between knowledge of nuclear weapons, conflict and cooperation, on the one hand, and equipping students with the skills to prevent and de-escalate conflicts on the other. It is neither nuclear weapons education nor nuclear education. Both of these are specifically in the realms of physics academia and research. Nor does nuclear war education assume all students will progress to become nuclear diplomats. More specifically, it aims to give an understanding of nuclear conflict and the skills to assist conflict resolution, enhance co-operation and promote mutual understanding. Thus its impact should be felt in local classrooms as well as national and multinational debating chambers. It would be foolhardy to believe that nuclear war education could be taught in isolation. The aims of nuclear war education require cross-curricular approaches. Indeed, it requires learning in a community setting to achieve the noble aims aforementioned. Thus nuclear war education can form part of a wider peace education package. The relationship between the two is symbiotic in many ways.

We are currently in a period of post–Cold War détente and indolent nuclear arms reduction. Despite reductions, multiple nuclear issues remain for the world to address. Nuclear proliferation is ongoing among countries that are not part of the Nuclear Non-Proliferation Treaty (NPT). India, Pakistan, North Korea and Israel all possess nuclear weapons and are out with the NPT. Iran's nuclear developments cause further concern in many quarters. Iran insists its nuclear research is a purely civilian programme. This has not convinced many and this includes council members of the United Nations. The UN Security Council has now passed six resolutions, including four imposing sanctions, in an effort to halt Iran's production of enriched uranium. Tensions between North and South Korea have been at their worst since the 1950–3 war. Central to the world's concern is the fact that North Korea is believed to have enough plutonium to make nuclear bombs. While it is unknown if they have been able to develop ballistic missiles to carry the warhead, nuclear tests have raised concern about that possibility. One means of control over North Korea has been sanctions, but even these have proved ineffectual.

The governments instrumental in passing those sanctions against both Iran and North Korea continue themselves to spend vast proportions of national budgets on nuclear weapons. This continues despite economic downturn and mass continued poverty evident all around us. United Kingdom expenditure on nuclear weapons, including Trident, was due to be £2 billion in 2009/2010 (Hansard, 2007). The US figure for the previous year was $52 billion (Schwartz and Choubey, 2009).

Education is constantly identified as a solution to economic revival, reducing poverty and international understanding and cooperation. However, while we continue to live in a world with new 'gunboat (nuclear) diplomacy', true diplomacy based on trust and co-operation cannot exist. This in itself is an unsatisfactory way for our next generation to view human interaction.

At the same time nuclear power is continually discussed as an alternative power source to fossil fuels. This also comes with a large yellow and black RADIOACTIVE hazard sign. The Chernobyl disaster (1986) is an example of dangers inherent in nuclear power. These are dangers which our next generation may face and have to deal with. The accident at the Chernobyl nuclear power plant in the Ukraine may result ultimately in the deaths of thousands of people. Estimates to the final figure vary widely and are still disputed. This accident has to be kept separate from the only two occasions nuclear weapons have been dropped in warfare. The American attacks on Hiroshima and Nagasaki in August 1945 also killed thousands. Again it is difficult to come up with a definitive final number of victims. The ongoing nuclear debate and threat of nuclear war justifies the requirement for nuclear war education. Any issue that causes such debate and presents such a threat must form part of our students' learning.

A history of nuclear war education

Organized peace education existed long before the bomb was dropped in 1945. Peace education can be traced as far back as 1912, when the School Peace League in the United States was formed. The league promoted peace when concern was growing about 'the European boiling pot' coming to a head. It could do little as the Great Powers entered into mechanized warfare on a scale never seen before. The carnage led to post-war disillusionment and a widespread revulsion or war. Despite the best efforts of peace educators, almost 20 years later, the world was engulfed in conflict again. World War II created a fresh focus on the desperate need for world citizenship after mankind's depravity plumbed to new depths with the Holocaust and the dropping of the atomic bomb. The despair and revulsion at mankind's ability to do harm to fellow man created a fresh impetuous for educators to have a role in resolving conflict and breaking the cycle of hate.

The education approach is different from country to country and changes from decade to decade. In fact, the presence of any nuclear war education is never guaranteed. Given the evolutionary nature of education and of the nuclear war issue, this is perhaps not surprising. The changes in the nuclear war education approach have been a suitable response to each social, economic and militaristic situation society has been dragged into. In the 1950s in Japan it was simply called 'A bomb education.' It was an education campaign led by teachers to educate not only the young people of Japan, but the whole world, about the horror of nuclear holocaust. Today it generally appears as part of wider peace education packages.

Nuclear war education was more obviously evident during the Cold War era. Nothing drives educators more than the fear of the horrors of history needlessly repeating themselves with catastrophic results, real or imagined. Most noticeably many western educators aligned themselves with anti–Vietnam War protesters.

Peace can seem as far away today as it must have seemed in the midst of Europe being set ablaze at the start and middle of the last century. Nuclear war education and wider peace education are now all the more pertinent given that conflicts seem to be arising all over the world and in very different and new forms from previous uses of violence. The age of global terrorism, religious fundamentalism and pan-nationalism has brought new threats. With them there is a new need for a suitable response from educators. Intra- rather than interstate conflicts have brought a new uncertainty to a world threatened by ultra-nationalism and religious fundamentalism. The broad peace message of those Japanese teachers has had no impact. Amid the turmoil nuclear weapons remain a threat. Thus nuclear war education is required and must evolve again.

The bureaucratic challenge to nuclear war education

W. R. Mitchell gave a concise summary of the overarching purposes of education:

> Education should help a person to develop spiritually, morally, socially, intellectually, physically, that he [or she] may fulfil his [or her] highest potential, qualify for suitable employment, make a suitable contribution to the welfare of the community, and lead a happy and satisfying life. (Mitchell, 1978, 11)

This succinct appraisal would gain broad consensus among modern educators. However, in a society bound by examinations, attainment figures and league tables, the high moral aims of Mitchell can be lost somewhere amid the clamour for statistics. This point is not lost by Harris: 'Educators whose priorities are preparing students for high stake tests in a capitalist competitive economic order are largely ignoring peace education theories and peace practice'(Harris, 2004, 17).

Khane also highlights the discrepancy between the bureaucracies that run many public schools and the status of sacred education principles (Khane, 1996). He argues that these bureaucrats, who judge education on attainment figures, would question the need for nuclear war education. However, it is clear that the ongoing forces of violence, disengagement and alienation make peace education necessary.

Whether nuclear war education promotes skills development and wider social goals is irrelevant to bureaucrats. The drive for measureable attainment is their sole aim. Can the two be reconciled? Can peace education deliver on both social and academic goals? Can peace education deliver outcomes at both a global and an individual level? In a world changing so fast and with depleted funding, education leaders are looking towards new delivery models and methods. For this to work bureaucrats have to look at coexistence, cooperation, partnership working beyond traditional education and more innovative approaches to delivery. The days of knowledge for knowledge's sake have gone. Albert Einstein would be pleased with this change in approach.

Educators are focused more than ever on the skills that complement knowledge, skills that will allow for the application and evolution of knowledge. Learning now centres on the application of skill, combined with knowledge, in real-life working and personal scenarios. Thus thematic learning is now more crucial to our educators and students. As such, nuclear war education would seem to fit in quite well with emerging approaches to education. Nuclear war education is capable of developing skills and also of enhancing knowledge of a contemporary and relevant issue. Of course thematic learning has been around for some time and is now back in vogue among cutting edge educators. In November 1983 the Director of Education for Avon County Council wrote:

> When, for the bulk of children and young people, education was confined to the three Rs, education was seldom a controversial issue. Education is accepted now as the process of preparing young people for life in the complex and often baffling world of the late twentieth century. It follows therefore, that education, in the interests of the pupils, has to tackle positively and honestly difficult and controversial issues. (Crump, 1983, 1)

This note was written as a foreword to Teacher's Guidance Notes on the teaching of controversial issues in the classroom. Inside those guidance notes was a section on the teaching of nuclear war. Then, as now, it was seen as a controversial issue in the classroom. Maybe as it becomes more engrained in the curriculum, it will lose its 'controversial' tag.

Politicization

Nuclear war education tends to exist in countries with existing peace (or anti-war) movements. Nuclear war education is no different as it requires organizations and individuals to champion and promote it. One might say this devalues the approach. By association with such movements the resources can be tainted, pigeonholed as 'political', and lose their effect. The resources could be viewed by some as attempting to achieve political rather than wider social, egalitarian and educational goals. Consensus can be particularly difficult to achieve in this area. Even seven experts working for UNESCO in the 1980s on a disarmament education project faced challenges in producing a teacher's handbook on the topic. Their work remains unpublished (Haavelsrud, 2004).

By placing nuclear war education under the much wider banner of peace education, it becomes politically, morally and educationally acceptable. This also aligns nuclear war education with wider educational aims and attempts at achieving citizens who have a moral and political conscience. However, without the impetus of pressure groups such as Campaign for Nuclear Disarmament (CND), nuclear war education would be crowded out in an increasingly cluttered education landscape. It is difficult for governments to preach peace education while the negative stalemate of collective security through nuclear deterrent exists at their behest. This dual responsibility of ruling powers creates an interesting dynamic. At a micro level, education authorities, schools and teachers can be guarded in what enters classrooms. Thus the politics of education take place both at policy and classroom levels.

Embedding nuclear war education across learning

As pedagogy evolves, there are still issues with curriculum models whereby teachers are responsible for a more holistic education. Some see this as eroding subject boundaries and specialism. Nuclear war education would never become a subject in its own right. It has a far wider cross-curricular appeal and can be taught in a variety of subjects using active-learning, student-centred decision-making models of teaching and learning. A cross curricular approach increases the likelihood of nuclear war education being properly embedded in the curriculum.

Nuclear war education initially appears to fit easiest in the history/social subjects curriculum although other curricular areas could benefit from it. Nuclear war education can also be relevant to English literature and media studies lessons. Texts such as *How I Live Now* (Rosoff, 2004) and *On the Beach* (Shute, 1957) are but two works that older students engage with. There is also a plethora of poetry which could act as stimulus at any level or age range. Media studies too can engage easily with nuclear war education. Many art projects in schools have been inspired by *Sadako and the Thousand Paper Cranes* (Coerr, 1977) This tells of 2-year-old Sadako Sasaki, who lived in Hiroshi at the time of the atomic bombing by the United States, and later developed leukaemia from the radiation. Sadako attempted to fold 1,000 paper cranes because according to Japanese legend, if 1,000 cranes are folded, a wish will be granted.

Sadako's wish was to live. She managed to fold 644 before she became too weak to fold any more; she died in 1955.

Regardless of the curriculum or the political system, students are often interested in the how, what, where, when and why of human conflict. My own experience as a teacher of history has seen many lessons on conflict 'fast forward' to nuclear annihilation at some point. This has always been instigated by students. Concern and interest about the topic is clear. However, is the teaching of nuclear annihilation appropriate and right? It is difficult to imagine a more emotive, disturbing or complicated subject. Despite this, teachers have a duty to simplify the challenging, dilute the inappropriate while still presenting the facts in a non-partisan manner. Educators must not merely give students the road map for life beyond the classroom. They must give them the skills to read the map, use the compass and event to redraw that map as their world changes.

If we are to give students ability to resolve conflict, educators must first have a common belief that all have a responsibility for the overarching aims of education. Any educational parochialism would sink those aims. Subject specialists must see their role as far more than just delivering subject knowledge. For example; the effective history teacher brings the world into the classroom. They act as a bridge between the past, the present and the future. A teacher teaching the Cold War should be teaching about political aspects, economic rivalry, geography, literature and citizenship. Most important of all, there should be a focus on learning about learning. Learning can be contextualized and made applicable by giving students challenges which relate to current affairs and future possibilities. Fortunately a range of resources are available which should help embed nuclear war education (cf. Scottish CND and CND web resources below).

Learning approaches and assessing nuclear war education

If one is to implement a cross-curricular programme of nuclear war education, then being able to assess the impact is vital. A set of closed questions in a traditional teaching and learning approach would not be befitting. Students engaging in nuclear war education would benefit from challenging tasks completed in collaborative groups rather than worksheets delivered by the teacher. Thus the method, outcome and aims are in line with cooperative and collaborative teaching pedagogies.

Students provided with background information, further learning resources and set criteria can then gain both academic assessed knowledge and also experience assessable skills. Time restrictions, limited resources and set criteria add to the realism of the challenge. It is important that students have the opportunity to experiment in various roles (giving them multi-perceptivity), communication modes and group work. Central to these active learning tasks, students take responsibility for their own learning and its outcome. To ensure outcomes are met, the criteria is best self-, peer- and teacher-assessed.

One important part of the learning process is having the opportunity to go back, retry and revisit a challenge after having obtained feedback. It is an important simulation for students to be able to experience successful outcomes after feedback. Realizing success increases students' ability to repeat that success in another context. Sadly, however, in the real world, challenging situations with regard to nuclear weapons may result in decisions whereby returning to 'try again' may not be a viable option.

Fortunately, in the classroom, the ability to rethink, reorganize and retry is possible. This is a vital part of skills consolidation and progression, as well as being a building block for knowledge transfer. The old adage 'Give me a fish and I will eat for a day, teach me how to fish and I will be able to eat forever' is appropriate to this learning approach. The issue of nuclear weapons is one where we must teach the next generation the skills to develop a peaceful and safer world. It is certain that this will not be handed to anyone on a plate.

A failed approach?

In conclusion, the need for nuclear war education will continue as long as the global threat exists. So, how do we assess nuclear war education? Is, 'no nuclear wars' an achievable target? If it was the assessment criteria, have we passed or failed?

At present we could say that nuclear war education has failed; there have been no nuclear wars but the associated threat and violence still exist. Can this be attributed to a failure of education? Essentially there has been no widespread acceptance of nuclear war education; so it is hard to measure its impact.

Nuclear war education has a specific and very general role to play in the education of our young people. In order to ensure this broader concept has a presence in school teaching and learning, it will require a 'hearts and minds' exercise to win over educators, students and the wider community to embed nuclear war education into curricular structures. Einstein said only two things were certainties in life: infinity and human stupidity. It would be stupid not to act upon the lessons first taught by Japanese teachers in the 1950s.

Suggested questions

- How can all curriculum areas contribute to nuclear war education?
- Does nuclear war education belong under the 'umbrella' of peace education?
- At what age should children be exposed to the ever-present threat of nuclear annihilation?

Further reading

- Harris, I. M. (1988), *Peace Education*. London: McFarland.
- Harris, I. M., and Morrison, M. L. (2003), *Peace Education* (2nd edn). London: McFarland.
- McGlynn, C., Zembylas, M., Bekerman, Z., and Gallagher, T. (2009), *Peace Education in Conflict and Post Conflict Societies: Comparative Perspective*. New York: Palgrave Macmillan.
- Raviv, A., Oppenheimer, L., and Bar-Tal, D. (eds) (1999), *How Children Understand Peace and War: A Call for International Peace Education*. San Francisco: Jossey-Bass.

References

Ardizzone, L. (2003), 'Generating Peace: A study of nonformal youth organizations', *Peace & Change*, 28, 420–45.

Avery, P., Johnson D. W., Johnson, R. T., and Mitchell, J. M. (1999), 'Teaching an understanding of war and peace through structured academic controversies', in A. Raviv, L. Oppenheimer and D. Bar-Tal (eds), *How Children Understand War and Peace: A Call for International Peace Education*. San Francisco: Jossey-Bass, pp. 260–80.

Bok, S. (1998), *Mayhem: Violence as Public Entertainment*. Reading: Addison-Wesley.

Boulding, E. (2000), *Cultures of Peace: The Hidden Side of History*. New York: Syracuse University Press.

Chomsky, N. (2002), *Media Control: The Spectacular Achievements of Propaganda*. New York: Seven Stories Press.

Coerr, E. (1977), *Sadako and the Thousand Paper Cranes*. New York: Putnam.

Crump, G. F. (1983), 'Peace Education: Guidelines for primary and pecondary schools', Avon County Council Education Department, Bristol County of Avon Public Relations and Publicity Dept.

Gallagher, T. (2009), 'Approaches to peace education', in M. McGlynns, Z. Zembylas and G. Bekerman (eds), *Peace Education in Conflict and Post Conflict Societies: Comparative Perspective*. New York: Palgrave Macmillan, pp. 5–7.

Haavelsrud, M. (2004), 'Target: Disarmament education', *Journal of Peace Education*, 1 (1), 37–58.

Hansard, (2007), Nuclear Weapons: Expenditure, Column 1357W, 30 October, http://www. publications.parliament.uk/pa/cm200607/cmhansrd/cm071030/text/71030w0066. htm#07110122000081 (accessed June 25, 2011).

Harris, I. M., (2004), 'Peace Education Theory', *Journal of Peace Education*, 1 (1), 5–22.

Khane, J. (1996), 'The eight year study: Evaluating progressive education', in J. Khane (ed.), *Retraining Education Policy: Democracy, Community and the Individual*. New York: Teachers College Press, pp. 119–46.

Mitchell, W. R. (1978), *Education for Peace*. Belfast: Christian Journals Ltd.

Raviv, A., Oppenheimer, L., and Bar-Tal, D. (eds) (1999), *How Children Understand War and Peace: A Call for International Peace Education*. San Francisco: Jossey-Bass.

Rosoff, Meg (2004), *How I Live Now*. London: Puffin.

Shute, Neville (1957), *On the Beach*. New York: Ballantine.

Schwartz, S., and Choubey, D. (2009), *Nuclear Security Spending: Assessing Costs, Examining Priorities*. Washington, DC: Carnegie Endowment Report.

Web references

Carnegie Endowment for International Peace, http://carnegieendowment.org/publications/ index.cfm?fa=view&id=22601&prog=zgp&proj=znpp.

CND education resources, www.cnduk.org/index.php/information/peace-education/peace-education.html.

SCND education resources, http://banthebomb.org/cndeducation.

Part 3
Genocide

The Unique and Universal Aspects of Modern Genocide

9

Stephen D. Smith

Chapter Outline

We still fail to grasp that we will never be able to fight against our tendency toward reciprocal annihilation if we do not study it and teach it and if we do not face the fact that humans are the only mammals that are capable of annihilating their own kind.

Yehuda Bauer (1998)

What's unique? What's universal?

At a first glance the unique and the universal are poles apart. A unique reading of history states of an event, 'this is unlike other events'. The universal view states, 'this is just like other events'. But all genocides are unique and all genocides are universal.

The fact that from 1915 to 1917 Armenians were rounded up from swathes of far-flung territory, walked into the desert, incarcerated in concentration camps and forced to march until they died was unique. The fact that Rwandans saw neighbours, friends and even family transformed into a highly localized killing network driven by orders from the radio was grotesquely unique. The fact that Jews were taken across Europe in trains to killing centres and processed through factories of death was unique beyond comprehension. Being unique in these contexts is to have individual and specific character. That individuality includes the fact that each has definable characteristics: fundamental underpinning causes, its own time, place in history, geographic location and political ideology in power, different ethnic group (or groups) affected, variation in the method of killing, duration of onslaught, intensity and intent.

Because historical events have *unique aspects* that define them as being different to other events, it does not follow that they are exclusive. The examples above all have commonalities, including the abuse of ideological power, the identification and segregation of victims, the lack of political intervention and the impact of the events on their survivors. It is in the *universal aspects* of an event in history that one may find the most complex, but also the richest, sources for understanding the unfolding of historical events and the principles of genocide in action.

On the surface, comprehending this is not complicated. Every genocide is different, but there are lessons we can learn from each of them which help us understand the nature, causes and consequences of genocide – and by extension human nature – in general. What then is problematic about the unique and universal aspects of genocide in the classroom? The challenge lies in approach. Is it more appropriate to teach genocide studies as independent unique histories or as a universal exploration of human behaviour? Are the approaches exclusive?

The uniqueness of the Holocaust

For a long time there were claims that the Holocaust was unique in history. In this context it was not a reference to its individuality but to its exclusivity. The Holocaust was seen as the genocide at the extreme to the extent that the word *genocide* itself did not sufficiently encompass it. There was '*the* Holocaust' and there were 'other genocides'. There were good grounds for this claim. The Nazis were totally intent on murdering all Jews without exception; policies were brutally applied, and it became a highly functional industrial operation. The Nazis intended to wipe out the existence of the Jews and all memory of Jewish presence in Europe and ultimately any geographical boundaries to which they could exert their influence. So severe was this onslaught that, in 1944 Raphael Lemkin, a Polish Jew and international lawyer, coined the term *genocide* in an attempt to describe the phenomenon and then to enshrine it in international law (Strom, 2008). On 11 December 1946 the United Nation General Assembly identified genocide as a crime and two years later, it adopted the Convention on the Prevention and Punishment of the Crime of Genocide, which provided a legal definition:

> . . . genocide means any of the following acts committed with intent to destroy, in whole or in part, a national, ethnical, racial or religious group, as such:
>
> (a) Killing members of the group;
> (b) Causing serious bodily or mental harm to members of the group;
> (c) Deliberately inflicting on the group conditions of life calculated to bring about its physical destruction in whole or in part;
> (d) Imposing measures intended to prevent births within the group;
> (e) Forcibly transferring children of the group to another group.

The Holocaust was in fact the *defining* genocide, but it was not the only one. The Holocaust was a genocide at the extreme. But that does not make it anything more than genocide. Claiming an exclusive status of one genocide over the other is counter-intuitive, counter-historical and counterproductive in the classroom. In the field of Genocide Studies it is now widely recognized that the Holocaust was indeed unprecedented[1] – there had never been an onslaught against a single group with such ferocious and sophisticated determination before, or since – but it is an entirely universal phenomenon also.

Claims of such exclusivity do not assist the exploration of universal values and behaviours. If the Holocaust is incomprehensible, then it will be too far removed from one's sense of reality. In this scenario the Nazis become monsters and the Jews sacred victims, at which point any valuable insights we might gain from the fact that the Holocaust happened in human history will be lost. The real challenge of the Holocaust was that it was actually an extraordinary event, with extraordinarily brutal intent and consequences. But it emerged out of an ordinary political process and was conducted by ordinary people. If the Holocaust truly is incomprehensible, then it is too far removed from our sense of reality to teach morality or justice or to inform our own lives and society (Gregory, 2000). We will not even be able to use it as being instructive for the prevention of genocide, when it is in fact the defining genocide of our time. Claiming its uniqueness suggests that everything should be compared to it and simultaneously nothing can compare to it, which sets it outside the experience of our students' lives. Rooting the Holocaust firmly in human history is critical to teaching success.

History or moral lesson?

There is however some confusion as to what rooting our learning firmly in historical study means in practice. Salmons states:

> The Holocaust should be studied not because it is redemptive, but because it is historically significant; it should be studied as history, not as a moral lesson; and we should recognize the very difficult questions about human beings that it may raise for young people and give space for them to reflect on these. (Russell, 2006, 38)

Salmons does not suggest that the Holocaust is exclusive, avoiding any redemptive or sacred reading of it. He does say that *because* it is historically significant it should not be taken out of its historical context and taught as a moral lesson. Salmons appears to caution about preaching rather than teaching the Holocaust. The underlying fear and concern that, were the Holocaust used as a proof text for a particular moral or ethical point of view or as a metaphor of human behaviour, the history would thereby be taken out of context is entirely justifiable. But this can lead to a most erroneous form of pedagogy, as clearly the Holocaust has many profound implications. It leaves too much to chance to give 'space for reflection' in the hope that the complex universal human implications will become apparent to students. Teaching about genocide can inspire social change for the better, but only if teachers can guide their students through the complex maze of possibilities.

Disentangling the past

The question is how to manage the intellectual tension between those features unique to a specific history and those common to all of us. There are several elements to consider when disentangling the past.

1. **Creating Distinction**. Making a distinction between historical scenarios and thematic issues is one way in which to disentangle the unique from the universal, while keeping both present in the classroom. Imagine a series of vertical columns. Each one of them represents an historical scenario. The first column represents Armenia, the next the Holocaust, the next Cambodia, the next Rwanda, and so on. In each column is a timeline which charts the historical scenario and documents linked to that timeline (primary and secondary sources). Then imagine across the historical columns a series of lateral lines. One is labelled 'propaganda', another 'ideology', 'mass killing', 'liberation', and so on. What emerges is a matrix in which unique historical scenarios can be taught independently of one another while each keeps its historical integrity, and the comparative themes, which raise universal implications, can be compared (Holocaust Centre, 2004).

2. **Establish Context**. Learning about genocide starts with understanding context. If 'lessons' are sought without first establishing a timeline, a grasp of key turning points and historical themes or if attention is not paid to ideology, socio-economic circumstances and the documentary sources that surround the history, then such lessons form no basis from which to draw conclusions. Teaching without context means that justice is not done to the subject matter. Students will be disorientated, basic historical building blocks will not be in place, and the implications will not be understood.

3. **Create Personal Links**. The history of genocide is overwhelming in scale. Its very nature is depersonalized killing. Humanizing the experience by exploring individual stories assists in exemplifying the circumstances people found themselves in as a result of the policies being implemented. It also overcomes the intent of the perpetrators to condemn whole groups – in which depersonalization is usually one of the first steps to their elimination. There is a moral task of teaching about victims of genocide as people before they became victims (Totten, 2004). The very fact that the Nazis turned names to numbers, or that regardless of their personal circumstances identification cards condemned Tutsis to death in Rwanda, demonstrates the need to make links to real people who faced such depersonalization.

4. **Focus on the Nexus of the Story**. One way to focus students when trying to understand the complex nature of genocide, is to find points in the historical narrative – the story – which reveal the complexity of the historical scenario but do not overwhelm the students. An example of the story nexus might be, 'Was

there an order given by Hitler to kill the Jews?' It focuses on whether there was clear intent, the documents that prove it (or fail to), the historical arguments, the possibilities, and allows questions around how much Hitler – and/or others – knew, let alone whether he was the principal architect of genocide. These in turn suggest questions about power and legal culpability. Such enquiry takes a big historical question. But on a more individual level, finding key moments in personal testimony also focuses the attention and creates a relationship between the learning and the subject – for example parents trying to decide whether to send their children into hiding, or the decision of families to split up to survive or to stay together only to be destroyed. The nexus in the story provides the point where questions and implications of both a specific and universal nature reside. The challenging questions that emerge from history provide the teacher as well as the student with key insights which can then be explored more fully together (Totten, 2004). Finding the dilemma in the history brings students deeper into the content and places them within the personal, ethical and political struggle.

5. **Empower Students with Their Own Voice**. There is general agreement that using student-centred teaching strategies directed towards personalized, deeper learning is the only effective way to teach about genocide (Facing History and Ourselves, 2010). There is wide acknowledgement that students need to identify closely with the history and to be able to form their own views and opinions. When learners in the classroom have context and are sufficiently empowered, the universal implications – that is, their own issues, challenges and interests – can best be explored. Using a range of creative responses – prose, poetry, art, drama, as well as digital media for presentations[2] – gives students their own voice in the clamour of thoughts that such histories surface. Without a mediated outlet for the learning experience, knowledge retention will be low, and ongoing engagement likely to be non-existent.

Cognitive links through empathy

A clear rationale needs to be established, one which states why students should learn this history, what the most important lessons are and what are appropriate and effective mediums of sources (USHMM, 2001). If one part of the learning experience is building knowledge, the other is making cognitive links to challenges and implications. Igniting the cognitive process needs a point of connection, one in which students begins to see themselves in relation to the history.

Survivors of the genocide make real connections. They are the would-be victims who made it through the hard link to the past. As the exception to the rule of genocide – total elimination – they have already demonstrated that the power of genocide can be overcome. They are ordinary people who experienced extraordinary things and whose very presence in the classroom demonstrates that survival is possible. The diminishing presence of survivors who are able to speak directly to students means there is an increasing reliance on audio-visual sources to deliver the personal story. Audio-visual testimony connects students through personal narrative to the people who suffered the consequences of the policies and the violence. The question is whether creating that connection creates emotional responses with no cognitive effects.

In a 2010 internal evaluation study conducted at the University of Southern California, the Shoah Foundation Institute asked students questions before and after they watched excerpts of video testimony. The study was a part of a usability trial to provide evaluation of the effectiveness of testimony in a new online learning platform during its prototype phase and to examine potential shifts in perception. Students watched excerpts of testimony on a contextualized and defined subject area. They were asked series of questions before and after the learning exercise. The idea behind the study was to examine how much cognitive impact the interaction with the life story had. In answer to the question 'the Holocaust is not relevant to my life,' there was a significant shift from the majority answering 'neutral' or 'moderately disagree' in the pre-exposure test to the majority answering 'strongly disagree' in the post-exposure survey. Over 90 per cent of students responded in the post-exposure questionnaire that their exposure to the life histories would 'influence how they perceive and treat others'.

This result seems to show that there is a link between empathy and cognitive learning. Students engaged with the life story and made cognitive links to their own attitudes and behaviours. It is essential if students are to change their perception and behaviour that they own the change process. They need to recognize that they are implicated in the implications. Involvement in the life and experience of the subjects of genocide – and their struggle to live through and live after genocide – develops a positive empathy, which does not drown out cognitive learning through overwhelming emotions. In fact there may be an argument that learning through history could be a barrier to the cognitive processes that leads to changed attitudes and behaviours. Historical enquiry provides a knowledge base about the unique aspects of genocide. But it is also safe, in that it does not demand a response. Personal stories are not safe, because the testimony implicitly asks the student, what if this happened to *you*? That demands a response, and that is universal.

Any exploration of the unique and universal aspects of genocide has to be interdisciplinary. *Where* we teach in the curriculum to a large degree conditions *what* we teach. The concern of those who propose an approach to teaching the Holocaust more orientated towards uniqueness is in deciding the point at which the historical substance of the Holocaust is diminished by using it to teach other disciplines (Goldenberg et al., 2007). In her survey of teachers in the United Kindgom, Russell found that the majority of teachers interviewed teach the Holocaust with a citizenship approach, focusing on values and morals, as opposed to straight history (Russell, 2006). The Holocaust is without doubt a question of moral issues, and it cannot be divorced from history. We have to manage both realities.

Lessons or implications?

Often the approach of teachers is rooted in their own moral concerns in pursuit of so-called lessons to be learned. Teaching must address social implications; but it is important not to structure teaching with the sole purpose of being the 'servant of moral instruction or social engineering' (Russell, 2006, 37). But that does not take away from the fact that teaching and learning about genocide does have the overall purpose of reducing its incidence. It is morally repugnant to think that one would teach about it without prevention being at the heart of the enquiry. Consider if medical students studied the pathology of diseases but never applied their knowledge to heal, how far would medicine have advanced over the ages if nothing was applied? Or imagine if environmental studies students never applied their knowledge to climate change. Learning is often – if not always – about applying the knowledge one obtains in different ways. However divorced school education appears to be from 'real life' at any time, it is in fact designed as a toolkit of basic skills and knowledge to equip students for living in the adult world on many levels. The same applies to learning about genocide. To remain in awe of the event, to know the historical detail and to refuse to engage with it, is both wilfully to turn our back on the suffering and degradation and by yet another kind of indifference to do nothing to avert the possibility of a repetition (Gregory, 2000b, 50).

But among the many disciplines in school education, it is the subject of history – and almost exclusively history – which can legitimately avoid being an applied subject. How do you apply knowledge about something past? Active pursuit of historical knowledge contains all the implications at the heart of enquiry. We do know that events that occurred in the past are highly instructive in the present. That is how societies learn. There is an organic process by which our collective action in the past informs our collective conscience in the present. Take learning about the abolition of slavery as an example. People no longer keep slaves in Western societies because action has been taken; implemented legislation forms the pattern of behaviour today. That in turn informs our value as individuals and as societies. Learning about how those values and societal norms emerged conditions human behaviours and expectations. The problem we encounter is what happens when events in the past, such as genocide, question our current social behaviours, or even the nature of society itself, with no apparent societal norms, laws or solutions. We know that events associated with genocide can happen in any society at any time. That is what makes the history of modern genocide so compelling, so difficult to understand, so sensitive to teach and absolutely imperative to apply.

When teachers bring the subject of genocide into the classroom, it is important to move beyond the polarized teaching methodologies represented by the unique and universal aspects of genocide. Both extremes create barriers to students' responses. And it is their responses that make the instruction effective. There is nothing exclusively unique about the incidence of genocide. Regrettably it happens all the time. There is also no single set of universal themes or lessons which apply to all cases all of the time. Genocide is not sacred; it is profane. Genocide is not easily contained; it disturbs who we are, what we believe, how we behave. But that does not mean it cannot be studied and understood. Genocide needs to be studied one day at a time, one story at a time, and its causes and consequences thought about deeply in a world in which genocide persists. To do this, students need to feel respected, empowered, drawn into the implications and responsible for their own responses.

This does not mean that students are trained to be political activists, anymore than teaching environmental issues involves membership in Greenpeace. But the knowledge developed in the classroom positions students in relation to similar human experience. Their knowledge may have a direct or indirect impact on how future events unfold. By empowering them with knowledge, engaging them through empathy and developing their critical and cognitive skills, students are provided with the tools to make their own decisions.

No one genocide is unique. All genocides have their unique aspects. All genocides have universal implications, and those implications are manifest and many. The key is to ask whether we are providing our students with the analytic and critical skills to understand themselves in relation to the past and to understand the past in their present.

Suggested questions

- To what extent do historical events have implications for the present?
- What is the educational purpose of learning about the history of genocides?
- Can individuals learn anything from the behaviour of societies?

Further reading

Facing History and Ourselves (2004), *Crimes Against Humanity and Civilization: The Genocide of the Armenians*. Brookline, MA: Facing History and Ourselves Foundation.

Strom, A. (2008), *Totally Unofficial: Raphael Lemkin and the Genocide Convention*. Brookline, MA: Facing History and Ourselves Foundation.

Totten, S. (2008), *Century of Genocide: Critical Essays and Eyewitness Accounts*. London: Routledge.

References

Facing History and Ourselves (2010), 'Teaching strategies', www.facinghistory.org/teaching-strategies (accessed 15 September 2010).

Goldenberg, M., and Millen, R. L. (eds) (2007), *Testimony, Tensions and Tikkun: Teaching the Holocaust in Colleges and Universities*. Seattle: University of Washington Press.

Gregory, I. (2000a), 'The Holocaust: Some reflections and issues', in I. Davies (ed.), *Teaching the Holocaust: Educational Dimensions, Principles and Practice*. London: Continuum, pp. 37–48.

—(2000b), 'Teaching about the Holocaust: Perplexities, issues and suggestions', in I. Davies (ed.), *Teaching the Holocaust: Educational Dimensions, Principles and Practice*. London: Continuum, pp. 49–60.

The Holocaust Centre (2004), *The Holocaust and Genocide: How Did It Happen?* London: Hodder Murray.

Russell, L. (2006), *Teaching the Holocaust in School History: Teachers or Preachers?* London: Continuum.

Strom, A. (2008), *Totally Unofficial: Raphael Lemkin and the Genocide Convention*, Brookline, MA: Facing History and Ourselves Foundation.

Totten, S. (ed.) (2004), *Teaching About Genocide: Issues, Approaches, and Resources*, Greenwich, CT: Information Age.

USHMM (2001), *Teaching About the Holocaust: A Resource Book for Educators*, Washington: United States Holocaust Memorial Museum.

Notes

1 Yehuda Bauer first stated that the Holocaust was not unique but was unprecedented in several speeches. Bauer had originally argued for the uniqueness of the Holocaust. His move to describe it as unprecedented was based on the fact that the scale, method and intent were unprecedented in history, but nevertheless they were not qualitatively unique, before or since.

2 University of Southern California Shoah Foundation Institute has developed an online resource, IWitness, where students can create their own online class work in response to the use of video testimony. This has been created specifically to bring together digital literacy, online work and assessment and genocide studies.

10 Teaching About Genocide

Ian Davies

This chapter is an overview of some of the issues that are important for educators who engage in teaching about genocides; contested issues are discussed and some practical ways forward are proposed. All this is done with a good deal of tentativeness and uncertainty.

In 1946, following work by Raphael Lemkin, Vespasian Pella, Henri Donnedieu de Vabres and others, the UN General Assembly affirmed that genocide was a crime under international law and the UN's Convention on the Prevention and Punishment of Genocide provided a legal definition (see previous chapter).

The weight of international law and associated moral condemnation are extremely important. And yet, the legal framework is not without controversy. Some, without necessarily going so far as to dispute the need for such a law, question its effectiveness. The Iraqi action against the Kurds (1988), the terrible events in Rwanda (1994) and the crimes in the former Yugoslavia (1990s) reveal that genocide is not to be prevented solely by legal statements of the international community. There are also questions about the details of what has been agreed. The question of what sort of group if acted against in particular ways would be considered as being subjected to genocide is not always easy to answer.

Further, the phrases 'intent to destroy' and 'in whole or in part', are seen by some as allowing for a level of disputation which is inappropriate. Perhaps most fundamentally there are a significant number of commentators who object to what has occurred when legislators have been felt to take the power and authority that they see as belonging to others. In a very challenging argument arising from several national cases and the European Parliament's resolutions in 2007 against racism, xenophobia and Holocaust denial (European Parliament, 2007). Cajani (2007) suggests that

> [a]lthough it is borne out of the necessary and just fight against racism and xenophobia, it affects – via a series of conceptual shifts – issues which are solely those concerned with historical research. On the contrary, it is necessary for historians and politics to remain autonomous, each in his own domain. Politics can decide which political use of history best serves its own ends, by instituting official memorials, for example; but it must not interfere – with the aid of judicial powers – in the work of historians. (Cajani, 2007, 18)

Such matters are not easy to resolve. The challenge for educators is to make sense of such matters and to act appropriately. Below, three areas are considered which are relevant to the work of educators: the aims of teaching about genocide, representations of genocide and teaching and learning about genocide.

The aims of teaching about genocide

It is necessary to develop a clear rationale for the teaching of genocide. This seeming truism is given cautiously as there are many sensitive issues that need very careful handling. For example, when *Teaching the Holocaust* was published (Davies, 2000), there was a need to consider whether the Holocaust should ever be something that can be 'taught' rather than being something over which there is a struggle to learn from. And yet, without some clarity about *what* and *how* to teach, it is possible that unanticipated and unwelcome practices will emerge. Broadly, when teaching about genocide, it will be helpful to aim for clearer understanding, the further development of humanistic dispositions and an enhanced range of skills that will allow for engagement. Genocide is in some ways not 'understandable' but it is necessary to argue against what could be seen as a hopeless position. Fackenheim (1978, 93) has, in my view, wrongly suggested that 'despite all the necessary attempts, to comprehend it, the Nazi system in the end exceeds all comprehension. One cannot comprehend but only confront and object'. Teachers have a responsibility not to provide all the answers and must avoid, in effect, declaring by use of logical explanation that genocide is somehow an almost inevitable part of human experience. But we do have to *know* and that requires a certain type and level of understanding about concepts, possible causation and forms of response (including emotional, psychological, political and so on). In terms of dispositions there is a necessary commitment to justice that is part of all teachers' responsibilities. Teaching is not a purely technical matter or an exclusively intellectual process. The intellect and the emotions are overlapping areas and an unemotional response to tragedy is simply wrong. But learners who are significantly upset simply cannot think, and if they reach that position, it is hard to focus on anything, including complex questions about what is right, what is wrong and what could have and should now be done. Familiarity with the notion of justice and how different formulations of it can lead to improvements in the human condition is useful (Sandel, 2009). Finally, there are skills of analysis and action which are normally part of many national curricula and the already stated aims of education systems. It is important for young people to know how in connection with their knowledge, understanding and dispositions they can persuade, organize and reflect on what could and should be done.

Representations of genocide

Broadly, there are two overlapping aspects to issues about representation: substantive questions of what genocide is or stands for and, questions of the form in which genocide can be shown. In relation to substantive issues it is important to be aware of who is involved and how that characterization is used. It has been said, 'Every Jew, after Auschwitz, knows that in some sense he is a survivor, an accidental remnant, and he shares that knowledge with every member of his people' (Sacks, 1995, 241). This is then a close step to making very particular links with one community and also connecting across several academic and political fields and across time. Genocide does not, of course, just affect Jews, Bosnians, Rwandans or any other specific group. It should also be remembered that inhabitants of individual countries will be variously affected and, obviously, have very different experiences as victims or perpetrators which at times occur in contexts that are variously interpreted (genocides in, e.g., Biafra 1966–7, East Timor 1975–99, Kosova 1999 are illustrative of some of these contested complexities). The decision to focus on one group or another has consequences for the meaning that is being ascribed to the study. This question of what genocide is 'about' goes to the heart of some very challenging issues. The fact that the Holocaust was not widely studied in the immediate aftermath of World War II and yet now receives greater attention (including the development of an annual commemorative day) is not necessarily something about which we should feel entirely comfortable. The use of a specific genocide as an example of discrimination with the perhaps associated perception that all acts of discrimination are linked on some sort of ladder that builds inexorably to genocide is reflective of a position in which events and issues are being seen as being *for* something and not only as significant in themselves. Lipstadt's position (1995) on the inappropriate elision of acts of discrimination (such as contemporary racism in America) with genocides needs to be considered carefully in order to avoid incorrect representations.

The issue of the form in which it is acceptable to represent genocide is similarly complex. Adorno's often quoted phrase 'no poetry after Auschwitz' shows the complexities of dealing with the ways in which it is possible to remember terrible events. The issue is thrown into sharper relief by the 1998 fictional film *Life is Beautiful*, which is variously described and has been referred to by some as a comedy. Whether or not such material should be used by teachers is hugely problematic but perhaps no more so than the standard use of the non-fictional diary of Anne Frank, which may be more about adolescence than about the Holocaust. The question of what genocide 'is' is a very significant challenge for teachers and learners.

Teaching and learning about genocide

As explained above, it is necessary to avoid an approach to teaching about genocide that seems to suggest a mechanistic, dehumanized set of 'techniques' that are directed towards a formulaic set of outcomes. What follows is necessarily loosely formulated in order to make clear that action should be considered dynamically and can be taken professionally. Preferences that individuals hold about the best ways ahead should not be formulated in inappropriately confident – or dogmatic – claims that a complete moral or pedagogical theory is in place or that one can always identify what specific action must occur in order to promote learning; the following should be seen as broad guidelines.

- Need for accuracy

Knowledge and understanding are elusive. Questions of what to include in any study of genocide brings issues of reasons why other events and issues have been excluded. Bias by inclusion is as problematic as bias by omission. But accuracy is easier to argue for. Simply, any teacher who educates about genocide must get the facts right. Not to do so is to abdicate responsibility to oneself and others. Information matters and helps us to approach the truth. Of course, this should not be interpreted as a call for simplistic assertions. There will always be a need, for example, to explore more deeply issues emerging from, for example, the 2008 Prague Declaration on European Conscience and Communism (which insisted on appropriate consideration of Soviet-led, as well as other, genocides), to accept the reality of what happened and to ask why particular facts are being highlighted and what interpretations are being developed in relation to them.

- Language

The way in which teachers and learners communicate about genocide is very important. The very word 'Holocaust', which literally means 'burnt offering', is controversial (with some preferring 'Shoah'), seeming to imply an acceptance of injustice by victims and to others to seem to have the potential to orient characterizations of particular contexts as 'belonging' more to one group than another. The very labelling of an event (as seen in the discussion about the action of members of the European Parliament and historians) is challenging. Would it help for teachers to introduce discussions of the slave trade, which was abolished in the British Empire in 1807 and is widely taught in English classrooms as genocide? There are some deliberate and worrying attempts, in Texas for example, to reposition slavery itself as something not necessarily connected with genocide at all by describing it as the 'Atlantic triangular trade' (McGreal, 2010).

There are many complex matters in relation to the use of language that cannot be reduced to a simple formula but the answer adopted by Leavis and Thompson – 'to discriminate and to resist' (Leavis and Thompson, 1942, 3) – is very important. It is probably necessary to interpret the guidance of the National Association for the Teaching of English – to allow 'as many voices as possible into the classroom.' (NATE 1988, 20) – with some caution. The interpretations that are seen as having some legitimacy are those that emerge from careful and proper academic consideration, a commitment to justice and the recognition of democratic process. As such, a useful classroom exercise could be to examine the language in, for example, the 1942 government memorandum 'Secret Reich Business' (McGuinn, 2002):

> Since December 1941, ninety-seven thousand have been processed by the three vehicles in service, with no major incidents. In the light of observations made so far, however, the following technical changes are needed.

It would also be useful to consider the ways in which the phrase 'ethnic cleansing' has been used. A 1993 UN Commission defined this as, 'the planned deliberate removal from a specific territory, persons of a particular ethnic group, by force or intimidation, in order to render that area ethnically homogenous'. Some will find the almost casual way in which 'ethnic cleansing' has been used as a label on occasions in the media to be disturbing. The seemingly easy distinctions that are made between 'removal' and killing, the extent to which any area could ever be 'ethnically homogeneous' and the use of the word 'cleansing' (with its closeness in sound and, normally positive, meaning of 'cleanliness') is, at the very least, potentially very worrying. The ways in which language may be used for evil purposes needs to be examined and (while making efforts to *avoid* thinking of simple ladders of discrimination which must inevitably lead to genocide) to consider the nature of everyday discourse in schools, the language and literature that are studied and the goals that are declared.

- ● Teaching controversial issues: Morality and genocide

Throughout the discussions referred to above is the fundamental issue of what sort of moral guidance may be given. Working from the position that teachers do not intend to and could not, in the face of the very many influences that act upon learners, indoctrinate students, it is necessary not to attempt to avoid bias but to find ways of dealing with it. Excellent guidance on how to deal with controversial material exists (e.g., Stradling's 1984 work was largely incorporated into the 1998 Crick report; and guidance exists for teachers of specific subjects, e.g., for history, see Historical Association, 2007). Care, however, needs to be taken in relation to several key points. The nature of what makes the issue controversial should be made clear. In many ways teaching about genocide is not at all controversial; it is wrong and there is no defence for it. In some cases what feels like controversy is actually a problem with the use of sensitive material (e.g., what sort of images should be shown to students? should the subject be treated academically?). Decisions made in relation to these matters can only be taken in context; in other words, existing professional practice should be adhered to as we make judgments about what is appropriate for the age and ability and previous experience of learners, the school ethos and so on. More fundamentally, teachers should operate with understanding of their fundamental principles. This does not mean that teachers will know all the answers but it does mean that they have a developed position in relation to justice. Sandel (2009) has discussed, in a very valuable way, the competing claims of different models of justice. The utilitarianism of Bentham, the process based models of Kant and Rawls and the virtue models of those who promote a particular version of the good society in practical circumstances probably need to be used in professional contexts in a blended, dynamic fashion. It is probably of little use to expect theory always to fit with the complex realities of a teacher's world. But once a teacher has thought through her own position about justice and knows which of the models presented by Sandel she finds most convincing, classroom practice will be more easily and effectively and appropriately established.

- School subjects

Teaching about genocide is included in a variety of school subjects but perhaps most obviously and frequently in history education. This historical connection is perhaps present insofar as societies are often unaware of genocide having taken place – either deliberately or otherwise – until it is in the past. History education rests fundamentally on a conceptual approach that develops understanding of substantive and procedural matters. Substantive concepts are those which are often related fairly directly to specific historical events. Revolution, for example, is often targeted by teachers who then use the examples of the French, Russian or American revolutions to make their points. Genocide is perhaps the concept that, as above, not without controversy, may lead to more specific case study work of the unique but nevertheless generally illuminating contexts of transatlantic slavery, Darfur, events in Armenia and so on. The procedural concepts are brought into focus with reflections on how historians work. If learners understand the past and the way the past is studied and created by historians, then there are opportunities to understand the nature of what is being studied and the ways in which these matters are constructed. Should those with spurious political motives decide to present unacceptable versions of the past, those who have had experience of this approach to learning history will be better able to defend what matters. More specifically, one of the procedural concepts that is relevant here is that of significance. If young people are able to understand the significance of genocide, then much can be achieved. This means that they need to consider the following:

1. Importance – how important was the event or issue judged to be by people at the time?
2. Profundity – how deeply were people's lives affected?

3. Quantity – how many lives were affected?
4. Durability – for how long have people's lives been affected?
5. Relevance – in terms of the increased understanding of present life. (Partington, 1980, 112–16)

These modes of enquiry can allow for people to be more informed and to be equipped to think more democratically about genocide.

Of course, other school curricular areas have their part to play. The relevance of English has been in part referred to above when considering the role of language and the use of literature, such as Anne Frank's diary. Religious education is obviously of crucial importance as it is vital to avoid stereotypes reflecting diversity and show that questions of genocide are related to living religions and ethnic diversity and not museum pieces. Geography is also of great importance to the understanding of how and why genocide occurs. This is not to suggest that engagement with these school subjects leads simply to knowledge about the causes and necessary responses to tragedy. Cooper's (2008) analysis, for example, in which there is an argument that specific contexts lead to action emerging from patriarchy will be persuasive to some and not others.

- Going beyond the classroom

It is important to consider how to ensure active engagement. It is often useful to reflect on how genocide is considered in places other than one's local or national context, whether (and, if so, how) visits can be made to memorial sites and whether witnesses and others can be invited into schools. Of course all of these approaches can take place with the use of new media within the classroom but, if it is possible to do so, there would be educational benefits in looking beyond teaching about genocide as something that can be done exclusively from one's own desk. It is an issue that affects society today and to see at least a part of that reality means that an effort should be made to go beyond the textbook.

Rathenow (2000) has discussed the ways in which the Holocaust has been characterized in Germany. In the East the socialist German Democratic Republic portrayed the events as something of which the workers were innocent. The communists were liberators in the struggle to achieve freedom. In the West the Federal Republic of Germany saw the problem as being one of Nazism; the German people were not to blame. All this of course was seen as far too simplistic a view of what had actually happened long before Goldhagen (1996) raised questions about individual responsibility and complicity. The historiography of genocide can take place by establishing links with international organizations and individuals. Visiting memorial sites is a discomfiting experience. Sensitive preparation is needed so that those who visit do not see it as a narrow worksheet-filled exercise, or as a ritual in which acts are expected and performed. Rather it is an opportunity to put one's knowledge and understanding into context, to see the reality of what happened (thus knowing that denial is not an option) and to experience that leap of imagination (one cannot say empathy in such circumstances) through which a more fundamental aspect of learning is developed. While great care must be taken in the selection of those chosen to talk with students and while many precautions must be taken so that learning occurs, the evidence provided by survivors and witnesses is essential.

Conclusion

Teachers and learners need to think about matters carefully and consider teaching approaches that lead to clearer understanding. Good educational work will be in place when there is a commitment to accuracy through a determination to enhance understanding of substantive and procedural concepts that are applied in context so that notions of victimhood and inevitability are not condoned. It is imperative that genocide is seen as something that we can understand and that requires a human response. It is something which individuals and societies are capable of and which must be faced squarely and resisted. As such it is something for which everyone must take responsibility in the sense of what we do and what we make of the history that we have. Questions need to be raised about contemporary as well as future and past societies. In short, it is necessary that it is tackled directly and explicitly.

Suggested questions

- Who should be entrusted with the responsibility of characterizing events as constituting genocide: professional historians, politicians, others?
- What reliance can be placed on what could broadly be described as emotional and/or cognitive matters? Should teachers look for emotional as well as cognitive responses? Does your answer include a consideration of whether assessment should take place? If so, how should it be done?
- What criteria could and should teachers and learners use when choosing *specific* content?

There is a large amount of web-based material. 'Teachers' TV' offers useful discussions, illustrations of practice and survivor testimonies; for example, www.teachers.tv/videos/55471 (accessed 18 May 2010).

Further reading

- Sandel, M. (2009), *Justice: What's the Right Thing to Do?* London: Allen Lane.
- Totten, S. (ed.) (2004), *Teaching About Genocide.* Greenwich, CT: Information Age.

References

Cajani, L. (2007), 'Political constraints on historical research: A recent European case', in E. Näsmän, A. Navarro, L. Cajani, I. Davies and M. Fülöp (eds), *Controversial Issues in Research.* London: Cice.

Cooper, A. D. (2008), *The Geography of Genocide.* Lanham, MD: University Press of America.

Crick Report (1998), *Education for Citizenship and the Teaching of Democracy in Schools.* London: DfEE/QCA.

Davies, I. (ed.) (2000), *Teaching the Holocaust: Educational Dimensions, Principles and Practice.* London: Continuum.

European Parliament (2007), www.europarl.europa.eu/meetdocs/2004_2009/organes/libe/libe_20070319_150_hearing.htm# (accessed 8 September 2010).

Fackenheim, E. (1978), *The Jewish Return into History: Reflections in the Age of Auschwitz and a New Jerusalem.* New York: Schocken Books.

Goldhagen, D. J. (1996), *Hitler's Willing Executioners: Ordinary Germans and the Holocaust.* London: Little, Brown and Company.

Historical Association (2007), *T.E.A.C.H: Teaching Emotional and Controversial History.* London: Historical Association.

Leavis, F. R., and Thompson, D. (1942), *Culture and Environment*. London: Chatto and Windus.

Levenson, E. (2009), 'A Shame on all humanity', *Guardian*, 31 March, www.guardian.co.uk/education/2009/mar/31/rwanda-genocide (accessed 9 September 2010).

Lipstadt, D. (1995), 'Not facing history', *New Republic* , 6 March.

McGreal, C. (2010), 'Texas schools board rewrites US history with lessons promoting God and guns', *Guardian*, 17 May, www.guardian.co.uk/world/2010/may/16/texas-schools-rewrites-us-history (accessed 25 January 2011).

McGuinn, N. (2000), 'Teaching the Holocaust through English', in I. Davies (ed.), *Teaching the Holocaust*. London: Continuum.

National Association for the Teaching of English (NATE) Language and Gender Committee (1988), *Gender Issues in English Coursewor*. Sheffield: NATE.

Partington, G. (1980), *The Idea of an Historical Education*. Slough: NFER.

Rathenow, H. F. (2000), 'How is the Holocaust taught in Germany,' in I. Davies (ed.), *Teaching the Holocaust*. London: Continuum.

Sacks, J. (1995), *Faith in the Future: The Ecology of Hope and the Restoration of Family Community and Faith*. Macon, GA: Mercer University Press.

Sandel, M. (2009), *Justice: What's the Right Thing to Do?* London: Allen Lane.

Stradling, R. (1984), *Teaching Controversial Issues*. London: Edward Arnold.

11 Pedagogical Issues in Teaching the Holocaust

Henry Maitles and Paula Cowan

Sixty-five years after the murder of more than 11 million people, the Holocaust is still very much an issue and at the fore in human memory. Thousands of books have been written on the experiences of the Holocaust, many of them from eyewitnesses and victims, and there has been an increasing amount of teaching about the Holocaust, with its compulsory inclusion in syllabuses in, for example, Belgium, England and parts of Germany and its official encouragement in many other countries, such as the Netherlands, France, Australia and some states in the United States.

Much of the Holocaust literature is moving and important. There had, of course, been barbaric massacres and mistreatments of peoples prior to the 1940s, but the Holocaust was the first time that the advanced technology of a major world power had been unleashed on racial groups – extermination by assembly line as twentieth-century industrial methods responded to unparalleled racial hatred. As Primo Levi put it:

> . . . notwithstanding the horrors of Hiroshima and Nagasaki, the shame of the Gulags, the useless and bloody Vietnam war, the Cambodian self-genocide, the desaparecidos of Argentina, and the many atrocious and stupid wars we have seen since, the Nazi concentration camp system

still remains a unicum, both in its extent and quality . . . never were so many human lives extinguished in so short a time, and with so lucid a combination of technological ingenuity, fanaticism and cruelty. (Levi, 1988, 9–10)

The fanaticism that Levi talks of here is hard to comprehend. The single-mindedness of the attempts to exterminate Jews often went beyond the actual needs of the war effort. For example, Gilbert (1986) points out that there were complaints from some factory owners that the constant changing of Jewish personnel made production for the war effort more difficult and that on the very day of the invasion of Normandy (6 June 1944), as the Red Army was about to renew its offensive in the east, the main order from German High Command was to round up 1,750 Jews from Corfu and deport them to Auschwitz.

The value of Holocaust education

There is a wide range of research that supports the positive contribution of Holocaust education to developing students' understanding of aspects of citizenship in developing their awareness of human rights issues and genocides, the concepts of stereotyping and scapegoating and general political literacy, such as the exercise of power in local, national and global contexts (Brown and Davies, 1998; Russell, 2006; Cowan and Maitles, 2007). The importance of knowledge cannot be underestimated, but it is only one side to citizenship; behaviour and action are another (Kratsborn et al., 2008). The European Union Agency for Fundamental Rights advocates that Holocaust education 'should encourage action against discrimination, racism and antisemitism' (FRA, 2010, 16). One of the lessons of the Holocaust, Bauman (1989) claims, is that evil 'can be resisted' as human beings have a choice, and during the Holocaust, some people exerted that choice by choosing 'moral duty' over 'self–preservation'. Landau (1989) asserts that Holocaust teaching 'perhaps more effectively than any other subject, has the power to sensitise them [pupils] to the dangers of indifference, intolerance, racism and the dehumanisation of others'.

Fried's survey of Swedish teachers' attitudes related to Holocaust teaching revealed that most teachers in Sweden used the Holocaust as a tool for discussions on broader ethical and moral issues and that more than 80 per cent considered that its teaching 'aroused more moral and ethical question than other areas' (Fried, 2009, 26). One history teacher from England who had participated in a teacher-only visit in 2009 stated that learning about Auschwitz could contribute to class projects on conflict resolution and diversity (TES, 2009). This is further backed up by large-scale survey evidence in England (HEDP, 2010).

Indeed, in an era of global discourse, Holocaust education has an impact beyond any national boundaries, although, as researchers in the field (von Borries, 2003; Cowan and Maitles, 2010) point out, there are peculiarities of each country's relationship to the events of the Holocaust that can make it difficult to transpose education needs in this area from one country to another. Further, in addition to each country's participation in World War II, Gundare and Batelaan (2003) consider that the delivery of Holocaust education varies according to the country's history of anti-Semitism. For example, although Oskar Schindler is widely recognized as a hero for saving more than a thousand Jews, Czechs who were affected by the German occupation of Czechoslovakia may view him as an enemy, as his enamel factory was on their land in the Sudetenland (now part of the Czech Republic). It is also likely that the Holocaust will have a different meaning for countries which have experienced genocide and ethnic cleansing since 1945, such as Kosovo (1999) and Bosnia (1995).

Three initiatives which have significantly impacted on Holocaust education in the United Kindgom are the Lessons from Auschwitz Project since 1997 (discussed in Chapter 12), the introduction of a national Holocaust Memorial Day (HMD) (since 2001) and the development of Citizenship Education (since 2002). HMD has led to the production of primary and secondary school and community resources using Holocaust survivor testimonies (among survivors of other genocides) and local authorities and schools commemorating HMD. Education for Citizenship has led to Holocaust teaching by providing a suitable context for learning in many key areas, such as human rights, the need for mutual respect, tolerance and understanding of a diverse and multicultural, multi-ethnic Britain. Cowan and Maitles's case study of predominantly white students in primary 7 (aged about 11 or 12 years, in their last year of primary school) showed an increase in students' positive attitudes to ethnic minorities, such as Gypsies and Muslims, and to other disadvantaged groups after learning about the Holocaust (Cowan and Maitles, 2007). Developing this into a longitudinal study, these students who had studied the Holocaust indicated that they had more positive values and attitudes one year later (in the first year of secondary) than their peers who had not studied the Holocaust in primary school. However it also showed that even after learning about the Holocaust, a small number of students considered there were 'too many Jews' in the United Kindgom.

Debates and difficulties

Basic knowledge of the Jewish faith and Jewish culture is key to understanding the Holocaust (Short, 2003). The reason for this is that during a study of the Holocaust, students may well ask, 'Who are the Jews'? The answer is complicated by the fact that while Jews belong to a particular faith, in the context of the Holocaust where the genocide of the Jews was a result of Nazi racist ideology and not simply religious persecution, both racial and the religious definitions require to be explained. Not all schools will teach Judaism as a world religion. Where Judaism is not taught as a separate topic, teachers who teach the Holocaust should consider how they can contribute to their students' concept of Jews and perhaps more importantly, how they can address any misconceptions that their students may have.

Holocaust education is part of the English National Curriculum in History at Key Stage 3 (12–14 years), and there are current debates as to its effectiveness. In particular, Russell (2006) suggests that history teachers are inconsistent in their methodologies; some teach it as history while others focus on the social and moral perspectives without applying historical inquiry. Linked in with this is the question of how to introduce anti-Semitism. Schweber (2004) found that teaching about the Holocaust emphasizes racism rather than anti-Semitism. Schweber found that in order to make Jewish people during the Holocaust seem normal to students, the history of anti-Semitism was overlooked or bypassed by teachers. While detailed information of the history of anti-Semitism is not appropriate for primary students, its meaning and some awareness of the historical context of European anti-Semitism might address students' lack of understanding of or difficulty in understanding contemporary anti-Semitism. This is of particular relevance to students, as one of the conclusions of the report of the 2006 All-Party Parliamentary Inquiry into Antisemitism in the United Kindgom was that there is a new awareness of the need to explain to school students the history of anti-Semitism. This is not to say that an understanding of anti-Semitism is an easy thing to develop. However, at the very least, it seems reasonable to expect students who hear or see the word *anti-Semitism* on TV or on the World Wide Web to know what it means if they have been learning about the Holocaust.

Linked to this are teachers' worries about their skills to handle open-ended discussions which they might not be able to control or direct. For example, there has been a report of one school in England whose history department 'avoided selecting the Holocaust as a topic for GCSE coursework for fear of confronting anti-Semitic sentiment and Holocaust denial among some Muslim pupils' (Historical Association, 2007, 15). There are also structural constraints in schools from the lack of tradition in discussion to the physical layout of classrooms. And there are worries about what parents might think about controversial discussion and the reaction of the mass media and politicians to what might be perceived as influencing students one way or another.

A further issue in primary schools is a perceived lack of teacher subject knowledge (Historical Association, 2007). The key findings of a study that involved more than 2,000 secondary teachers in England indicated that while teachers perceived themselves to be 'knowledgeable' about the Holocaust, responses to knowledge-based questions revealed 'important gaps in historical understanding' (HEDP, 2009, 6). This led to the development of a Continued Professional Development Programme in Holocaust education for secondary teachers, which comprises a two day workshop presented by the Holocaust Education Development Programme (HEDP).

Paradoxically, in secondary schools a study of political consciousness in 28 European countries (Torney-Purta et al., 2001) found that in many countries, teachers are afraid to tackle controversial issues because, almost by definition, the discussion becomes multidisciplinary, and they are uncomfortable in that zone. However, in analyzing how high school students understood the place of classroom discussion, Hahn

(1998) found that students in the Netherlands did not try to persuade each other, even when discussing highly controversial issues that they felt strongly about, whereas in German and US state schools and English private schools there was strong argument and persuasion. Interestingly, she found that there was virtually no discussion on political issues in the state sector in England even in social science classes, where she gathered that 'the primary purpose was to prepare for examinations'.

The role of the teacher in this is crucial. As Agostinone-Wilson (2005) and Ashton and Watson (1998) suggest, the teacher needs to be confident enough and have the honesty to suggest to students that they are not just independent observers but have a point of view, which also can and should be challenged. While this is an area of some discussion in Britain, Wrigley (2003) points out that in Germany, teachers are encouraged to allow discussion around controversial issues, present a wide range of views and be open about their own standpoint while allowing for all views to be challenged. Indeed, it is crucial, according to Ashton and Watson (1998), that teachers understand their proactive role where necessary, otherwise backward ideas can dominate the discussion. Students have little problem with this and are not as dogmatic as adults when it comes to changing attitudes and political understanding.

Another difficulty is that teaching areas such as the Holocaust, genocide and the abuse of children's rights is upsetting for many students. It is a matter of debate as to whether these areas can effectively be taught to students without some level of distress. Role play can be used to develop empathy by, for example, giving students a choice of scenarios or allowing them to devise their own scenario where they can apply what they have learned about racist Nazi policy. One common example used in primary schools is when students role-play a scenario where an employer interviews an applicant with the required skills and experience but does not give him the job because he is Jewish. This example arouses emotions in the students and can develop their empathy for victims of prejudice in an appropriate way. The most famous and controversial simulation is that of Jane Elliott. In response to the assassination of Martin Luther King Jr. (now over 40 years ago), Elliott devised the controversial and startling 'Blue Eyes/Brown Eyes' exercise (Peters, 1987). This famous exercise labelled participants as inferior or superior based solely upon the colour of their eyes and exposed them to the experience of being a minority. It was designed to show the impact of discrimination on both victims and bystanders. It was controversial at the time and is still discussed today. While it is not necessary to link the Elliott experiment to genocide per se, it is clearly possible to link the two and try to suggest the ultimate horrors that can develop from discrimination. It is still in use and has been the subject of much debate, as has been the Gestapo Holocaust simulation, which tries to show what happened during the Holocaust by involving the players in life and death decisions, which most do not 'survive' (Narvaez, 1998; Elliott, 2009).

The critique is that simulation debases the memory of the Holocaust and does not reflect what really went on. For example, an eighth-grade teacher in the United States called upon his colleagues to be involved in the experiment on discrimination as 'a day of sheer pleasure for the staff being themselves as Nazi officers and becoming Adolfs . . . because staff need the stress relief and entertainment' (Elliott, 2009). Critiques of such simulations come from individuals and organizations heavily committed to Holocaust education. Dawidowicz (1990) and Totten (2002), for example, argue that they reflect poor pedagogy and oversimplify Holocaust history. Totten is particularly critical and argues that

> [f]or students to walk away thinking that they have either experienced what a victim went through or have a greater understanding of what the victims suffered is shocking in its naivety. Even more galling is for teachers to think that they have provided their students with a true sense of what the victims lived through – and/or to think they have at least approximated the horror and terror the victims experienced. (Totten, 2002, 122)

The Anti-Defamation League in the United States further claims that simulations can trivialize the experience, stereotype group behaviour, distort historical reality, reinforce negative views, impede critical analysis and disconnect the Holocaust from its historical context. It cites one simulation (in Florida) where children were very distressed and crying; one child reported that 'the only thing I found out today is that I don't want to be Jewish'. In other words, this approach can have exactly the opposite impact than teachers want. Further, there is a fear of psychological scarring shown by the blue eyes/brown eyes children experiencing stress and disengagement for a period afterwards. Nonetheless, there are those who argue that using simulation is an issue of pedagogy and can encourage students to consider the Holocaust from the perspectives of bystanders, victims and perpetrators (Drake, 2008; Schweber, 2004). Jane Elliott, an advocate of such simulations, expresses caution. She argues that it needs experienced teachers, extensive debriefing, experienced facilitators and a strong rapport between students and teachers for it to work (Drake, 2008).

Holocaust literature is commonly used in schools to engage students, and there is a wide range of material available across the primary and secondary sectors. While Holocaust fiction can be beneficial to a young person's understanding of the Holocaust and of Holocaust-related issues and, in particular, can motivate student interest in this area, teachers require to be mindful that they are 'made up' stories and, as such, are likely, in the interests of a good story, to contain historical inaccuracies. Teachers cannot assume that every Holocaust fictional publication can potentially aid their students' understanding of this subject, as such literature may provide young people with incorrect information which can lead students to forming misconceptions of the Holocaust and of genocide. Kokkola (2003) emphasizes the ethical considerations that such writers should adopt, but Holocaust fictional writers are not required to comply with this, as their principal aim is to get their books sold and read. One widely acclaimed Holocaust novel, *The Boy in the Striped Pyjamas* (Boyne, 2006), has received much criticism. Gilbert describes this novel's climactic sequence of events as 'contrived' and 'implausible' and the book as 'dishonest' and reports that its author, John Boyne, 'admitted that he changed many facts to suit the story' (Gilbert, 2010). By doing so Boyne is claimed to have distorted history (Cesarani, 2008) and conveyed Auschwitz as 'real' as a fantasy context such as Harry Potter's Hogwarts School (Eaglestone, 2007, 52). This novel has undoubtedly engaged large numbers of young people throughout the world who would not normally be interested in this topic; but its lack of acknowledgement of basic facts about the Holocaust raises questions regarding the popularization and trivialization of the Holocaust.

The points raised in this chapter suggest that teaching about the Holocaust is complex, and methodologies need to be well thought through. Students need understanding of concrete historical events,

Jewish history and lessons that can be drawn for current and future terms. It is difficult but rewarding.

Suggested questions

- Is there an optimum age for exposing students to the Holocaust?
- Do simulations/role play/films enhance or trivialize the Holocaust?
- How accurate and truthful does fiction that teachers use to teach the Holocaust need to be?

Further reading

- Cowan, P., and Maitles, H. (2011) 'Teaching the Holocaust: To Simulate or Not?' *Race Equality Teaching*, 29 (3), 24–36.
- Davies, I. (ed.) (2000), *Teaching the Holocaust: Educational Dimension, Principles and Practice*. London: Continuum.
- Short, G., and Reed, C. (2004), *Issues in Holocaust Education*. London: Ashgate.

References

Agostinone-Wilson, F. (2005), 'Fair and Balanced to Death: Confronting the cult of neutrality in the teacher education classroom', *Journal for Critical Education Policy Studies*, 3 (1), www.jceps.com/?pageID=article&articleID=37.

Ashton, E., and Watson, B. (1998), 'Values Education: A fresh look at procedural neutrality', *Educational Studies*, 24 (2), 183–93.

Bauman, Z. (1989), *Modernity and the Holocaust*. Cornwall: Polity.

Boyne, J. (2006), *The Boy in the Striped Pyjamas*. Oxford: David Fickling Books.

Brown, M., and Davies, I. (1998), 'The Holocaust and Education for Citizenship', *Educational Review*, 50 (1), 75–83.

Cesarani, D. (2008), 'From the Pulpit: Striped Pyjamas', *Literary Review*, 359, 3.

Cowan, P., and Maitles, H. (2007), 'Does Addressing Prejudice and Discrimination through Holocaust Education Produce Better Citizens?' *Educational Review*, 59 (2), 115–30.

—(2010), 'Policy and Practice of Holocaust Education in Scotland', *Prospects*, 40, 257–72.

Dawidowicz, L. (1990) 'How They Teach the Holocaust', *Commentary*, 90 (6), 25–32.

Drake, I. (2008), 'Classroom Simulations: Proceed with caution', *Teaching Tolerance*, 33, 1–3.

Eaglestone, R. (2007), 'Boyne's Dangerous Tale', *Jewish Chronicle*, 23 March, 53.

Elliott, E. (2009), 'Teacher's Holocaust E-Mail Raises Concerns', *Baltimore Jewish Times*, 25 June 2009.

Foster, S., and Mercier, C. (2000), 'The Jewish background and the religious dimension', in I. Davies (ed.), *Teaching the Holocaust*. London: Continuum, pp. 25–36.

FRA (2010), 'Discover the Past for the Future: A study on the role of historical sites and museums in Holocaust education and human rights in the EU', European Union Agency for Fundamental Rights (FRA), http://fra.europa.eu/fraWebsite/attachments/Main/Results-Discover-the-Past-for-the-Future.pdf (accessed 8 July 2010).

Fried, E. (2009), 'Surveying Teachers' Experiences and Perceptions in Relations to Holocaust Education', *Canadian Diversity*, 7 (2), 23–7.

Gilbert, M. (1986), *The Holocaust*. London: Collins.

Gilbert, R. (2010), 'Grasping the Unimaginable: Recent Holocaust novels for children by Morris Gleitzman and John Boyne', *Children's Literature in Education*, 41, 355–66.

Gundare, I., and Batelaan, P. (2003), 'Learning About and from the Holocaust: The development and implementation of a Complex Instruction Unit in Latvia', *Intercultural Education*, 14 (2), 151–66.

Hahn, C. (1998), *Becoming Political*. Albany: State University of New York Press.

HEDP (2009), *Teaching About the Holocaust in English Secondary Schools*. London: Holocaust Education Development Programme, www.hedp.org.uk (accessed 7 July 2010).

Historical Association (2007), *T.E.A.C.H. Teaching Emotive and Controversial History, 3–19*, www.haevents.org.uk/PastEvents/Others/Teach%20report.pdf (accessed 14 May 2010).

Kokkola, L. (2003), Representing the Holocaust in Children's Literature. London: Routledge.

Kratsborn, W., Jacott, L. and Öcel, N. P. (2008), *Identity and Citizenship: The Impact of Borders and Shifts in Boundaries* (Children's Identity & Citizenship in Europe: London).

Landau, R. (1989), 'No Nazi war in British history', *Jewish Chronicle*, 25 August.

Levi, P. (1989), *The Drowned and the Saved*. London: Abacus.

Narvaez, A. (1987), 'Role-playing revives Holocaust horror', *New York Times*, 23 May.

Peters, W. (1987), *A Class Divided: Then and Now*. New York: Yale University Press.

Russell, L. (2006), *Teaching the Holocaust in School History*. London: Continuum.

Schweber, S. (2004), 'Simulating Survival', *Curriculum Inquiry*, 33 (2), 139–88.

Short, G. (2003), 'Holocaust Education in the Primary School: Some reflections on an emergent debate', *London Review of Education*, 1 (2), 119–29.

TES (2009), 'Eyes wide open', *Times Educational Supplement*, 10 July 2009.

Torney-Purta, J., Lehmann, R., Oswald, H., and Shulz, W. (2001), *Citizenship and Education in Twenty-Eight Countries*. Amsterdam: IEA.

Totten, S. (2002), *Holocaust Education: Issues and Approaches*. Boston: Allyn and Bacon.

von Borries, B. (2003), 'Research on the Attitudes of Pupils and Teachers Towards the Shoa in Germany', *Intercultural Education*, 14 (2), 201–14.

Wrigley, T. (2003), *Schools of Hope: A New Agenda for School Improvement*. Stoke-on-Trent: Trentham.

Teaching the Holocaust in the Multicultural Classroom

Geoffrey Short

Introduction

Until fairly recently, there was little academic interest in teaching the Holocaust in multicultural classrooms. Over the past few years, however, the issue has become more important, influencing the work of Yad Vashem, the Holocaust memorial and educational centre in Jerusalem (Avraham, 2008), and guiding the efforts of individual researchers (e.g., Short, 2008). In April 2009, a three-day seminar on the impact of cultural diversity on Holocaust education was hosted by the Anne Frank House in Amsterdam. It attracted in excess of 30 participants, both academics and practitioners, from a dozen countries.

The multicultural classroom, depending on its composition, can create any number of problems for teachers of the Holocaust. In this chapter I have chosen to focus on what might be considered one of the more challenging, namely, manifestations of anti-Semitism from

Muslim students. A priori, many of these students can be expected to react negatively to lessons on the Holocaust, for it seems that hostility towards Jews, largely fuelled by events in the Middle East, is widespread and growing in Muslim communities across the world. In Britain, for example, the All-Party Parliamentary Group Against Antisemitism (2006) claimed that the anti-Semitic views of radical Islamists were 'entering mainstream discourse' (26). It noted that Arabic translations of *Mein Kampf* and the Protocols of the Elders of Zion[1] were freely available on the streets of London and it highlighted the findings of an opinion poll published in the *Times* in 2006 showing that over a third of the 500 Muslims interviewed considered the Jewish community in Britain 'a legitimate target (in) the struggle for justice in the Middle East' (ibid., 30). The situation is no better elsewhere in Europe. Certainly not in Sweden, where the city of Malmo witnessed an upsurge in anti-Jewish incidents after the Gaza war of 2008/2009 that was widely attributed to Muslim youth (Meo, 2010). In France, too, according to the Algerian-born politician Rachid Kaci (2007, 212), 'the deep-rooted hatred that some Muslims, or so-called Muslims, feel for Jews cannot be denied'. Voicing a similar concern, the Canadian feminist and committed Muslim Irshad Manji (2005), in her much-publicized critique of Islam, argues that anti-Semitism has become a troubling cornerstone of the faith. It may thus be no coincidence that in Australia, Suzanne Rutland (2010) has identified a positive correlation between increasing anti-Jewish sentiment and an expansion of the country's Muslim population. Rutland comments at length on the problem in schools where Muslim students are alleged to have harassed their Jewish peers as well as Jewish members of staff.

The central question that this chapter seeks to address is whether learning about the Holocaust can have a beneficial effect on Muslim students. Some authorities clearly have their doubts. Rutland (op. cit.), for example, describes an interfaith initiative in Australia, Together for Humanity, that aims to combat racism by stressing the shared moral values that inform the three Abrahamic faiths: Judaism, Christianity and Islam. It deliberately eschews any reference to the Holocaust on the grounds that to do otherwise could be counterproductive, especially for

Muslim participants. In an interview with Rutland, the programme's national director justified this decision as follows:

> On a theoretical level, my concern with the Holocaust as the primary message to combat prejudice, at least with the Arab/Muslim children, is the connection in people's minds between the Holocaust and the State of Israel. . . . Essentially the view that is reported by Muslims is that the Jews have stolen the land of the Palestinians with the support of the West as compensation for the Holocaust. (Rutland, op. cit., 86)[2]

To treat Holocaust education as an impediment to tackling racism among Muslim youth or, worse, as likely to inflame existing tensions between Muslims and Jews is in my view, a profound error of judgement and seemingly little more than an article of faith. I will argue, on the basis of findings from my own research (Short, op. cit.) and other studies, that as far as the majority of Muslim students are concerned, learning about the Holocaust can be an effective antidote to racism in general and anti-Semitism in particular.

Research findings

The sampling frame in my study comprised the Head of History in every maintained, non-selective and predominantly Muslim secondary school in five local authorities in south-east England. The 18 schools selected were predominantly Muslim in the sense that either the majority of students were Muslim or, where this was not the case, such students constituted the largest single ethno-religious group within the school. For reasons that are unknown, three schools refused to allow their staff to participate. The sample of 15 consisted of 6 men and 9 women, a third of whom taught in single sex schools. They were interviewed between January and September 2007.

In order to assess the impact of anti-Semitism on the students' willingness to learn about the Holocaust, the teachers were asked two questions.

- How do your students respond to learning about the Holocaust?
- Have you encountered any opposition to teaching the Holocaust from parents?

For the most part, the students responded positively. They were variously described as 'really interested', 'very receptive' or 'reacting with horror [and] repugnance'. There had been no opposition of any kind from parents and roughly half the teachers reported no anti Semitism at all when discussing the subject with students even though, in a couple of schools, anti Semitism was said to be rife. The following comments are representative:

> [There has been no] denial or any form of anti-Semitism even though I think anti-Semitism is quite prevalent in this school. I've had resistance to teaching Judaism in RE [Religious Education] but not when teaching the Holocaust.

> Because of the television they watch at home etc. the Bangladeshi pupils get exposed to quite a lot of information about the Middle East, about Palestine especially, so there's quite a lot of anti-Jewish sentiment that is expressed but not usually when we're teaching the Holocaust. When learning about the Holocaust they do realise that it's racism and they've been taught since they were very little that racism is wrong.

Three teachers stated that a minority of Muslim students had made anti-Semitic remarks when starting work on the topic but that they had stopped doing so as the work progressed.

Questions relating to the amount of time devoted to the Holocaust, the areas of the curriculum in which it is taught and the schools' response to Holocaust Memorial Day (HMD) provided further evidence (albeit circumstantial) that staff engaging with the Holocaust in predominantly Muslim schools do not necessarily find it stressful. If they did, one might expect them to devote as little time to it as possible. However, in this study they did not hold back; quite the contrary. The Holocaust was taught in every school in Year 9 (to 13- and 14-year-olds) for an average of eight and a half hours, considerably longer than in two comparable studies conducted in Britain in the 1990s in which Muslim students were not the primary focus (Brown and Davies, 1998; Short, 1995). Again, if teachers find addressing the Holocaust especially demanding in schools with a largely Muslim catchment area, one might anticipate that in addition to minimal coverage in the history curriculum, it would be entirely absent from those areas of the curriculum where its inclusion is not mandatory.

Once more, however, the findings confounded the prediction as the Holocaust was taught exclusively as history in only four schools. Elsewhere, it was covered most often in religious education and citizenship and, from time to time, in English. With regard to Holocaust Memorial Day, a handful of schools did nothing to mark the occasion, but most (two-thirds of the total) either held an assembly, placed posters around the school or attempted something more ambitious. For example:

> When we do the Auschwitz trip we try to get those pupils [who went on it] to actually do something on HMD. A few years ago we spent the whole day on equal opportunities but focusing on the Holocaust and we had a survivor who came in and spoke and then the two students did their presentation.
>
> When it is HMD we teach what happened to all students from Year 7 all the way up to Year 11. In that week, when we [the history department] see the students, we devote the lesson to the Holocaust. Also, the library puts a display up in the corridors.

Schools are not obligated to acknowledge HMD. The fact that many of them did (especially at a time when the Muslim Council of Britain was boycotting official ceremonies) strengthens the view that most Muslim students are willing to learn about Jewish suffering in Nazi-occupied Europe.[3] They seemed able to keep their views on the Holocaust separate from those on the conflict in the Middle East. Their 'hostility towards Jews', in other words, was more a case of anti-Zionism than anti-Semitism.

The findings from this study clearly undermine the contention that Muslim students will inevitably react badly to learning about the Holocaust because of the Holocaust's perceived link with the re-establishment of Israel. The contention is cast further into doubt by research conducted in a number of other countries. For example, in a small-scale study in Toronto, Canada's most cosmopolitan city, Reed and Novogrodsky (2000) examined the inclination of teachers in multicultural classrooms to broach the Holocaust as part of an antiracist initiative. They administered a questionnaire to 12 teachers who they subsequently interviewed. Seven taught in secondary schools and 5 in middle schools. Nine of the classes reflected the ethno-cultural diversity of the city, with one including immigrants from Poland, Greece, India, Vietnam, Korea and the Caribbean. Although the researchers did not set out specifically to monitor the reaction of Muslim students to learning about the Holocaust, they did comment on

> [a teacher who] wrote that a few of her Muslim students were a little reluctant at first to start the unit but almost immediately became 'interested and enthralled by the new knowledge.' (Reed and Novogrodsky, 2000, 516)

Also in Canada, Short and Reed (2004, 38) recall survivors telling them 'that students from all kinds of background eagerly respond to their Holocaust narratives' and that they frequently receive warm embraces from Muslim students. In Australia, a programme designed to combat anti-Jewish sentiment among young Muslims, Courage to Care, makes explicit reference to the Holocaust in that it utilizes survivors and focuses on rescuers. It has been evaluated very positively (Cohen, 2005). More surprisingly, perhaps, a course on the Holocaust for Arab and Jewish students run by the Centre for Humanistic Education in Israel has also produced a favourable outcome. An evaluation of the short-term impact of the course on Arabs (many, if not all of whom were presumably Muslim) stated that

> [m]ore and more students began to absorb the significance of the Holocaust as an attempt to 'annihilate a nation', the meaning of the term genocide, and some of them even retracted the comparisons they had initially made between the Holocaust and the Nakba. (Kalisman, 2010, 80)

Comments from the various adults involved in these reports (if taken at face value) undermine any suggestion that Muslim youth are bound to object to learning about the attempted annihilation of European Jewry. That said, a readiness to learn about the Holocaust offers no guarantee that its teaching will be as effective as it might be in diminishing anti-Semitism and racism more generally. To ensure that that happens, teachers must take fully into account the needs and characteristics of their students. I turn now to consider the extent to which those taking part in my study complied with this fundamental canon of sound pedagogy.

Teaching the Holocaust effectively?

Teachers were asked whether the fact that there was a high proportion of Muslims in their school affected the way they approached the Holocaust. Just over half the sample claimed that it did. As illustrated in the following statements, some were keen to ensure that their Muslim students saw the Holocaust as relevant to their own lives.

> I make a point of highlighting tabloid newspaper headlines related to Islamophobia to make the Holocaust more personal for those students.
>
> It's made us search for resources like the school version of Schindler's List where Spielberg introduces the Holocaust and mentions Bosnia.

Another teacher was keen to minimize the risk of the Arab/Israeli conflict influencing his students to side with the perpetrators rather than the victims of the Holocaust. He said, 'I am very conscious to hammer home the distinction between being Jewish and the perception of Israel in the Middle East'.

I have argued elsewhere (e.g., Short and Reed, op. cit.) that teachers ought to familiarize themselves with the knowledge of Jews that their students possess prior to formally encountering the Holocaust. The importance of uncovering this knowledge and contesting it if necessary, is self-evident, for students will not automatically recoil in horror as a result of discovering the full extent of the Nazi persecution of the Jews. How they react will depend, in large part, on how they regard Jews, and should they regard them as in some sense 'bad people', their response to learning of their fate may be less one of revulsion than of joy at the perceived triumph of good over evil. The danger in such a response is that students fail to see Nazism for what it is and specifically the threat that neo-Nazi political parties continue to pose to *all* ethnic minorities.

In the West, Muslims are likely to share not just the anti-Semitic myths and stereotypes in widespread circulation, but also those that are restricted to their own communities. The latter might well relate to tensions in the Middle East, but equally, they might derive from the Koran which contains a number of unflattering references to Jews (e.g., Lewis, 1987). There were just a few teachers in my study who took advantage of the opportunity the Holocaust affords to challenge some of the ill-informed beliefs of their students.

> [The main advantage of teaching the Holocaust is] getting rid of some of the perceptions that some pupils have. I have had pupils say to me 'I think Hitler was brilliant because he killed the Jews'. The way we teach it I think educates them out of that mindset.
>
> The particular pupils who make those comments. . . . They're always Muslim pupils.
>
> [Studying the Holocaust helps develop] an understanding of hate, of how it could happen in this area in particular; how lack of tolerance can get out of hand and be manipulated.. . . Also the conversations that arise as a result of teaching [the Holocaust] are about the Palestinian question and the prejudices and misinformation that some of the kids have received. We can address and tackle some of the specific anti-Jewish racism . . .

The fact that the majority of teachers did not explore the possibility of their students harbouring misconceptions about Jews detracts from, if it does not entirely nullify, the potential benefits to the students of learning about the Holocaust. It is thus of concern that a number of them may have completed the course with their anti-Semitic prejudices more or less intact.

To diminish further the prospect of this happening, teachers should draw their students' attention to Muslim rescuers of Jews. Enquiring whether they did so, I asked, in particular, if they were aware of this phenomenon in North Africa and, if they were, whether they made a point of referring to it. Not a single teacher knew of the protection offered by Muslims to their Jewish neighbours in countries such as Tunisia (Satloff, 2006) and none spoke either about Muslim rescuers of Jews in Europe (Mughal and Rosen, 2010). This omission is unfortunate and especially so in respect of anti-Semitic students, for having been made aware of the facts, they may come to reflect on them and, in the process, abandon their prejudice in order to make sense of the rescue. That said, in the interests of historical truth students should also be told about the Mufti of Jerusalem's role in the formation of a Muslim SS unit (the Handschar division) in the Balkans in 1943 (e.g., Dalin et al., 2009). Informing them that this unit was responsible for the murder of most of Bosnia's Jews will, of course, do nothing to lessen any anti-Semitic feeling. However, if discussed in conjunction with rescue, it might prompt students to appreciate that there was not at the time, as there is not now, a monolithic Muslim attitude towards Jews, a useful insight in the present climate of strained relations between the two groups.

When Holocaust education fails

My research suggests that the majority of young Muslims are prepared to study the Holocaust and, if taught properly, can benefit from it in the same way and to the same extent that other students do. There can be no doubt, though, that there are schools in which *some* Muslim pupils will present serious difficulties for their teachers. This is certainly the case in France, according to Georges Benoussan, author of a study of contemporary anti-Semitism in the country. In an interview in 2004 he said,

> The problem [of anti-Semitism] goes back to the early 90s, when teachers began to encounter verbal violence while trying to teach the Holocaust in schools with large concentrations of North African students. The students would stop the teachers and say, 'This is an invention'. I know of cases in which the teacher mentioned Auschwitz and Treblinka, and students clapped.
>
> Of course, there were also North African kids who really took an interest. . . . We are talking about a minority here. (Friedman, 2004, 48)

In Britain, Joyce Miller (2004) referred to something similar in her description of the Enhanced Citizenship Curriculum for Bradford schools set up in the wake of the 2001 disturbances in the city. She found that

> some teachers in Bradford consider the Holocaust to be a difficult subject to approach with Muslim pupils. Anti-Semitic literature appears in Bradford, as it does elsewhere, and is too readily given credence.

My own study reinforced this anecdotal evidence, for it drew attention to a couple of teachers who claimed that the attitude of some of their Muslim students towards Jews caused major disruption in the classroom. As one of them put it, the Holocaust proved 'a hugely difficult topic to teach'. That said, she was sure that the problem was limited to a vociferous minority who intimidated the others. Believing the recalcitrants to have been influenced by extremists who had infiltrated the local mosque, she described their behaviour:

> It was . . . abusive comments and defacing the books. They were simply brainwashed with phrases that they couldn't explain. For example, they would shout out . . . 'they're corrupt' and you'd say 'what do you mean by that?' but they couldn't tell you. They're just told these things and they'll repeat it. You couldn't get into a conversation about it. It was just bite-sized phrases that they'd been taught that they'd shout out constantly.

There is little point in encouraging these students to engage with the Holocaust, for their resistance is seemingly impenetrable, their distorted image of Jews acting as an insuperable barrier. Whether a way can eventually be found to reach them will have to await the outcome of further research, but in the short term there appears to be no known antidote to this depth of hostility. Over the longer term an answer might be sought in antiracist education, preferably conducted in the primary school, where it is thought to be most effective (with relatively little opposition from the peer group). One of the main aims of this approach to education (evident, e.g., in UNESCO's Project Aladdin) is to inoculate students against those who would peddle hatred against any racial or ethnic group. For young Muslims in the United Kingdom, such malign influences will include elements within their own community intent on promoting an anti-Semitic agenda.

Suggested questions

- Should schools with a substantial number of ethnic minority students be required to teach the Holocaust?
- Are there any lessons to be drawn from the Holocaust that are of particular relevance to ethnic minorities?
- How would you respond to students who asked why they were studying the Holocaust rather than a genocide committed against their own people?

Further reading

- Gill, L. (2004), 'How the Holocaust was more than just racism,' *Times* (T2), 21 January.
- Gryglewski, E. (2010), 'Teaching the Holocaust in Multicultural Societies: Appreciating the learner', *Intercultural Education*, 21 (Special Supplement), S41–S50.
- Nates, T. (2010), 'But apartheid is also genocide. . . . What about our suffering?' Teaching the Holocaust in South Africa', *Intercultural Education*, 21 (Special Supplement), S17–S26.

References

All-Party Parliamentary Group Against Antisemitism (2006), *Report of the All-Party Parliamentary Inquiry into Antisemitism*, London: The Stationery Office.

Avraham, D. (2008), 'The Challenge of Teaching the Holocaust in a Multicultural Classroom', *Yad Vashem Jerusalem Quarterly Magazine*, 51 (October), 4.

Brown, M., and Davies, I. (1998), 'The Holocaust and Education for Citizenship: The teaching of history, religion and human rights in England', *Educational Review*, 50 (1), 75–83.

Cohen, S. K. (2005), 'Courage to Care': A first encounter between the Holocaust and Australian school students', *Australian Journal of Jewish Studies*, 19, 121–33.

Dalin, D. G., Rothmann, A. F., and Dershowitz, A. M. (2009), *Icon of Evil: Hitler's Mufti and the Rise of Radical Islam*, New Brunswick, NJ: Transaction.

Friedman, M. (2004), 'It began with students denying the Holocaust', *Jerusalem Report*, 13 December, 48.

Kaci, R. (2007), 'Antisemitism is the legitimate child of Islamism: The real cancer of Islam', in S. Fineberg, S. Samuels and M. Weitzman (eds), *Antisemitism: The Generic Hatred. Essays in Memory of Simon Wiesenthal*. London: Vallentine Mitchell, pp. 212–17.

Kalisman, R. (2010), 'Examples of Best Practice 2: Holocaust education as a universal challenge', *Intercultural Education*, 21 (Special Supplement S1), S78–S80.

Lewis, B. (1987), *Semites and Anti-Semites*, New York: Norton.

Manji, I (2005), *The Trouble with Islam Today*. Edinburgh: Mainstream.

Meo, N. (2010), 'Race-hate attacks drive Jews to turn their back on liberal Sweden', *Sunday Telegraph*, 21 February, 32.

Miller, J. (2004), 'Community Cohesion', www.insted.co.uk/bradford.pdf (accessed 28 July 2010).

Mughal, F., and Rosen, E. (2010) (eds), *The Role of Righteous Muslims*, London: Faith Matters.

Reed, C., and Novogrodsky, M. (2000), 'Teaching the Holocaust in a multiracial, multicultural, urban environment in Canada', in F. C. DeCoste and B. Schwartz (eds), *The Holocaust's Ghost: Writings on Arts, Politics, Law and Education*. Edmonton: University of Alberta Press, pp. 513–21.

Rutland, S. D. (2010), 'Creating Effective Holocaust Education Programmes for Government Schools with Large Muslim Populations in Sydney', *Prospects*, 40 (1), 75–91.

Satloff, R. B. (2006), *Among the Righteous: Lost Stories from the Holocaust's Long Reach into Arab Lands*. New York: Public Affairs.

Short, G. (1995), 'The Holocaust in the National Curriculum – a survey of teachers' attitudes and practices', *Journal of Holocaust Education*, 4 (2), 167–88.

Short, G. (2008), 'Teaching the holocaust in predominantly Muslim schools', *Holocaust Studies: A Journal of Culture and History*, 14 (2), 95–110.

Short, G., and Reed, C. A. (2004), *Issues in Holocaust Education*. Aldershot: Ashgate.

Notes

1   The Protocols of the Elders of Zion is a notorious czarist forgery that first appeared in St Petersburg at the end of the nineteenth century. It purports to show how the leaders of international Jewry intend to dominate the world.

2   In the course of Israel's war of independence (1948–9) and the civil war that preceded it, approximately 725,000 Palestinians fled or were expelled from their homes. The Palestinians use the term 'Nakba' to refer to this catastrophic outcome of the conflict.

3   The Muslim Council of Britain (MCB) is an umbrella organisation established in 1997 by representatives of more than 250 Muslim organisations from all parts of Britain. Until December 2007, it boycotted Holocaust Memorial Day, calling instead for a more inclusive ceremony commemorating deaths in Palestine, Rwanda and the former Yugoslavia, alongside those of the Holocaust.

13 Visiting Auschwitz – Valuable Lessons or Holocaust Tourism?

Paula Cowan

Chapter Outline

Introduction

Auschwitz has become the ultimate symbol of the Holocaust, of genocide and of man's crimes against humanity. Its complex of camps became the epicentre of the genocide against the Jews and the site of the largest mass murder in modern history. Set up by an act of the Polish Parliament in 1947 and designated a UNESCO world heritage site in 1979, the Auschwitz-Birkenau Memorial and Museum (ABMM), as its title suggests, is both a memorial and a museum, comprising Auschwitz 1 concentration camp and Auschwitz-Birkenau death camp. It is in fact the largest cemetery in the world with a collection that includes thousands of deportees' personal effects and extensive grounds that include barracks, camp blocks, guard towers, the infamous railway tracks and ruins of the gas chambers.

In its original form, Auschwitz was

> . . . a mundane extension of the modern factory system. Rather than producing goods, the raw material was human beings and the end-product

was death, so many units per day marked carefully on the manager's production charts. The chimneys, the very symbol of the modern factory system, poured forth acrid smoke produced by burning human flesh. The
brilliantly organized railroad grid of modern Europe carried a new kind of
raw material to the factories. It did so in the same manner as with other
cargo. In the gas chambers the victims inhaled noxious gas generated by
prussic acid pellets, which were produced by the advanced chemical industry of Germany. Engineers designed the crematoria; managers designed
the system of bureaucracy that worked with zest and efficiency more backward nations would envy. Even the overall plan itself was a reflection of the
modern scientific spirit gone awry. (Feingold, in Baumann, 1989, 8)

Today, the ABMM is a reproduction and 'simultaneously a tourist attraction and a memorial site' (Wollaston, 2005) with travel operators popu-
larizing it to attract customers or tourists. For example, Viator tours
market ABMM as 'the best known cemetery and place of genocide in
the world'; the company's promotional material states 'that this sobering
half day trip will have a lasting impact' and rates the museum with 4½
(out of 5) stars (Viator website, 2010). Sometimes referred to as 'dark
tourism' or 'Holocaust tourism', this is the context that today's visitors to
the ABMM find themselves and indeed contribute to. They pose in front
of the 'Arbeit Macht Frei' gatepost, take photographs and recordings of
each other, sit 'on the ruins of the crematorium eating sandwiches'
(Lennon and Morley, 2000, 61) and purchase items from the shop. Some
may perceive this experience as 'commercial, political and religious
exploitation of the site' (Wollaston, 2005, 66), but this chapter will argue,
on the basis of findings of research in Scotland, that the ABMM can
provide a meaningful learning experience for students and teachers that
impacts on their individual personal and professional development as
well as on their schools and communities. While this chapter focuses on
one specific memorial site, it raises questions that are relevant to educators who take their students to visit any memorial site and to educators
in countries such as Germany, Poland and Austria who regularly take
their students to Holocaust memorial sites and/or camps.

Rationale and considerations

One central principle is that preserving the ABMM bears witness to the
fate of its victims. Another principle, one advanced by Clemitshaw

(2008) and Garside (2008), is that a visit to a museum or memorial site 'brings history closer to the visitor' (FRA, 2010). While the actual people, victims or perpetrators are in reality no closer to the students than in a classroom, book or film, the student's emotional response can stimulate interest and learning. This common view partially explains why the former Secretary of State for Scotland, Jim Murphy, facilitated the first one-day Scottish schools visit to Auschwitz for students and teachers (East Renfrewshire Parliamentary Office, 2005), although it should be noted that findings from a BBC survey that revealed that 60 per cent of those under 35 had not heard of Auschwitz, also contributed to the Minister's thinking (ibid.).

In the United Kingdom, school visits to the ABMM have been organized by the Holocaust Educational Trust (HET) since 1999 and are an integral component of their Lessons from Auschwitz Project (LFAP). Aware of possible cynicism towards a one-day visit to Auschwitz, the HET incorporated this visit into a wider educational programme that comprises a seminar where students hear from a Holocaust survivor prior to visiting the ABMM, take part in a seminar on their return and undertake a Next Steps component , where students pass on what they have learned from the LFAP experience to their school and/or community. The Trust's rationale is that the experience provided by the LFAP empowers young people to challenge Holocaust denial, anti-Semitism and racism inside and outside their schools.

Yet teachers and educators need to consider the specific learning content of a visit to the ABMM. The architectural historian and expert witness for the defence in the libel case *DJC Irving v. Penguin Books Ltd and Deborah Lipstadt* (1998–2001), Robert Jan van Pelt, argues that the Auschwitz complex should be left standing until the last survivor dies and at that point it should be closed, left to nature and forgotten (BBC 2009). His reasoning is based on the fact that as the Auschwitz complex is now a reproduction, there is little that can be learned from it in its current form. It is uncertain whether his comments refer to something *new* being able to be learnt from it or to young people's learning. Certainly, several writers have highlighted educational concerns by recognizing that museums (i.e., designers, curators, government representatives) choose to present or construct a historical narrative in a particular way (e.g., Blum, 2004; Gross, 2009; Marcus, 2007; Williams,

2007) and recommending that young visitors have some knowledge of the historical context of the Holocaust prior to their visit (Rathenow and Weber, in Holden and Clough, 1998). One may additionally recommend that visitors have some knowledge of the historical context of Auschwitz in particular. Cowan and Maitles (2011) additionally point out that the visit component of the LFAP is so highly structured and quick paced that some young visitors to the ABMM may require more time than they are allocated to absorb its contents. However it is widely recognized that much can be learned from a visit to the ABMM.

School- and community-group visits to Auschwitz

Visiting the ABMM as part of a school or community group can be beneficial, as participants can provide each other with support. For example, a senior scout leader who accompanied a group of 20 Boy Scouts to the ABMM as part of a week's visit to Poland commented that the scouts in his group 'talked to each other, asked each other questions, and gave each other emotional support' (Cowan and Maitles, 2010). Similar to including a visit to the ABMM as part of a trip to World War II- or Holocaust-related sites, this visit has the advantage of placing the ABMM in a wider context. Another obvious advantage is that the youth leader or teacher will know the participants and therefore be able to tailor the visit to participants' needs and be more able to respond to participants' emotional and educational requirements.

The LFAP was expanded in 2005 when the British Government recognized the value of the project and provided funding to allow two students, aged between 16 and 18 years, from every secondary school in England to participate. This financial governmental support enabled thousands of young people across England to participate in this project. Following this, the Scottish Government agreed to subsidize the LFAP in Scotland in 2007. Usually in this project, on arrival at the ABMM two students from one school are organized in a larger group with another eight or ten students from four or five schools. Teacher participants walk round in the group with their students. Hence, in this model, students from the same school may not necessarily know each other, and apart from meeting at the orientation component in the project prior to the visit, students will not know the students in their group, and some students will be accompanied by their teachers. The HET trains educators to support students on the visit and with their Next Steps, and each group is accompanied by a trained educator and a museum guide. The HET also provides participants with literature to assist with their preparation for the visit.

Research findings

Findings are taken from two studies: a pilot study comprising five students from one authority who had participated in the first Scottish schools visit to Auschwitz in 2005, and a larger study comprising 105 students and 42 teachers from 27 authorities in Scotland who had participated in the first LFAP in 2007. Feedback in the pilot study was obtained by individual interviews, and feedback from the larger study was obtained from student and teacher responses to an online questionnaire and nine follow-up individual-student interviews. Interviews from the pilot study were conducted almost two years after the students had visited the ABMM, questionnaires from the larger study were distributed between March and April 2008 and interviews were conducted between December 2008 and April 2009. The majority of teachers taught history, modern studies and religious, moral and philosophical studies, and English, with a small number teaching psychology, sociology and classical studies. Though the student cohort were of a wide range of ability, the majority were academic and studied history at Higher level ('Highers' are the university entrance qualifications in Scotland).

The research aimed to investigate:

1. the impact the experience had on students with regards to their personal growth (in the pilot study the visit to the ABMM was the main element; in the larger study the visit to ABMM comprised one element of the LFAP);
2. the impact this experience had on teachers' professional growth (in the larger study only);
3. the range of student follow-up activities in their school and wider community.

Data from both studies strongly challenges van Pelt's view that little can be learned from the ABMM although it should be noted that the data in the larger study focused on the LFAP and not just the visit component. Students from this larger study perceived that there were different types of gains in their personal development. First, data from the questionnaires showed that they perceived gains in their understanding of anti-Semitism, genocide, the plight of refugees, human rights and World War II . Secondly, a small number of students reported that extrinsic gains had been achieved, as the work that they had undertaken in the Next Steps had contributed to folio and unit work for their external examinations (Cowan and Maitles, 2011). Thirdly, data from the interviews gave more insight into the breadth of student personal growth extending to contemporary issues. While students infrequently referred to 'anti-Semitism', they frequently spoke about broader issues such as genocide, refugees and sectarianism. The following quotation is evidence of this:

> It has made me more aware of other things that are going on in the world. It has changed my attitude towards genocide. I am a lot more aware of it now than I was before. I think that it helped me a lot to understand how it must have felt to have been Jewish at the time and what it would have been like not to be Jewish, and either be at risk of supporting Jewish people or just going along with the crowd. I think going into the camp helped me understand the mass scale it was on. (Cowan and Maitles, 2011)

One student from the pilot study had continued to read about the Holocaust after her visit to the ABMM and some two years later was still reading Holocaust literature as she had not realized how 'big' an issue it was. She commented,

> It wasn't till coming back home that you realized how big it was, cos two pages – that's what I was used to – two pages of a textbook, that's all it was. (Cowan, 2008)

Teachers too reported gains in *their* personal development although one should point out that the LFAP is not designed for teachers. Even though teachers considered that they were well aware of the educational issues and had sufficient knowledge of the Holocaust prior to the visit, they perceived gains in their knowledge of Auschwitz and the Holocaust, human rights, anti-Semitism, refugees and genocide. Teachers further perceived that the visit contributed to their professional development by providing impetus in their teaching of human rights, prompting further reading of the Holocaust and putting a new perspective on their lessons (Maitles and Cowan, 2011). Teacher-only visits to the ABMM have been organized by the HET since 2006. These visits prepare teachers for their students' participation in the LFAP, allow teachers to share the experience with their professional peers and the opportunity to pose questions to the guides that they would not want to ask in front of their students, for fear of upsetting them. However, a teacher-only visit can potentially impact on the student experience by upsetting the equilibrium of the student–teacher relationship. The equal balance of this relationship which was achieved by student and teacher equally sharing the experience, was a feature that some teachers recognized to be beneficial.

One of the concerns of a visit to any Holocaust memorial or museum is the intensity of the student's emotional response. The following student quotes show that the artefacts displayed at the ABMM personalize the Holocaust.

> We went into the concentration camp and saw the pyjamas they wore. And we just stood thinking, how could they have survived the cold let alone all the labour? . . . I saw all the hair, all the shoes and it's a lot of shoes, I had my arctic socks and my thermals on and I was STILL freezing. (Cowan, 2008)

> I found the rooms in Auschwitz 1 filled with human hair, shoes, suitcases, and baby clothes very moving. All of these made me start thinking about all these people who had their full lives ahead of them and its all been taken from them through no fault of their own. And it made you wonder, if this was your family back then, it would have been them. (Cowan and Maitles, 2011)

These artefacts are also upsetting to look at. Yet, some may argue that it would be unusual for any visitor, young or old, not to be upset by such an experience. This supports the idea that preparation for this visit should include emotional preparation as well as background knowledge. However there is a danger that too much preparation can reduce the impact of the experience. One recommendation would be for teachers or head teachers to take the maturity and emotional needs of their students into consideration when choosing their students for participation in the LFAP, as should teachers who take a group of their own students. Students who have a direct connection with the Holocaust due to their religious or cultural backgrounds should be given special consideration, as they will be additionally learning about their heritage. At the other end of the emotional spectrum are young people whose interest in the Holocaust or World War II may be rooted in fascination of the cruelty that occurred or even voyeurism. Hence teachers and educators must exercise caution.

Students perceived that the experience impacted on their personal growth in additional ways which affected their behaviour. Student comments reported that they perceived they were now more likely to do the following:

- challenge an offensive comment made towards an individual because of his or her religious or cultural background or race or sexual preference;
- challenge separation on religious grounds (sectarianism, e.g.);
- explain about the Holocaust when the view that 'holocausts are still happening' in the world is expressed;
- not go along with the crowd;
- value their family.

Students on their return from the ABMM engaged in a wide range of school and community activities as part of their Next Steps. Common school-based activities were assemblies, photograph displays, Power-Point presentations to different year groups, and articles in school magazines. More innovative activities included a debate for the school and wider community on the effects of technology in conflict with guest speaker Professor Heinz Wolff. The student brought five students from different year groups together to organize this event. There were also student talks to Rotary groups* a parent council meeting, college students and primary teachers; and in one school two students devised an eight-week cross-curricular lesson plan in English, history and religious, moral and philosophical studies for a year 2 group that focused on the

---

* Rotary is a worldwide organization whose main objective is service in the community and workplace throughout the world.

Holocaust, discrimination and racism. It is evident that some of these activities focused on broader lessons that could be described as learning *from* the Holocaust rather than learning *about* the Holocaust.

Further, the experience can be viewed as life changing for two students who reported that after their visit to the ABMM they changed their mind about their choice of career; one decided to study journalism and another joined the police force. This together with the examples described elsewhere in this chapter suggests that the valuable lessons that can be taken from a visit to Auschwitz are diverse and far-reaching. Yet are these lessons shared by all participants? For example, what impact does the experience have on students who visit the ABMM on a Thursday and have a school trip to a theme park the following day? Such extraordinary timetabling trivializes the visit to the ABMM and reduces students' perception of the experience, and their schools can arguably be seen as complicit in making 'dark tourism' acceptable.

Suggested questions

- Can one ever be prepared for visiting a memorial such as the Auschwitz-Birkenau Memorial and Museum?
- How can teachers assist students with their Next Steps activities?
- How should teachers choose students to participate in the LFAP?

Further reading

- Rees, L. (2005), *Auschwitz: The Nazis and the Final Solution*. London: BBC.
- Shuter, J. (2000), *Auschwitz, Visiting the Past*. London: Heinemann.
- Williams, P. (2007), *Memorial Museums: The Global Rush to Commemorate Atrocities*. New York: Berg.

References

Bauman, Z. (1989), *Modernity and the Holocaust*. Cambridge: Polity.

BBC (2009), 'Cash crisis threat to Auschwitz', http://news.bbc.co.uk/1/hi/7827534.stm (accessed 25 November 2010).

Blum, L. (2004), 'The Poles, the Jews and the Holocaust: Reflections on an AME trip to Auschwitz', *Journal of Moral Education*, 33 (2), 131–48.

Clemitshaw, G. (2008), 'Citizenship Without History? Knowledge, skills and values in citizenship education', *Ethics and Education*, 3 (2), 135–47.

Cowan, P. (2008), 'Seeing, hearing and feeling – how can a visit to Auschwitz encourage young people to practise citizenship?', in A. Ross and P. Cunningham (eds), *Reflecting on Identities: Research, Practice and Innovation*. London: London Metropolitan University, pp. 511–20.

Cowan, P., and Maitles, H. (2010), 'Policy and Practice of Holocaust Education in Scotland', *Prospects*, 40 (2), 257–72.

—(2011), 'We Saw Inhumanity Close Up: What is gained by school students from Scotland visiting Auschwitz?' *Journal of Curriculum Studies* (forthcoming 2011).

East Renfrewshire Parliamentary Office (2005), *Scottish Schools Visit to Auschwitz-Birkenau*. Glasgow: East Renfrewshire Parliamentary Office.

FRA (2010), *Excursion to the Past – Teaching for the Future: Handbook for Teachers*. www.fra.europa.eu/fraWebsite/attachments/Handbook-teachers-holocaust-education_EN.pdf (accessed 17 November 2010).

Garside, R. (2008), 'News and Comment', *Race Equality Teaching*, 26 (2), 5.

Gross, Z. (2009), 'Analysis of Holocaust Discourse While Visiting the Auschwitz-Birkenau Museum', *Canadian Diversity*, 7 (2), 97–100.

Lennon, J., and Foley, M. (2000), *Dark Tourism: The Attraction of Death and Disaster*. London: Continuum.

Maitles, H., and Cowan, P. (2011), 'It Reminded Me of What Really Matters': Teacher responses to the Lessons from Auschwitz Project, *Educational Review* (forthcoming 2011).

Marcus, A. S. (2007), 'Representing the Past and Reflecting the Present: Museums, memorials and the secondary history classroom', *Social Studies*, May/June, 105–10.

Rathenow, H. F., and Weber. N. H. (1998), 'Education for Auschwitz: A task for human rights education', in C. Holden and N. Clough (eds), *Children as Citizens: Education for Participation*. London: Jessica Kingsley, pp. 95–112.

Viator (2010), www.viator.com/tours/Krakow/Auschwitz-Birkenau-Museum-Half-Day-Trip-from-Krakow/d529-2145IT3 (accessed 17 November 2010).

Williams, P. (2007), *Memorial Museums: The Global Rush to Commemorate Atrocities*. New York: Berg.

Wollaston, I. (2005), 'Negotiating the Marketplace: The role(s) of Holocaust museums today', *Journal of Modern Jewish Studies*, 4 (1), 63–80.

14 Why Study Rwanda When We Have Learned About the Holocaust?

Andy Lawrence

The difficulties of teaching the Rwandan genocide

At the time of writing (2011), very few schools across the United Kingdom taught the Rwandan genocide. Of those that did, most did not explore the subject in any great depth. Why is this so?

There are, of course, many obstacles to be negotiated when teaching about any genocide, whether it be the Holocaust or more recent genocides, such as Rwanda's (1994). A recent study at the Institute of

Education, carried out as part of the Holocaust Education Development Programme, unearthed the nature and depth of many of these problems (HEDP, 2009). Limited curriculum time and dealing with emotional content and 'very limited' content knowledge were recognized within the report's findings as reasons why teachers lack confidence in their teaching of these difficult topics. Further to these issues, in the Rwandan context, is the politicization of the events before, during and after the genocide. Even the political issues surrounding the story of Paul Rusesabagina, the shooting down of President Habyarimana's aircraft and recent stories of unrest and repression within Rwanda, cloud the narrative and make teachers wary of approaching the subject.

In order to get a sense of the situation regarding the teaching of the genocide in Rwanda, the Survivors Fund (SURF) conducted a research survey, albeit on a limited scale. Their survey revealed that similar issues afflict the teaching of the Holocaust; a scarcity of time, resources and knowledge all hinder teaching about the genocide.[1] One important challenge to teaching about the Rwandan genocide in particular is the scarcity of suitable material that teachers feel comfortable using. Over 70 per cent of teachers surveyed had not found any suitable external resources and had created their own. A similarly high proportion chose to make use of the 2004 film *Hotel Rwanda* as a resource – for many teachers this film was their only teaching aid to teach the topic. While there are obvious dangers in using a feature film to teach the complexity of the genocide, the wider point is that resources are not readily available. Crucially, only 10 per cent of teachers made use of any survivor testimony.[2] Time devoted to this subject is also short, with more than 60 per cent of teachers spending fewer than three hours on this subject. Teacher confidence is also clearly an issue – over 80 per cent of teacher respondents rated their subject knowledge as being either 'average' or 'poor'. This depicts a fairly stark picture of lack of time, resources and knowledge.

Are comparable studies of the Holocaust and Rwanda wise?

At a first glance it may appear that one 'easy way out' in terms of teaching the Rwandan genocide would be to compare it to the causes, course and consequences of the Holocaust. Indeed, the Taskforce for International Holocaust Education, Remembrance, and Research explicitly demonstrate the merits in comparing the Holocaust with the Rwandan genocide (ITF, 2010). From the point of view of studying the latter, students' conceptual knowledge, gained through an examination of the Holocaust, will enhance their investigation of the events in Rwanda in 1994. An understanding of the term 'genocide' will help students contextualize the situation in Rwanda. Similarly, a knowledge of how genocidal situations are brought about by regimes gained through a study of what occurred in Europe in the 1930s and early 1940s may provide a base from which an analysis of the administration in Rwanda may benefit.

However there are pitfalls in this approach that must be guarded against and call the approach into question. Chief among these is the temptation to diminish the status of either the Holocaust or the Rwandan genocide as historically unique events. As many details divide them as tie them together – a study of the discriminatory policies of categorization of the 'other' genocide adopted by both regimes can be meaningful only if it goes beyond, for instance, saying that 'they were the same because the Jews were made to wear a Yellow Star and the Tutsis were called *Inyenzi* (cockroaches)'. Paper-thin comparisons negate a meaningful, in-depth study of what happened in Europe in the 1930s and in the Great Lakes region in the early 1990s. The danger with a comparative approach is that students can easily make facile comparative judgements that miss the point of the bigger questions that teachers are asking them to consider. Who was the bigger rescuer: Paul Rusesabagina or Oskar Schindler? Where would it have been worse to have been: Babi Yar or Bisesero? This approach does not work.

Teaching the Rwandan genocide and better citizens

One obvious, well intentioned, yet ultimately misguided justification for embarking on the teaching of the Rwandan genocide asserts that it provides us with moral lessons that our students can take out into the modern world. This line of thinking – that we can create 'better' young people by studying the behaviour of those in Rwanda in 1994 – is inaccurate. First, it runs the risk of bending the history of the genocide to fit a modern-day purpose. It would be easy to settle the students in class, press 'play' on the *Hotel Rwanda* DVD and have the students leave the room determined to start acting like Paul Rusesabagina. Secondly, why choose the Rwandan genocide to try to alter perceived problems in our society today? The two don't fit together in any but a superficial way – the first is a unique historical event; the second is a contemporary issue born of circumstances inherently different to those seen in 1994.

While the pedagogical scene around the teaching of the Rwandan genocide has yet to be fully explored and mature, there are debates around the teaching of the Holocaust that are instructive. The discussion that took place in several publications was initiated by Nicholas Kinloch, who claimed that the same teaching approaches used to teach the Holocaust can be applied to teaching the Rwandan genocide. In essence Kinloch's position was that the sole aim of history teachers should be to help students become better historians and that the attempt to extract moral lessons from the study of the Holocaust is doomed to failure (Kinloch, 1998). Kinloch was criticized for not aiming high enough and for restricting the ambition of the teaching at hand (Illingworth, 2000), and for presenting a perpetrator-led narrative that essentially dehumanizes the victims of the genocide under consideration. We must, however, remain careful. Approaching the teaching of the Rwandan genocide with overtly moral objectives is to lessen, if not cheapen, the history that we are teaching. Any attempt to use the events of 1994 to impose notions of right and wrong or to have our charges walk out of the classroom as better people simply because they have watched a film or DVD is laden with difficulty. Besides, teaching through the lens is a simplified, subjective, contested, fictionalized, narrative which is not subject to the rigour of historical scrutiny. Hence discussions around morally complex issues and decisions should not be reliant on such a resource.

The unique historical nature of the Rwandan genocide, like the Holocaust, surely means that it will not be repeated and, therefore, any lessons that we seek to learn from it and 'apply' to our world are false ones (Kinloch, 2001). Used in isolation *Hotel Rwanda*, like *Schindler's List* offers a distorted view of the genocides that they speak of – largely Jews and Tutsis were not rescued, they did not escape. Similarly, these films have been used widely as a tool to elicit some kind of empathetic response on the part of students. If teachers aim for these outcomes, then any number of blockbuster films will suffice. Any tragedy in history can be used to portray human beings at their best and at their worst – the Rwandan genocide does not necessarily need to be burdened with an artificial task.

A quick internet search readily throws up examples of well-meaning educational manuals based around these films that seek to, for example, 'raise questions of guilt, punishment, forgiveness, and reconciliation.' Even if these questions were based on historically reliable footage, surely the transposing of such issues from the tumult of Rwanda in 1994 to the United Kingdom in the second decade of the twenty-first century is a step too far. 'Guilt', 'punishment', 'forgiveness' and 'reconciliation' are all words whose meanings are simply too different to translate from a genocidal context to that of the United Kingdom at this present time.

Reasons for teaching about the Rwandan genocide

The obstacles to teaching about the Rwandan genocide may be legion but it can provide the following benefits:

Build on good Holocaust teaching

While it is not preferable to have students compare the Rwandan genocide with the Holocaust, there is clearly scope for a study of the former to build on that of the latter both in terms of skills and conceptual knowledge. The quality of Holocaust teaching is improving markedly thanks to the work of educational institutions such as the Holocaust Educational Trust, and the Holocaust Memorial Day Trust and other initiatives, such as the Imperial War Museum's Holocaust Education Fellowship and the Holocaust Education Development Programme. Debate within professional publications, such as *Teaching History*, as evidenced above and below, helps development of this subject. Therefore there is enough good practice available for teachers who are interested in teaching about the Rwandan genocide.

The Rwandan genocide highlights a historically unique episode

Simply put, students should study the Rwandan genocide because it happened . . . and happened only very recently. The killing of so many men, women and children in such a short space of time under the glare of the world's media spotlight is surely worthy of study. There is the temptation for students to assume that, after studying the Holocaust, something as terrible could never and would never happen again. It is instructional for them to see that it did.

The genocide tells us something about how the world works today

In an increasingly networked world, global institutions, such as the UN, play leading roles in international relations. A critique of the action (or inaction) of the United Nations in 1994 is a useful case study that needs to be brought to the attention of students, who will feel the influence of such organizations throughout their lives. Similarly, the attitudes of nation states to the suffering of their fellow human beings highlight the true nature of international relations that students may not have previously come across.

Elements of good practice

There are an increasing number of resources that allow the teaching of the Rwandan genocide to be undertaken with confidence. In addition to the previous points made in this chapter, the use of *Hotel Rwanda*, in isolation, is not particularly suitable. While elements of the film can help set context of the genocide and introduce essential elements of the narrative, the film just shows one atypical story. For the central character the film ultimately has a happy ending with his wife and children safe – something that was not the case for the vast majority of Tutsi or mixed Hutu/Tutsi families of the time.

The most effective teaching resources that cover the Rwandan genocide all encompass the use of survivor testimony. It is very important that students see the victims of genocide as more than nameless, emaciated figures. The establishment of personal connection, of lives that contained the same likes and ambitions, is key to students humanizing those that the genocidaires wished to dehumanize. Breaking away from the narrative of the perpetrator is essential instead of just seeing the Tutsi victims simply as broken and bloodied bodies or lines of skulls in present-day memorials.

Below is a case study of what a relatively short series of activities based on survivor testimony looks like. The key point with this example is that much of the work was done by students themselves in interviewing survivors. The process of building background knowledge, understanding the sensitive and serious nature of their task, formulating questions and analysing responses all goes towards accumulating in-depth subject knowledge and developing meaningful, transferable historical skills. Furthermore, in terms of building a sense of 'active' citizenship, there is little better catalyst than interaction with a human being, not much older than the students themselves, who has been through the trauma that a survivor has. While there is no prescribed 'learning outcome', it is surely right that we trust our students to take something meaningful from the encounter. It is not insignificant that at least one group of students who interviewed a survivor then went on to collect 1,100 pairs of shoes from their school community to send to survivors battling to put their lives back together in Rwanda.

Case study: Student-generated resources

During 2010 students from four schools in England, Hampton School, European School Culham, Bilton School and Sandhurst School, were given the opportunity to film interviews with survivors of the Rwandan genocide who are now based in the United Kingdom. The students helped design learning activities that were specifically produced to complement the recording of survivors' testimony. The students interviewed survivors who reside in different parts of the United Kingdom before meeting up at the Imperial War Museum to hold a workshop to plan how the interviews could help other students learn about the genocide and its aftermath. The use of survivor testimony should enable students to make meaningful connections and allow them to investigate the multiple narratives that the events of 1994 have to relate. What, then, might a viable scheme of work look like? Below is a simple, short scheme that includes the essential elements that will allow students to enhance their knowledge of the causes, course and consequence of the genocide as well as developing historical skills (SURF online, n.d.).

Here there is a clear contrast between the traditional teaching approach and the reality of everyday life in a history or citizenship or religious studies classroom. The resources that the students help produce do not require a huge amount of curriculum to get through – a scheme of work that incorporates lengthy study of the background to the genocide would obviously be preferable. However, as all the available research suggests, time is limited. Here a prior study of the Holocaust may well help students to quickly understand the nature of genocide and some of the circumstances that might bring it about. While there are useful lesson plans and resources in existence that provide background information, an in-depth understanding of Rwanda's domination by German and then Belgian colonial powers is not necessarily obligatory (SURFa, online, n.d.). Choices have to be made by teachers and it is surely preferable that they have the opportunity to confront their students with words of survivors rather than in-depth studies of the consequences of the Congress of Berlin in 1884.

Lesson 1: Before

A lesson that looks at what life was like in Rwanda before the genocide. Content includes a brief film giving an overview of Rwanda's immediate pre-genocide history and filmed testimony from three survivors: Simeon, Cassien and Daphrose. The activities contained within the lesson ask pupils to consider the nature of the discrimination that Tutsis faced before 1994. The card sorting activity approach is one that focuses on students analysing and thinking about information.

Lesson 2: During

Again using the testimonies of Simeon, Cassien and Daphrose, this lesson looks at the dreadful 100 days in 1994 when the genocide was unleashed in Rwanda. Activities ask pupils to consider the nature of the survivors' experiences within the context of everyday language that they use themselves.

Lesson 3: After

The story of Simeon, Cassien and Daphrose concludes with a look at their lives after the genocide and whether they have had positive experiences since. Further to this the pupils are asked to assess whether the survivors have received justice in the years after 1994.

Conclusion

If the teaching of the Rwandan genocide is to become a more common feature of classrooms in the United Kingdom (and the case here seems to be compelling), the problems created by a lack of time, knowledge and inclination need to be solved. Nevertheless, the beginning of the process of providing solutions starts with the establishment of a solid pedagogy built on the good practice that currently exists in much teaching about the Holocaust and in the creation of good resources that will interest teachers to explore the genocide further. An attempt to highlight such resources has been made above and, as the twentieth anniversary of the genocide approaches, the hope that there is more to come is certainly realistic.

Suggested questions

- Should the Rwandan genocide be taught in all schools as the Holocaust is in England?
- Is 17 years long enough to gain an accurate perspective on such emotive content?
- Do time restrictions mean that some controversial topics can never be taught properly?

Further reading/resources

- Frontline, 'The Triumph of Evil', www.pbs.org/wgbh/pages/frontline/shows/evil/.
- Ghosts of Rwanda', www.pbs.org/wgbh/pages/frontline/shows/ghosts/video/.

- Human Rights Watch,.www.hrw.org/legacy/reports/1999/rwanda/.
- BBC, http://news.bbc.co.uk1/hi/world/africa/1288230.stm
- An online forum debate, www.schoolhistory.co.uk/forum/index.php?showtopic=12053&hl=schindler&st=0.

References

HEDP (2009), *Teaching About the Holocaust in English Secondary Schools*. London: Holocaust Education Development Programme, www.hedp.org.uk (accessed 31 March 2011).

Illingworth, S. (2000), 'Hearts, Minds and Souls: Exploring values through history', *Teaching History*,100, Thinking and Feeling Edition, 20–4.

ITF (2010), *Holocaust, Genocide and Crimes Against Humanity*. www.holocausttaskforce.org/images/itf_data/EWG_Holocaust_and_Other_Genocides_copy.pdf (accesses 31 March 2011).

Kinloch, N. (1998), 'Learning About the Holocaust: Moral or historical question?', *Teaching History*, 93, History and ICT Edition, 44–6.

—(2001), 'Parallel Catastrophes? Uniqueness, redemption and the Shoah', *Teaching History*, 104.

SURF (n.d.), www.survivors-fund.org.uk (accessed 31 March 2011).

SURFa (n.d.), www.survivors-fund.org.uk/resources/education/lesson-plans.php (accessed 31 March 2011).

Notes

1 This online survey about the teaching of the Rwandan genocide was conducted between September 2009 and May 2010 and completed by 50 teachers.
2 The resources produced by Survivors Fund are based on video clips of interviews with survivors. Further information at www.survivors-fund.org.uk/education/.

Part 4
Racism and Discrimination

Islamophobia

Geri Smyth

15

Chapter Outline

Introduction

> The Commission notes a particularly dramatic aspect of social exclusion, the vulnerability of Muslims to physical violence and harassment. (Runnymede Trust, 1997a, 3)

Nearly 15 years after the Runnymede Trust's report (1997a), some may argue that this challenge has grown and is greater than ever. Islamophobia is not a new phenomenon but the European Monitoring Centre on Racism and Xenophobia (EUMC) reported that

> [a] greater receptivity towards anti-Muslim and other xenophobic ideas and sentiments has, and may well continue, to become more tolerated. (Allen and Nielsen 2002, 46)

The report recommended that it would be increasingly relevant for monitoring of Islamophobic incidents to be maintained in the future.

The EUMC has since 2007 become the European Union Agency for Fundamental Rights, and this body has produced regular monitoring reports on discrimination faced by minorities across Europe. The 2009 EU-MIDIS Report (FRA, 2009) found that on average one in three Muslims surveyed in 14 member states of the EU had experienced discrimination in 2008. This survey also found that the majority of Muslims were unaware that discrimination against them might be illegal and were not aware of organizations that might support them if they faced discrimination.

The growth in the recognition and reporting of Islamophobic activity can partly be seen as a result of media and politicians' responses to events such as the bombing of the World Trade Center in 2001, the London transport bombings in 2005 and the attempted bombing at Glasgow airport in 2007. Although these acts were carried out by Muslims, the ways in which these events have been reported have led to a confusion in the minds of many between the religion of Islam and a political Islamist movement. These terms are controversial, but it is clear that every Muslim is not responsible for the above bombing attacks, in the same way as, for example, not every Christian can be held to account for Nazism. In January 2011 Baroness Warsi, co-chair of the UK Conservative Party, argued that Islamophobia is seen as normal and uncontroversial and that attempts to divide Muslims into moderates and extremists have fuelled misunderstandings.

The Runnymede Trust's summary report (1997b, 1) defines Islamophobia as fear, hatred or hostility towards Islam, Islamic culture and Muslims. Islamophobia also refers to the practice of discriminating against Muslims by excluding them from economic, social and public life. It includes the perception that Islam has no values in common with other cultures, is inferior to the West and is a violent political ideology rather than a religion. Islamophobia affects all aspects of Muslim life and can be expressed in a range of ways that include direct attacks, abuse and violence against Muslims and those perceived to be Muslim, and attacks on mosques, Islamic centres, Muslim cemeteries and businesses owned by Muslims. Islamophobia can result in Muslims experiencing discrimination in education, employment, housing, and delivery of goods and services, as well as a lack of provisions and respect for Muslims in public institutions.

This chapter explores the reasons why it is relevant and important for teachers to confront and challenge Islamophobia and suggests how this might be done. The chapter is written from a Scottish perspective, but its implications are relevant for the wider UK and European contexts.

The Scottish context

In the 2001 census, Islam was the most common faith after Christianity with 42,600 people (0.84% of the population) describing their religion as Islam. In England the Muslim population recorded in the 2001 census was 1,525,000 (3.1% of the population). Fifty per cent of Muslims in Scotland at the time of the census were born in the United Kingdom. The majority of Muslims in Scotland are of Pakistani ethnic origin with around 8 per cent being of white ethnicity.

The majority of schools in Scotland are non-denominational. Alongside Roman Catholic state provision there is also one Jewish state school in Scotland (identified as non-denominational) and three Episcopalian schools. In England there are a small number of voluntary, state-aided Muslim schools (six with primary and five with secondary provision). These cater for a very small proportion of the pupil population. There have been calls for a state-funded Islamic school in Scotland. This has been supported by Scotland's First Minister, Alex Salmond, with the provisos that the school remain within the state school system and that there be sufficient support for such a school. The Commission on British Muslims and Islamophobia, established by the Runnymede Trust, recommends that there be state funding for Muslim schools. The European Commission on Racism and Intolerance (ECRI) in fact considers that the bar on establishing Muslim schools is an ongoing problem of discrimination. Debate on the issue of religious schools should be held in classrooms as well as in the media and among policymakers. Teachers and students need to discuss the meaning and purposes of education and the reasons why some members of some faiths may consider that a 'non-denominational' education is not adequate.

Islamophobia manifests itself across Europe. Many Scots are complacent about the lack of racism in the country, where there is a myth that integration is easier. There have been successful recent campaigns against racism, notably One Scotland Many Cultures and Show Racism the Red Card (SRtRC), which have had an influence in schools. SRtRC has produced excellent resources for schools and teachers on challenging Islamophobia. Yet it is only too easy to find incidents of Islamophobia in Scotland, many of which directly affect children and young people. For example, a manager of a childcare centre was found guilty of misconduct for posting Islamophobic comments on her blog page (Islamophobia Watch, 2010). Further a group of youths threw eggs into an Islamic Centre in Scotland (*Paisley Daily Express*, 2010). In 2011, STV reported a rise of 20.4 per cent of racist incidents recorded in Scotland in 2009/10 to the number reported in 2008/09 (STV, 2010). Figures for 2010 showed that 48 per cent of race-hate victims were of Pakistani origin.

With the opportunities presented by the Scottish *Curriculum for Excellence*, teaching about Islam and Muslims should not be left to religious education, as all young people should be engaged in developing critical literacy skills which will allow them to challenge the prejudice often conveyed by the media.

Case study

The relevance of teaching about Islamophobia is demonstrated by the following conversation from a group of six 10- to 13-year-olds at a seminar event (March 2009) for young people. No adults were present during this conversation:

> Girl 1: Some white people think all black people are bad and some black people think all white people are bad.
>
> Boy 1: Black people get a lot of bad press and one of the reasons people feel prejudiced towards them is terrorism . . .
>
> Boy 2 :That was Muslims.

Here the boy speaking is making a distinction between 'black people' and 'Muslims' and indicating a belief that 'Muslims' are responsible for 'terrorism'.

Boy 3: But dinnae say it was Muslims cos not all Muslims are bad.

Girl 1: Yeah it's just it was those people whether they were black or Muslim or spotted. You can't just say it's all those people with blue eyes are going to kill us.

Boy 1: That's like Hitler.

Anti-Muslim sentiment is used as a generic racist insult, targeting all who are seen to fit with this image of 'all black people are bad' as is suggested in the opening line of the above conversation.

These young people showed a sophisticated understanding of the way in which the media can influence attitudes by connecting stories of terrorism and Islam and also showed that such attitudes can lead to dangerous generalization and stereotyping. The opportunity to express their views led to the young people's development of understanding. However, there are misunderstandings in their conversation, such as that all Muslims are black. It is important for teachers to allow such conversations and understandings to evolve in the classroom and to tackle the misunderstandings.

The generic nature of the insult led to a 9-year-old Christian girl from Iran being called a 'Paki' on the street. When writing for the Save the Children (Scotland) CARIS project, she expressed how she could not understand why she was being called this as she did not come from Pakistan. She was doubly confused as she was popular with her schoolmates and involved in a wide range of school and community based activities, so she wondered why she was verbally abused on the street (Save the Children [Scotland], 2005). The answer lies in prejudice and ignorance, which teachers need to address. Gaine explains that

> Children (and adults) may simultaneously hold images of frightening Muslims alongside friendship with a Muslim in their class. 'You're all right, but it's all the others' or 'You're like one of us' are some of the mechanisms employed to resolve these contradictions. (Gaine, 2005, 19).

Such attitudes reflect the dangers, referred to by Baroness Warsi, of attempting to label and divide the Muslim community and show the overarching view among the indigenous non-Muslim population that integration should mean assimilation, rather than a two-way integration which adapts to change. Gaine also points out that a 'common perception' is 'that Muslims are all inflexible fundamentalists and hence a threat to British culture' (ibid., 11). For this reason the curriculum needs to include reference to and discussion of Muslim contributions to and achievements within Scotland and the United Kingdom.

The British Council (Homes et al., 2010) survey of perceptions of and by Muslims in Scotland found there was more tolerance of Muslims in Scotland than in other parts of the United Kingdom. While this is heartening, there is a danger that this can lead to a complacency and an acceptance that Islamophobia is not a problem in Scotland. Islamophobia may well be less obvious in Scotland where the Muslim population is smaller than in England, as indicated above. Instead, as is evident from the above discussion, there is such a problem and teachers need to confront it.

The media

Interestingly this survey found considerable differences in attitudes to Muslims among those sections of the respondents who read tabloids and those who read broadsheets, with readers of the *Guardian* (a national UK newspaper) being the most accepting of Muslim values, suggesting a link between the media and attitudes. The report of the British Council survey quoted from Muslims in Scotland about how they felt they were perceived. There was a belief expressed that media coverage, particularly sensationalism regarding Muslim extremism in the tabloid press, did not help perceptions of Islam, although one male Muslim also commented that the reports in the media meant that Muslims were led to believe by negative media reporting that all non-Muslims held Islamophobic views:

> 30% of people think wrong about us, but we think 100% do. – Male Muslim, Glasgow (Homes et al., 2010, 37)
>
> I think in the eye of the media . . . every Muslim is a terrorist. – Male Muslim, Dundee (Homes et al., 2010, 35)

Although both national and local media are indeed perpetrators of Islamophobic attitudes in contemporary society, there is also an increase in reporting Islamophobic incidents and in condemning such incidents.

Newspaper reports of Islamophobic incidents may tend to concentrate on vicious and violent assaults by members of organized extremist racist groups, such as the Scottish Defence League (SDL), English Defence League (EDL) and the British National Party (BNP). However, Muslims are also subjected to the effects of Islamophobia by individuals who act in a climate of xenophobia which is perpetrated and upheld by the media. The website Islamophobia Watch documents Islamophobic material in the public domain and is a useful resource for teachers wishing to generate debate in the classroom. The Hate Crimes Survey on Islamophobia (Human Rights First, 2007) reports on the increase of Islamophobia across Europe, referring to the under-reporting and under-recording of such incidents. It is important that teacher input on Islamophobia comprise a range of media articles and reports on Islamophobia that include investigation of bias and generalization and stereotyping of Islam and of Muslims, alongside past and contemporary reports of other religious and culturally based hate crimes.

Forms of discrimination

A discussion of the effects of Islamophobia can be helped by considering the following four levels of discrimination that interact and overlap.

- **Structural discrimination** – this refers to the ways in which different statuses and access to benefits in society are structured into society physically, politically and legally.
- **Institutional discrimination** – this operates when normal institutional procedures and practices work against the interests of certain groups even though there may be no conscious decision to discriminate; for example, religious observation in school for only one faith.
- **Cultural discrimination** – this arises when there are shared assumptions about normality and unquestioned ideas leading to prejudice against those who do not match with these ideas. The often unconscious use in teaching about religion of the terms 'us' and 'them' is a form of cultural discrimination towards those who do not fit with the assumed Christian norm.
- **Personal discrimination** – this refers to individual acts of stereotyping, abuse, harassment and physical assault and can include name-calling and bullying in school based on Muslim identity, assumed or actual.

As with the young person quoted earlier in the chapter, another Muslim compared the treatment of Muslims in contemporary media with the treatment of Jews in the Holocaust. Scapegoating is a further area to be explored among young people.

> It's like in the days of the Nazis they used to always go on about the Jews all the media, and it's like the Muslims are the new Jews. – Male Muslim

The Muslim women in the British Council focus groups frequently mentioned specific negative and incorrect impressions they believed non-Muslims held about Muslim women.

> They are often really, really surprised that you actually wear the scarf of your own choice. – Female Muslim

> People assume that women aren't allowed to get an education or something if they're Muslim or they're expected to just get married. – Female Muslim

Such perceptions highlight the need for teachers to discuss these views. Interestingly the British Council report (Homes et al., 2010, 7) also investigated Muslims' perceptions of non-Muslim Scots and argues that increased dialogue is required between Muslims and non-Muslims to aid understanding of issues around identity. The report acknowledges that in schools there are opportunities for mixing the two groups but that these opportunities may not go beyond the school gates. Community education therefore has a role to play in breaking down stereotypes.

What teachers can do

So there is a responsibility for schoolteachers but also a need for more informal education networks to challenge and counter Islamophobia and other cross-cultural negative stereotyping. In fact this report argues that education is key to this challenge, with one male Muslim respondent suggesting (Homes et al., 2010, 31) that school teaching should include teaching about Islamic belief and worship, which would lead to 'quite a bit more tolerance towards our (the Muslim) religion. More of an understanding of who Muslims are and what we stand for'. This is particularly relevant given the British Council report (ibid., 2010) finding that 66 per cent of respondents were less tolerant towards Islam since the 2007 attack on Glasgow airport.

One requirement of teachers in Scotland when achieving the Standard for Initial Registration is to demonstrate an understanding of principles of equality of opportunity and social justice (GTCS, undated). The Code of Conduct and Practice for Registered Teachers incorporates similar principles in England (GTC, 2009). It is important that initial teacher education and continued professional development are conducted in a policy context and that the history of racism in general and Islamophobia in particular is considered alongside the development of legislation.

It is perhaps more difficult to specify exactly how teachers will act to challenge and confront the specifics of Islamophobia. Richardson (2004) has written about the need for teachers to have a framework of concepts and big ideas to help in challenging Islamophobia. These include the need for teachers to acknowledge shared humanity by discussing issues of similarity, sameness and universality while at the same time recognizing difference and diversity by sharing contrasting stories and ways of doing things. Teachers must also enable young people to recognize that there is excellence everywhere and that the peoples of the world are interdependent, borrowing and mingling ideas and creating mutual influence. At the same time it is essential that teachers recognize individuals' personal and cultural identity and allow this to flourish in the classroom, while being aware of concepts of race and racism and how these can impact negatively on students in their classrooms. Richardson's Big Ideas can be incorporated in small ways such as incorporating cultural reference points into texts, activities, materials and assignments. Displays, exhibitions, signs and visual materials in classrooms and public areas of the school should reflect the identities of society, as should visiting speakers, artists, musicians and storytellers. Teachers with few or no Muslim students should not be complacent about the perceived absence of Islamophobia in their school but should actively seek links with schools where there are Muslim students and teachers.

The Open Society Institute (2005) make a number of recommendations, targeted at schools, education authorities and teacher educators, for consideration in challenging Islamophobia in the classroom. These include the need for all teachers to respect young people's Muslim identity; avoid negative perceptions and less favourable expectations of Muslim students and avoid stereotypical thinking about Islam and Muslims. Muslim educational achievement needs to be considered in teacher education and possible reasons for underachievement identified. Curricula need to be considered in terms of linguistic and cultural bias, by omission as well as more overt bias. Teachers should also be trained to offer support to Muslim students who are victims of Islamophobic behaviour, to deal appropriately with offending students and should be encouraged to adopt assessment practices that respect cultural diversity. This requires an ability to recognize Islamophobia and not to trivialize students' concerns.

Suggested questions

- Consider the texts used in your classroom across the curriculum: is there any mention of Muslim achievement or influence? Are there any Muslim authors referred to? If there are children with Muslim names, is there any added value to this or is it tokenistic?
- Collect newspaper stories which discuss Islam or Muslims and consider the forms of discrimination which are documented therein. How might such examples be used to help people understand Islamophobia?

Further reading

- Lambert, R., and Githens-Mazer, J. (2010), *Islamophobia and Anti-Muslim Hate Crime: UK Case Studies 2010*. University of Exeter, European Muslim Research Centre, http://centres.exeter.ac.uk/emrc/publications/IAMHC_revised_11Feb11.pdf.
- Show Racism the Red Card Islamophobia Education Pack, www.srtrc.org/uploaded/ISLAMOPHOBIA%20ED%20PACK%20FINAL%20PDF.pdf.

References

Allen, C., and Nielsen, J. S. (2002), *Summary Report on Islamophobia in the EU After 11 September 2001*. European Monitoring Centre on Racism and Xenophobia (EUMC) (2002) http://fra.europa.eu/fraWebsite/attachments/Synthesis-report_en.pdf (accessed 25 February 2011).

FRA, (2009), *EU-MIDIS Data in Focus Report 2: Muslims Publications Office*, European Union Agency for Fundamental Rights.

Gaine, C. (2005,) *We're All White Thanks: The Persisting Myth About 'White' Schools.* Stoke-on-Trent: Trentham Books.

General Teaching Council for England (2009), *Code of Conduct and Practice for Registered Teachers*, www.gtce.org.uk/teachers/thecode/fulltext/fourth (accessed 4 April 2011).

General Teaching Council for Scotland (n.d.), *Standard for Initial Teacher Education*, www.gtcs.org.uk/standards/standard-initial-teacher-education.aspx (accessed 4 April 2011).

Homes, A., McLean, C., and Murray, L. (2010), *Muslim Integration in Scotland: Final Report.* British Council.

Human Rights First (2007), *Islamophobia 2007 Hate Crime Survey*, www.humanrightsfirst.org/wp-content/uploads/pdf/07601-discrim-hc-islamophobia-web.pdf (accessed 25 February 2011).

Islamophobia Watch (2010), www.islamophobia-watch.com/islamophobia-watch/2010/12/4/childcare-manager-ran-racist-blog-claimed-that-muslims-smell.html (accessed 31 March 2011).

Open Society Institute (2005), *Muslims in the UK: Policies for Engaged Citizens.* www.fairuk.org/docs/OSI2004%20complete%20report.pdf (accessed 25 February 2011).

Paisley Daily Express (2010), *Racist attack on Islamic centre*, 12 May, www.paisleydailyexpress.co.uk/renfrewshire-news/2010/05/12/racist-attack-on-islamic-centre-87085-26424413/ (accessed 31 March 2011).

Richardson, R. (2004), 'Curriculum, ethos and leadership: Confronting Islamophobia in UK education', in B. van Driel (ed.), *Confronting Islamophobia in Educational Practice.* Stoke-on-Trent: Trentham Books, pp. 19–33.

Runnymede Trust (1997a), *Islamophobia: A Challenge for Us All.* Runnymede Trust, London.

—(1997b), *Islamophobia: A Challenge for Us All.* Summary report, Runnymede Trust, London.

Save the Children (Scotland) (2005), CARIS, www.savethechildren.org.uk/caris/index.html (site no longer available; last accessed 24 November 2008).

STV (2011), *Racism on the rise in Scotland*, http://news.stv.tv/scotland/227562-racism-on-the-increase-in-scotland/ (accessed 31 March 2011).

16 Homophobia

Barry van Driel and Michele Kahn

Hatred and prejudice are such destructive forces. They destroy human beings, communities and whole societies. And they destroy the hater, too, from the inside. A parent who brings up a child to be a racist damages that child and damages the community in which they live. A teacher who educates a child that there is only one sexual orientation and that anything else is evil denies our humanity and their own too.

Archbishop Desmond Tutu, 2007

Introduction

Teaching and learning about lesbian, gay, bisexual and transgender (LGBT) issues remains a controversial issue in schools across the globe. Just how much work needs to be done in schools around this issue is illustrated by the extent to which LGBT-identified individuals experience overt and subtle intolerance in schools and the extent to which fundamental human rights appear to be violated.

In a recent study by the organization Stonewall on homophobic hate crimes in the United Kingdom, 1,145 gay and lesbian youth were interviewed about their experiences. The report, published in 2007, revealed that, in general, schools were not perceived by LGBT youth as being safe and accepting spaces. The study showed that 65 per cent of young gay, lesbian and bisexual youth had experienced direct bullying (75% in faith schools) in school environments. More than three in five young gay and lesbian individuals felt that there was neither an adult at home or at school who they could talk to about being gay. Furthermore, only 23 per cent indicated that they and their peers had been told in school that homophobic bullying was wrong, and some 35 per cent did not feel safe or accepted at school. The fact that the same study showed that close to 100 per cent of the youth had heard insulting homophobic remarks at school shows how much work still needs to be done in schools in the United Kingdom to raise awareness about LGBT issues.

Such alarming findings are not confined to the United Kingdom. In the United States, the influential Southern Poverty Law Center reported in the spring of 2007 that 75 per cent of gay students had reported being verbally assaulted at school, and more than a third said that they had been physically harassed. A study in the same year by the Gay, Lesbian and Straight Education Network (GLSEN) in the United States showed that when LGBT students were asked about experiences with bullying, 86.2 per cent of LGBT students reported being verbally harassed and 44.1 per cent physically harassed and 25.1 per cent reported being physically assaulted at school in the past year because of their sexual orientation (Kosciw et al., 2008, 30). More than 80 per cent of the youths surveyed stated their teachers never, or rarely, interrupted homophobic remarks. In fact, and perhaps even more concerning, nearly two-thirds of students heard school staff make homophobic remarks (ibid., 21). It is not surprising therefore that the number of students who did not feel safe or accepted at school was even higher than the United Kingdom: 60.8 per cent of the students indicated they did not feel safe in school because of their sexual orientation (ibid., 25).

At the European level, survey research conducted by the International Lesbian and Gay Association (ILGA)-Europe and IGLYO[1] looked at mechanisms of social exclusion affecting LGBT youth in everyday life across Europe. In the 37 countries surveyed, no less than 61 per cent indicated they had had negative personal experiences in school environments because of their LGBT identity. No less that 53 per cent reported verbal or physical bullying. Finally, some 43 per cent of respondents to their study 'found that their school curriculum expressed prejudice or included discriminative elements targeting LGBT people' (Takács, 2006, 55).

All of the data above point to a widespread sense of discomfort that is experienced by LGBT-identified individuals in school environments in both North America and Europe. The data point to the prevalence of bullying and the fact that it is not only the other students that are responsible for creating an intolerant climate; it is often the teachers, staff and the curriculum itself that promote intolerance.

Addressing sexual diversity in schools: General patterns

The opportunities and barriers to address a topic as potentially controversial as teaching about sexual diversity in classrooms are highly dependent on a variety of factors. Multiple factors at the national level, including the budget (or lack of it), political changes in governments, the constitution and laws, the national curriculum and the impact of traditional religious institutions, influence what happens in education. Furthermore, the lens through which LGBT issues are viewed in societies is related to established cultural and religious patterns which often have the effect of oversimplifying sexual orientation and gender identity into 'manageable' binary categories. These include references to behaviour as being masculine or feminine, gay or heterosexual, normal versus abnormal, deviant versus acceptable and healthy versus unhealthy. There are also multiple factors at the local and even school level.

At the level of the schools themselves, it can be useful to identify several approaches when it comes to education about sexual-diversity issues.

1. *Avoidance*. Studies such as the ones referred to in the introduction to this chapter indicate that this is the most common approach in multiple countries

and that such avoidance might actually be growing. In the short term, avoidance appears to be the easiest way of dealing with a controversial issue such as homosexuality. The reasoning is rather simple in many cases: if we pretend that homosexuality does not exist, we can therefore ignore it. Sexual diversity then remains invisible. Other arguments along these lines are that schools should be teaching the three Rs and not provocative social issues, or that schools should not be 'promoting sex'.

2. *Condemnation*. Especially religious schools that base their teachings on scripture are more likely to discuss homosexuality as immoral and sinful behaviour. However, negative images of LGBT-identified individuals are pervasive in both public and private schools, often surfacing in textbooks and literature and reinforced by staff and students.

3. *Marginalization*. Seeing LGBT issues as unimportant or rare and devoting as little attention as possible to them.

4. *Separation*. Treating LGBT issues separate from broader discussions of sexual behaviour and love relationships and treating homophobia as unconnected to other forms of intolerance, such as sexism.

5. *Compartmentalization*. Here, LGBT issues are tackled in one subject area such as sex education or teachers rely on what is written in a textbook, usually with little discussion. The alternative is to work across subject areas, with teachers in different disciplines bringing in other resources, such as literature and film, to develop understanding in a range of contexts and thus deepen the discussions.

6. *A-historical versus historical approach*. Only focusing on the situation today versus understanding that there is a long history of persecution (human rights violations) of the LGBT community (and other minority communities), but also presenting positive examples from the past (e.g., a timeline of LGBT human rights gains).

7. *Local versus global*. Seeing the issue as only local or global instead of recognizing both as being important.

8. *Whole-school approach*. Including after-school activities, research, exhibitions, gay-straight alliances, anti-bullying campaigns, guest speakers and specific school policies to protect LGBT students and teachers (within perhaps a broader human rights context). Whole-school approaches demand significant resources but can have a more profound impact.

9. *Whole-community approach*. Bringing the community into the school and the school into the community (e.g., service learning). It is difficult to influence student attitudes when the outside community and parents adhere to an intolerant belief system and even promote homophobia. Such approaches can be effective, but are also quite challenging and carry the risk of a backlash (especially in more conservative communities).

What about LGBT staff?

LGBT equity for students will never make significant advances until there is equity for LGBT educators. Teachers and other school staff who are known or suspected of being LGBT can face significant employment repercussions (i.e., being fired or reassigned) and social marginalization and harassment from parents, colleagues and students (Eckes and McCarthy, 2008; Ferfolja, 2008; Jackson, 2007; King, 2004; Macgillivray, 2008). For example, in 2009 in Washington, DC, a parent filed a complaint against her first grader's teacher for allegedly corrupting her child's innocence after hearing that she announced her wedding to another woman to the class and was reading books like 'Uncle Bobby's Wedding', which is about two gay guinea pigs. When educators do not feel safe to disclose their sexual orientation and/or gender identity, their overall job performance is substantially affected. Jackson (2007) documented how homosexual teachers in various stages of being out were influenced by how they felt perceived in terms of their sexual orientation, as well as how they addressed social justice issues in the classroom. Teachers in supportive school environments were more likely to have an integration of their identities as a homosexual and as a teacher, which in turn made them more effective educators. However, for this to happen, schools must have written policies that specifically address LGBT issues that protect educators from employment discrimination and harassment. Additionally, fostering an accepting and welcoming school climate must accompany legal policies in order for conditions to improve. In 2003, the United Kingdom passed the Employment Equality (Sexual Orientation) Regulations (SI 2003/1661), which forbids discrimination on the basis of sexual orientation, and in 2008 an amendment to the Sex Discrimination Regulations of 1975 (SI 2008/656) provided additional protection for transgender individuals having had or undergoing reassignment surgery. This legislation has allowed teachers to come out as bisexual, knowing that they have legal protection to conduct their lives just as heterosexual teachers do (Tackling Homophobia, 2003). Without legal backing, LGBT educators are more likely to remain closeted and students who may themselves be struggling with their identity and/or beliefs about sexuality and gender are denied LGBT role models. Persons who are at a loss in how to enact change in their schools can turn for guidance to GLSEN and Stonewall and also local organizations. These groups already have a framework and plan for change and typically need volunteers to help reach their goals for safer and welcoming schools. Without activism it is unlikely that conditions will change.

Addressing LGBT issues in education: A closer look at the objections

The controversy that surrounds objections to talking about LGBT issues seems to stem from four general perspectives: (1) Children are sexually innocent; (2) religious and/or cultural beliefs clash with non-heterosexual orientations; (3) talking about LGBT issues means talking about sex and that to talk about sex is to promote it; (4) LGBT issues are not relevant to the curriculum. The notion that children are sexually innocent has been countered throughout the psychological literature. A number of researchers (Maccoby and Jacklin, 1974; Garvey, 1984; Lively and Lively; 1991) have expressed that childhood innocence, in the sense that children are unaware of gender and sexuality, is a myth. Children are aware of their own gender and gender roles as early as 2 years of age. By extension, children already come to school with ideas about how boys and girls should behave and this by extension is intertwined with sexuality as normative gender roles assume heterosexuality. De Palma and Jennett (2010) describe the 'No Outsiders' project in the United Kingdom, which addresses homophobia at the primary school age. They cite various evidence that points to the need to address this phenomenon early on. For instance, they cite data from Childline, a child protection helpline, that '60% of the young people who called to talk about sexual orientation, homophobia or homophobic bullying were 12 to 15 years, and 6% were 11 years or under' (ibid., 18).

Some individuals believe that LGBT matters are not relevant to the curriculum. De Palma and Jennett (ibid.) comment on the situation in the United Kingdom as follows:

> LGBT equality still remains largely unaddressed in schools despite the fact that this pressing human rights issue is officially recognized by the Department for Children, Schools and Families (DCSF), the Office for Standards

in Education (Ofsted) and the General Teaching Council for England (GTC) (De Palma and Jennett , 2010, 15–16).

An example from the United States can prove illustrative. In Alameda, California, in 2009 parents sued the school board over the district's decision to incorporate six lessons a year on the harm that teasing does, including a 45-minute lesson that specifically addresses LGBT topics (also known as Lesson 9). Some parents called it the gay and lesbian curriculum and many felt that it was unfair for their children to have to learn something in school that conflicted with their religious values (www.ednews.org/articles/ca-schools-phase-out-gay-friendly-curriculum.html).

In fact it would be difficult to teach certain lessons without discussing gender and sexuality – especially in subject areas such as history, biology, literature and citizenship/civics. For example, the fact that women were not allowed to vote until the early and mid-twentieth century must include a discussion about the underlying beliefs about gender roles. Furthermore, attitudes towards same-sex couples have changed through time and teachers need to discuss topics such as the Stonewall riots, Plato, or even Nazi persecution policies within the context of same-sex relationships.

Potential for change

Despite resistance towards discussing or introducing LGBT topics in schools, there are a presently a vast array of materials that can be used by teachers to supplement their textbooks. For example, the Council of Europe's education kit *Compass* (Council of Europe, 2002) (especially unit 2.24), banned in Poland for several years for its mention of LGBT issues, is widely available in multiple languages and uses a human rights lens (*Compass* is a manual on human rights education for use in Europe. This can be found online at http://eycb.coe.int/compass/en/contents.html). The documentary *It's Elementary* (Chasnoff and Cohen, 1996) from the United States shows several schools which incorporate LGB issues into the curriculum through (a) Gay and Lesbian Pride Day, (b) teacher-led discussion about LGB stereotypes, (c) a photography exhibition of LGB families, (d) LGB guest speakers, and (e) stories with LGB people and/or kids with LGB parents. These activities occur from the first grade on to secondary school.

For many across the globe, sex education in the Netherlands has served as an inspiration. It has the lowest teenage pregnancy rates in Europe; youth start to engage in sexual activity at a relatively late age and attitudes towards homosexuality are very accepting.[2] It was the first nation to recognize same-sex marriage (in 2001). Referred to as 'The Dutch Model' by UNESCO (2000), almost all secondary schools and more than half of primary schools address sexuality and contraception. Homosexuality is almost always included in these lesson plans, despite the lack of a national curriculum as such. Nevertheless, improvements are constantly being made. In August 2010, the largest publisher of school books in the Netherlands, Nordhoff, decided to include examples of LGBT couples in a variety of math examples and problems, in assignments and in general discussions in a variety of subjects. Homosexuality is already discussed in biology and history lessons. But until now textbooks did not include examples of LGBT couples when discussing more general themes. It is usually dad and mom who shop together for groceries (already reflecting a certain amount of gender equality in the country). In the future, the examples will include either two men or two women shopping together (as couples).

The publishing company also recently indicated it would not create separate books for conservative Christian schools, though they do anticipate objections from such schools. In an interview with Radio Nederland Wereldomroep (2010), the director of Nordhoff, Frans Grijzenhout, compared giving in to such pressure to creating separate books that would not include other minorities, such as immigrants. He emphasized that the school books should reflect modern reality.

Though the Dutch government has long supported education about LGBT issues, recent hate crimes have led to an even more active stance. In a letter from the minister of education, culture and science, the Dutch government, in February 2010, confirmed that education about LGBT issues will be a priority area (*kerndoel*) in both primary and secondary education (Brief van de Minister van Onderwijs, Cultuur en Wetenschap, 2010).

Concrete recommendations for action

Ideally, addressing homophobia should be part of a whole-school approach that starts at a young age. De Palma and Jennett put it as follows:

> Both homophobia and transphobia are cultural phenomena and can only be addressed by purposefully promoting the equality of LGBT people as part of a broader whole school ethos that celebrates diversity and challenges inequities of all kinds. In short, the institutional culture of school must be transformed as a whole, and this must begin at the beginning, as soon as children first walk through the school gate. (Palma and Jennett, 2010, 16)

With this comment in mind, we would like to present recommendations for educators wishing to address LGBT issues.

1. Know what kind of exposure students have already had. Get a sense of their attitudes, knowledge and misconceptions. Some ideas to open these discussions include,

    a. Open-ended surveys in class that could include simple, 'non-threatening' questions; for example, 'In your opinion, is there a social group which experiences more discrimination than other social groups?' This can serve as a discussion tool especially for teachers who are reluctant to initiate these conversations.
    b. Assigning a book with a character who is gay and getting reactions that way.
    c. Current events about 'gay' issues, embedded in other social issues.
    d. Talking about human rights and human rights violations in society and then addressing particular targets of human rights violations, such as the LGBT community.

2. Be aware of any previous attempts in school – failures and successes – to address LGBT issues. Investigate who has been the longest at the school and perhaps invite alumni who were homophobically bullied at school to speak to students at school about their experiences.
3. Seek out multiple ways of addressing intolerance against sexual minorities. Discuss international human rights documents, human rights violations today or the history of the Holocaust and related crimes. Though not the main target

of the Nazis, for instance, thousands of LGBT individuals were persecuted and killed by the Nazis because of their sexual orientation or gender identity (a good book for young people is *Damned Strong Love*, by Lutz van Dijk, 1995).

4. Establish a framework for discussion. The difference between facts and opinions needs to be explained and understood by students, perhaps first with non-controversial topics and then with controversial ones. The difference should be visible – for example, on a poster or the writing board where students can regularly add to, discuss and reflect-upon.

5. Practise debating various issues using debate methodologies, and gradually move towards debating more controversial topics, such as LGBT issues. Ideally, the debate questions would not be phrased in ways that would increase intolerance but would explore a variety of solutions. For instance, debate questions could include 'Do you agree with the statement that the best way to tackle homophobia is to have a zero tolerance policy on insulting language?', or 'Do you agree that people who use homophobic language should be forced to apologize in public?' Such debates revolve around the desirability of specific solutions to homophobic utterances. They run less risk of provoking homophobic and otherwise intolerant comments.

6. Get students to actively find information (students as researchers). For instance, students can research laws, interview LGBT organizations, research the media online for examples of hate crimes and do other tasks that empower them to make informed decisions about their beliefs and behaviours.

7. Complicate issues. Avoid simple answers to complex issues and be prepared for some things to remain ambiguous (such as definitions). For example, in terms of explaining sexual orientation, educators may find sexual-orientation models, such as the Klein (1993) model, useful for showing that sexual orientation can be fluid and is multifaceted (i.e., involving emotional and sexual attractions, past present and ideal attractions, etc.).

8. Establish a support network before approaching the principal/director. This includes talking to other teachers who might want to work towards a cross-curricular approach. Contact local agencies that support LGBT issues and other allies (parents, colleagues, etc.).

9. If requesting permission to start a schoolwide activity, come prepared with facts that establish the need. Organizations such as the Gay, Lesbian, Straight Education Network and the Human Rights Campaign in the United States and Stonewall in the United Kingdom have resources that can speed up this process.

The recommendations we have provided are only a starting point and must be implemented taking into consideration the context of the school and community in which they are presented. Undoubtedly, introducing LGBT topics will disturb those with homophobic leanings, which may include staff, students and parents. Educators should be prepared for such backlash and remember that where there are detractors, there are also community members who advocate supporting *all* students. And more and more national governments are taking this stand as well. The increasing number of countries accepting both heterosexual and homosexual marriage, where there were none a dozen years ago, is an indication that something fundamental is changing for the better.

Suggested questions

- Think of the way you learned about LGBT issues in primary and secondary school. Which of the approaches discussed here (avoidance through the whole-community approach) come closest to the ones used in your schooling? Why do you think this was the case?
- If you work in a school, what measures has the school taken to combat homophobic bullying, if any? Are they sufficient in your view?
- Imagine that you have to justify including LGBT issues into the curriculum to a colleague who doesn't believe this is necessary. What would you say? What do you think your colleague would say? Practise the dialogue with a partner.

Further reading

- Goldman, L. (2008), *Coming Out, Coming In: Nurturing the Well-being and Inclusion of Gay Youth in Mainstream Society*. New York: Routledge.
- Jackson, J. M. (2007), *Unmasking Identities: An Exploration of the Lives of Gay and Lesbian Teachers*. Lanham, MD: Rowman and Littlefield.
- Sears, J. T. (ed.) (2005), *Gay, Lesbian, and Transgender Issues in Education: Programs, Policies, and Practices*. New York: Harrington Park Press.
- Van Dijk, L., and van Driel, B. (eds) (2007), *Challenging Homophobia*. London: Trentham Books.

References

Brief van de Minister van Onderwijs (2010), *Cultuur en Wetenschap* (Letter from the Minister of Education, Culture and Science, 5 February), https://zoek.officielebekendmakingen.nl/kst- 27017-66.html (accessed 6 August 2010).

Chasnoff, D., and Cohen, H. (1996), *It's Elementary: Talking About Gay Issues in School* [Film]. San Francisco: Women's Educational Media.

Council of Europe (2002), *Compass: A Manual on Human Rights Education for Young People*. Strasbourg: Council of Europe Publishing.

De Palma, R., and Jennett, M. (2010), 'Homophobia, Transphobia and Culture: Deconstructing heteronormativity in English primary schools', *Intercultural Education*, 21(1), 15–26.

Eckes, S., and McCarthy, M. (2008), 'GLBT Teachers: The evolving legal protections', *American Educational Research Journal*, 45(3), 530–54.

Ferfolja, T. (2008) 'Discourses That Silence: Teachers and anti-lesbian harassment', *Discourse: Studies in the Cultural Politics of Education*, 29(1), 107–19.

Garvey, C. (1984), *Children's Talk*. Cambridge, MA: Harvard University Press.

Hemenway, M. (2009), *The Real Purpose of Gay Marriage*. 14 December, http://pfox-exgays. blogspot.com/2009/12/real-purpose-of-gay-marriage.html (accessed 5 December 2010).

Jackson, J. (2007), Unmasking Identities: An Exploration of the Lives of Gay and Lesbian Teachers. Lanham, MD: Lexington books.

King , J.R. (2004), 'The (im)possibility of gay teachers for young children', Theory into Practice, 43(2), 122–7.

Klein, F. (1993), *The Bisexual Option*. New York: Haworth Press.

Kosciw, J. G., Diaz, E. M., and Greytak, E. A. (2008), *The 2007 National School Climate Survey: The Experiences of Lesbian, Gay, Bisexual and Transgender Youth in our Nation's Schools*. New York: GLSEN.

Lively, V., and Lively, E. (1991), *Sexual Development of Young Children*. Albany, NY: Delmar.

Maccoby, E. E., and Jacklin, C. N. (1974), *The Psychology of Sex Differences*. Stanford, CA: Stanford University Press.

Macgillivray, I. (2008), 'My Former Students' Reflections on Having an Openly Gay Teacher', *High School Journal of LGBT Youth*, 5(4), 72–89.

Radio Nederland Wereldomroep (2010), 'Homostellen in Nederlandse Schoolboeken' (Homosexual couples in Dutch school books), 6 August, www.rnw.nl/nederlands/article/ homostellen-nederlandse-schoolboeken (accessed 1 December 2010).

Stonewall (2007), *The School Report: The Experiences of Young Gay People in Britain's Schools*. Report authored by Ruth Hunt and Johan Jensen.

'Tackling homophobia' (2003), *Secondary Teachers*, 33, www.teachernet.gov.uk/teachers/issue33/ secondary/features/Tacklinghomophobia_Secondary/ (accessed 1 December 2010).

Takács, J. (2006), *Sexual Exclusion of Young Lesbian, Gay, Bisexual and Transgender (LGBT) People in Europe*. Report for ILGA-Europe and IGLYO.

UNESCO Courier (2000), 53 (7), 19.

Van Dijk, L. (1995), *Damned Strong Love: The True Story of Willi G. and Stefan K*. New York: Henry Holt.

Notes

1 International Lesbian, Gay, Bisexual, Transgender and Queer Youth and Student Organisation
2 In fact various international studies have shown the Dutch to have the most accepting attitudes of all nations towards homosexuality – followed by several Scandanavian countries. See, e.g., Kelley, J. (2001), 'Attitudes Towards Homosexuality in 29 Nations', *Australian Social Monitor*, 4, 15–22.

17 Anti-Semitism

Paula Cowan

Introduction

Commonly referred to as the longest hatred (Wistrich, 1994), anti-Semitism is generally defined as prejudice, hatred or hostility towards Jews and/or Judaism. The kidnapping and decapitation of American journalist Daniel Pearl (2002) and the torture and subsequent murder of Ilan Halimi, a young Jew in Paris (2006), are reminders that extreme anti-Semitism persists in the twenty-first century. The Halimi murder additionally highlights institutional anti-Semitic attitudes, as the French police did not initially recognize the anti-Semitic nature of this crime.

Anti-Semitism is complex as it exists in many forms and guises. Historian Robert Wistrich has commented that it is 'morphing all the time' (*Jerusalem Post*, 2010), and it can be argued that some of these emerging forms are difficult to recognize. Learning contexts in which discussion of anti-Semitism would enhance student learning include genocide, racism, far-right politics, Judaism and the Holocaust. Further, because of its complexities, educators may be unsure as to how they should address anti-Semitic behaviour or attitudes in their workplaces, and this may be one reason why such behaviour persists in our society.

Wilhelm Marr (1819–1904) is attributed to coining the word 'anti-Semitism' by naming his organization 'The League of Anti-Semites'. This was one of the earliest anti-Jewish political organizations. Marr used the word 'anti-Semitism' to distinguish between the historical religious hatred and the (then) new racial hatred towards Jews. This chapter aims to show that from the 1870s when anti-Semitism entered the lexicon, its meaning is far from simple. Focussing on contemporary manifestations of anti-Semitism, this chapter will explain the reasons for this by examining the many facets of anti-Semitism and the issues these raise for teachers and educators.

Anti-Semitism and Holocaust education

Short and Reed state that the purpose of Holocaust education is

> to inoculate the generality of the population against racist and anti-Semitic propaganda and thereby restrict its appeal to a disaffected and politically insignificant rump. (Short and Reed, 2004, 6–7)

For the following reasons a harmonious relationship between Holocaust education and anti-Semitism cannot be assumed. First, students should understand that although anti-Semitism was a fundamental aspect of national socialism in Germany in the 1930s and 1940s, it is not a German phenomenon (Short and Reed, 2004). Indeed the earliest manifestations of anti-Semitism predate Christianity, as it existed in Hellenistic and Roman times (Runnymede Trust, 1994). The rise of Christianity and the subsequent charge of deicide led to Jewish people being regarded as less than human, an enemy and a threat. In the Middle Ages, Jews were blamed for the Black Death and excluded from most occupations; thousands were victims of persecution and massacres in the Crusades. Jews were expelled from many countries; for example, England in 1290 (for 350 years) and Spain in 1492. As happened during *Kristallnacht* (1938), in which Jewish-owned shops and synagogues across Germany and Austria were destroyed by fire attacks, the German priest Martin Luther's dictate of 1563 was that synagogues should be set alight. As in the ghettos of the Holocaust, Jews were confined to ghettos in Italy between the sixteenth and eighteenth centuries; and as with the yellow star worn in Germany and Nazi-occupied Europe in the 1930s and 1940s, Jews in the Middle Ages were required to wear distinctive clothing. Although anti-Semitism in Europe existed centuries before the actual word was coined and the features commonly associated with the Holocaust were neither unique to the Holocaust nor to Germany, early anti-Semitism originated from religious or theological attitudes and not race theories. Jews were, in the main, exempt from hostility if they converted to Christianity, but the development of racial anti-Semitism led to new definitions of Jews, with no concessions being granted to non-practising, secular Jews. This culminated with the Nuremberg laws (1935), which stated that any individual who had three or four Jewish grandparents was a Jew. The complexity of these forms of anti-Semitism justifies the conclusion made by the the All-Party Inquiry into Antisemitism in the United Kingdom (2006) that there is a need to explain the history of anti-Semitism to school students.

Secondly, teaching the Holocaust may unintentionally promote anti-Semitism by introducing students to anti-Jewish stereotypical images and propaganda that they would not previously have encountered and to the perception of Jews as a race, thereby reinforcing the stereotype of Jews as victims of persecution (Short and Reed, 2004). It may also set a precedent which can act as an incentive for future anti-Semitic individuals (Kochan, 1989).

Thirdly, teachers cannot assume that students can easily transpose their understanding of anti-Semitism in the context of the Holocaust to recognition and understanding of anti-Semitism today. Students may well be of the view 'that was then; this is now', and view anti-Semitism as something that primarily involves extreme measures such as a loss of citizenship, expulsion, segregation or murder of Jewish people. Such a perception can hinder students' recognition that some traditional anti-Semitic themes 'have found their way into Arab or Islamic anti-Zionist discourse' (Laqueur, 2001, 25). The rise in anti-Semitism in Europe in this century is closely linked to the conflict in the Middle East between Israelis and Palestinians (Laqueur, 2001, 6). Teachers must ensure that their political views, which may include political allegiances that stem from their religious backgrounds, do not influence their teaching and recognize that such views and allegiances may influence the learning of their students.

Finally, during a study of the Holocaust, there is a tendency for teachers 'to emphasise racism *rather* than anti-Semitism' (Short and Reed, 2004). The complicated nature of the relationship between teaching the Holocaust and anti-Semitism has been indicated in previous research where students in Scotland who had studied the Holocaust perceived that this had not developed their understanding of anti-Semitism (Cowan and Maitles, 2005; Maitles and Cowan, 2007). While it can be argued that the Holocaust can be taught effectively without directly using the term 'anti-Semitism', one may ask, If this term is not used in a study of the Holocaust, then in which learning contexts is it most likely to be used? This is especially relevant to students who visit the Auschwitz-Birkenau Memorial and Museum. Findings of one small-scale study were that students who participated in the Lessons from Auschwitz Project in 2007 discussed their experience of visiting Auschwitz on their return to school. While 98 per cent of the study cohort discussed the Holocaust, a significantly smaller number, 57 per cent, discussed anti-Semitism (Cowan and Maitles, 2010).

Anti-Semitism and other school contexts

Aside from history, the other principal curricular area which easily benefits from focus on anti-Semitism is religious and moral education. This is because anti-Semitism is relevant to understanding theological tensions between Judaism and Christianity, as Christian anti-Semitism is one consequence of the charge of deicide against the Jews. Anti-Semitism can also be relevant to English literature, where it can contribute to understanding fictional characters of popular texts, such as Shylock (*Merchant of Venice*) and Fagin (*Oliver Twist*); real people such as Anne Frank (*The Diary of Anne Frank*); and anti-Jewish sentiments as expressed by T. S. Eliot (in the poem 'Burbank with a Baedeker: Bleistein with a Cigar'). Another aspect of anti-Semitism is the censorship of literature where Jews (and Israel) are portrayed favourably. It is disconcerting that in 2009, the UNESCO World Book Capital City was

Lebanon, a country where Holocaust literature such as *Schindler's List* and *The Diary of Anne Frank* and books by many Jewish authors are banned.

In modern studies, politics and citizenship education, a study of anti-Semitism is important to understanding its association with the politics of the far Right and to the fundamental importance of universal human rights. The case of Sven (not his real name) highlights the potential challenges between teaching democracy, human rights and anti-racism.

Eighteen-year-old Sven was a member of an established Nazi group who expressed his sympathies with their ideas by writing Nazi slogans at his school in Sweden and met with school peers after school to discuss these views (Orlenius, 2008). Sven had a negative influence on his school peers, and some students, in particular foreign students and those from ethnic minorities, were offended by his behaviour. The school suspended him although there was no evidence of him bullying or being violent to anyone. When the County Administrative Court disagreed with this decision, the case was taken to the national Supreme Administrative Court, who decided that based on the circumstances presented, the school was not allowed to suspend Sven and that he be reinstated.

While there is no definitive response to behaviour like Sven's, this case raises the issue as to whether freedom of speech should be, as it is in the Swedish constitution, guaranteed to every citizen. The central issue is that of competing rights, as students from ethnic minorities have the right not to be intimidated. Conditions of freedom of speech therefore, require to be identified. Teachers cannot ignore a racist comment, anti-Semitic or otherwise, made by a student or anyone in their school or educational institution. It follows that teachers require clarity in such matters as to how they are to respond to a student who displays such behaviour.

The following incident is an example of anti-Semitism in a different school context:

A group of secondary school students run to catch the school bus. Some money falls out of one of the boys' pockets. As he stops to pick up his money, one boy stops running, points at the Jewish boy and shouts out:

'Oh look everybody, here is a Jew picking up his money. Jews like money'.
The teenagers stop, crowd round and laugh at the Jewish boy and then get on the bus.

A few days later, the father of the Jewish boy makes an appointment with the year tutor. He explains the situation and names the boy who made the remark. The year tutor is sympathetic and explains that he cannot do anything about it until his son comes to him (the teacher) to report the incident and provide the names of the teenagers who witnessed the incident. Only once these are provided will the school investigate the matter.

The teacher's response puts the onus on the victim to come forward and provide key information that may alienate him further from his peers. Clear evidence will make it easier for the teacher because if there are no witnesses, then it will be one student's word against another. If the victim does not provide the information or if the parent did not approach the school, then the above behaviour would go unnoticed. This strategy is as relevant in addressing bullying and other forms of racism as it is to responding to anti-Semitism.

Toolkits and other resources that advise educators on how to deal with such issues are helpful, but their impact is dependent on the commitment of educators to create an ethos that sensitively and effectively tackles racism in its many forms, recognizing that anti-Semitism is one of those forms. In such an ethos, the students who witnessed this incident would, as responsible citizens, on their own volition report it to the school.

It is also worth noting that young people may use the word 'Jew' as a general insult. An example of this is reported by David Burrowes, MP, when he stated in the Westminster Parliament that 'Jew' had been etched onto his son's locker at secondary school (House of Commons, 2011). While this incident may be an isolated case, it does suggest that schools need to be proactive in preventing such racist language from becoming widespread in their playgrounds and encourage their students to speak out against it.

Global anti-Semitism

Leading figures who have publicly condemned anti-Semitism in the twenty-first century include Canadian Prime Minister Stephen Harper

(2010), German Chancellor Angela Merkel, and Foreign Minister Guido Westerwelle (2010), Barack Obama (2008, prior to his presidency) and Pope Benedict XVI (2009). In contrast, in 2003 Mahathir Mohammad, the Prime Minister of Malaysia, spoke at the first conference of Muslim leaders since the terrorist attacks of 9/11 and remarked that 'the Jews rule the world by proxy'. The keynote speaker at the Organisation for Security and Cooperation in Europe (OSCE) regional conference in Romania in 2008 stated that the anti-Semitic climate in Hungary by the media, Magyar Garda organization, Fidesz political party and clergy on Hungarian National Day that year was such that

> [t]he President of the [Hungarian] Jewish community recommended that Jews stay at home for their own safety. (Shapiro, 2008)

Denis MacShane, MP and Chair of the UK All-Party Inquiry into Antisemitism (2005–2006), claims that the 'strongest, formal organized political expression of anti-Semitism' is found in the European Parliament (MacShane, 2008, 30). This claim is supported by the election to this parliament of members from parties that are openly anti-Semitic: the National Front in France, the Greater Romania Party, the Ataka Party in Bulgaria and the British National Party in the United Kingdom. Further, individual politicians are anti-Semitic. One such example is the Polish MEP Maciej Giertych, who in 2007 brought out a booklet bearing the European Parliament's logo in which he argued that

> Jews are unethical, want to live obsessed with separateness and are a tragic community because they don't accept Jesus as the Messiah. (MacShane, 2008, 31)

One of the findings of the UK All-Party Parliamentary Inquiry into Antisemitism in Britain was that anti-Semitism today

> is focused on the role of Israel in the Middle East conflict. . . . Jews throughout the world are seen as legitimate targets in the struggle to establish a Palestinian state or to eliminate the State of Israel. (All-Party Parliamentary Inquiry, 2008, 3)

This adds a subtle dimension to anti-Semitism as it allows anti-Semites to hide behind a political ideology that sympathizes with Palestinians and opposes the establishment and/or policies of Israel, the state that was established, after the Holocaust, as a homeland for the Jewish people.

There is nothing wrong with anti-Zionism as such, or indeed criticism of the (Jewish) state of Israel. In addition, not all critiques of Israel are anti-Semitic and not all forms of anti-Zionism are rooted in anti-Semitism. Many anti-Zionists would argue that their desire for a democratic, secular, bi-federal state in this area, which would mean an end to Israel as an independent Jewish state, is based on political ideology and not racism. However when the terms 'Zionists' and 'Jews' are used interchangeably and then justified by insisting that the criticism is directed specifically against Israel and not Jews; and/or when criticism of Israel leads to denying Israel's right to exist in any form and encouraging violence against Israel and Jews in general, then the distinction becomes blurred and unacceptable. Several Jewish communal organizations have allegedly been 'justifiably' targeted in the interests of anti-Zionists. The bombing of the Argentine-Israeli Mutual Association, in Buenos Aires (1994), in which 85 people were killed and hundreds were injured is one example of this. Educators therefore, need to exercise caution and recognize the possible link between anti-Zionism and anti-Semitism.

The UK Community Security Trust (CST) data show that the number of recorded anti-Semitic incidents rises when there are 'trigger events' in the Middle East. In 2006, when there was war between Israel and Hezbollah, this number rose sharply from 459 to 598. In 2009, when there was conflict between Israel and Hamas in Gaza, the number rose from 546 to an unprecedented 924 (CST Online, 2010). Similarly, the report that documented the rise in anti-Semitic incidents in France in 2005, concluded that

> disaffected French North African youths were responsible for many of the incidents, which French officials linked to tensions in Israel and the Palestinian territories. (Cited in Judaken, 2008, 543)

While it is unacceptable to call for the destruction of an entire country, Iranian President Mahmoud Ahmadinejad continues to call for the destruction of Israel. He also expounds Holocaust denial, an anti-Semitic ideology that rejects established historical facts of the Nazi genocide of the Jews by dismissing documents and testimonies as unreliable or as lies. Holocaust denial first appeared in the late 1940s claiming that the Holocaust was a hoax perpetrated by the Jews to secure the establishment of the state of Israel. Historian Deborah Lipstadt refers to this as a 'growing assault on truth and memory', 'totally irrational' and 'rooted in anti-Semitism' (Lipstadt, 1994). Alongside this is a 'softer variant', which includes minimization and relativization of facts and events in order to cast doubt on the authenticity of the Holocaust (Laqueur, 2001). This similarly is an expression of anti-Semitism. Several countries have legislated against Holocaust denial, and countries where it is illegal include Germany, Austria and Hungary.

Holocaust deniers refer to themselves as 'revisionists', a group whose origins are historians who claimed that Germany was 'unjustly held responsible for the (1914–1918) war' (Lipstadt, 1994, 20). Lipstadt argues that all historians are to some extent revisionist, as they continually investigate and interpret the past, but that Holocaust deniers are not revisionists in this sense, as they distort irrefutable historical evidence. Revisionists blame the deaths of Jews during the Holocaust on wartime deprivations and disease and not on Nazi anti-Semitism. The first (Holocaust) Revisionist Convention (1979) was attended by 'neo-Nazis, philo-Germans, right-wing extremists, anti-Semites, racists, and conspiracy theorists' (Lipstadt, 1994, 65). Holocaust deniers, the historian David Irving, and Nick Griffin MEP, the leader of the British National Party, have also publicly expressed fascist and/or anti-Semitic views. Irving additionally was branded a 'racist' and an 'anti-Semite' by a High Court judge in 2000, when he lost his libel case against Deborah Lipstadt.

One of the challenges that Holocaust denial brings to teachers and educators is whether they should discuss it with students or not. It is likely that primary teachers do not discuss it with their students (when studying the Holocaust) for fear of confusing them. Yet their students can easily access internet material such as the International Holocaust Cartoon Contest (2006), which challenges accounts of the Holocaust and uses Holocaust imagery to criticize the West and the state of Israel. This is a matter of great concern, as educators will rely increasingly on technology, as Holocaust survivors are not present to bear witness. The key issue is that any discussion of Holocaust denial will lead to it being regarded by young people as a legitimate discourse, while not discussing it can allow young people to be influenced by this assault on historical reality which is taking place worldwide on the Web. In 2009 the social networking site Facebook deleted two Holocaust denial groups from its site but to date has refused to delete numerous others that promote hatred of Jews (and of Israel) because it claims 'these groups are engaging in legitimate discourse over a controversial issue' (*Guardian*, 2009).

The World Wide Web is presently the major source for the dissemination of anti-Semitism and propagation of such views. Online discussion forums and blogs have recently become tools that express racism and anti-Semitism. In Scotland, inciteful comments such as 'Jews are not fit to breathe our air' and 'Jews got what they deserved' appeared respectively on the online forums of the Scottish national newspapers the *Scotsman* and the (Glasgow) *Herald* (Cowan, 2010). Online platforms assure anonymity and can encourage engagement and participation and empower individuals. They can also cause offence and foment hostility and racism. The successful prosecution in 2010 of the author of one of the above comments emphasizes the importance of the individual to report such material to the police.

It is clear that present-day anti-Semitism is extensive and comes in different forms: from Christians and Muslims, from the political Left and the political Right. The Runnymede Trust states that

> the level of antisemitism in a European country has been a valid indicator of intolerance and injustice on a wide range of other issues also, affecting non-Jews as well as Jews. (Runnymede Trust, 1994, 11)

This suggests that anti-Semitism adversely affects society as a whole and not just one particular group of people. MacShane goes further and encourages people to reflect on their values. He refers to the new anti-Semitism as *neo-anti-Semitsm* and states:

> Today's neo-antisemitism is not about Jews. It is about us. (MacShane, 2008, viii)

Suggested questions

- Does freedom of speech include the freedom to express racist and/or anti-Semitic views in your school? If you are a teacher, are you clear as to what your response should be to such behaviour?

- Are student behaviours and attitudes affected by events in the Middle East? Should Holocaust denial be discussed in class?

Further reading

- Bloomstein, R. (1993), *The Longest Hatred: The History of Anti-Semitism*. VHS.
- Office for Democratic Institutions and Human Rights (ODIHR) (2007), *Addressing Anti- Semitism: Why and How? A Guide for Educators*. www.osce.org/documents/odihr/2007/12/28962_en.pdf.
- Wistrich, R. (2010), *A Lethal Obsession: Anti-Semitism from Antiquity to the Global Jihad*. London: Random House.

References

All-Party Parliamentary Inquiry into Antisemitism (2006), *Report of the All-Party Parliamentary Inquiry into Antisemitism*. London: The Stationery Office.

Cowan, P. (2010), 'Scotland's New Approaches to Learning about the Holocaust and Racism', *Race Equality Teaching*, 28 (2), 27–30.

Cowan, P., and Maitles, H. (2005), 'Values and Attitudes – Positive and Negative: A study of the impact of teaching the Holocaust on citizenship among Scottish 11–12-year-olds', *Scottish Educational Review*, 37 (2), 104–15.

—(2010), 'Policy and Practice of Holocaust Education in Scotland', *Prospects*, 40 (2), 257–72.

CST (2010), *Antisemitic Incidents Report January–June 2010*, www.thecst.org.uk/ (accessed 6 October 2010).

Guardian (2009), *Facebook Protests over Holocaust Denial Groups*, 11 May, www.guardian.co.uk/technology/blog/2009/may/11/facebook-holocaust-denial (accessed 6 October 2010).

House of Commons (2011), *Anti-Semitism*, 20 January 2011, www.publication.parliament.uk/pa/cm201011/cmhansrd/cm110120/halltext/110120h0001.htm (accessed 12 February 2011).

Jerusalem Post (2010), *Anti-Semitism Is Worse in 2010 Than 1910* www.jpost.com/Features/InThespotlight/Article.aspx?id=184274, 10 August (accessed 17 September 2010).

Judaken, J. (2008), 'So What's New? Rethinking the "New Antisemitism" in a global age', *Patterns of Prejudice*, 42 (4), 531–60.

Kochan, L. (1989), 'Life over Death', *Jewish Chronicle*, 22 December.

Laqueur, W. (2001), *The Holocaust Encyclopedia*. New Haven, CT: Yale University Press.

Lipstadt, D. (1994), *Denying the Holocaust: The Growing Assault on Truth and Memory*. London: Penguin.

MacShane, D. (2008), *Globalising Hatred: The New Antisemitism*. London: Weidenfield and Nicolson.

Maitles, H., and Cowan, P. (2007), 'Does Addressing Prejudice and Discrimination Through Holocaust Education Produce Better Citizens?' *Educational Review*, 59 (2), 115–30.

Orlenius, K. (2008), 'Tolerance of Intolerance: Values and virtues at stake in education', *Journal of Moral Education*, 37 (4), 467–85.

Runnymede Trust (1994), *A Very Light Sleeper: The Persistence and Dangers of Antisemitism*. London: Runnymede Trust.

Shapiro, P. A. (2008), *What's in the Air?* www.european-orum-on-antisemitism.org (accessed 3 November 2010).

Short, G., and Reed, C. A. (2004), *Issues in Holocaust Education*. Aldershot: Ashgate.

Wistrich, R. S. (1994), *Antisemitism: The Longest Hatred*. New York: Schocken.

18 Gypsy and Roma Families

Martin Myers

In 1967 the Plowden Report was commissioned by the Conservative Education Minister, Sir Edward Boyle, to consider primary education in all its aspects and the transition to secondary school. It stated that Gypsy children are

> probably the most severely deprived children in the country. Most of them do not even go to school, and the potential abilities of those who do are stunted. (Plowden Report, 1967)

Prior to Plowden it had been over 30 years since any comparable attempt had been made to assess education in England. For Gypsy children and their families Plowden is important because for the first time it both identified and in some respects attempted to quantify the problems associated with Gypsies and education. In recognition of the severity of problems, the report devoted an entire appendix to the subject, noting that Gypsy children's educational needs are

> extreme and largely unmet. Moreover the economic and social handicaps of the group from which they come arise to a large extent from the

fact that successive generations of gypsy children are deprived of the education that would enable them to compete on equal terms with the rest of the community. Extreme as they are, the needs of gypsy children cannot be effectively met by measures of the kind we recommend for the more general problems of urban deprivation. They will require special attention and carefully planned action. (Plowden Report, Appendix 2, 1967)

In 2003 the Pupil Level Annual School Census (PLASC) included for the first time the ethnic categories 'Gypsy/Roma' and 'Travellers of Irish Heritage' when gathering information about educational performance. While there are many doubts about the accuracy of statistics relating to Gypsy children at school (Acton, 2004; Myers and Bhopal, 2009), the inclusion of these ethnic categories represents a significant step forward in quantifying Gypsy experiences of school education. To date, the PLASC figures have highlighted significant concerns about levels of achievement and attendance for around 12,000 students identified in these two categories (DCSF, 2008).

The PLASC categories also highlight the difficulties of identifying often quite disparate communities within generic umbrella terms such as 'Gypsy' and 'Traveller'. Such terms can describe a lifestyle as well as signify ethnic status, on occasion doing both simultaneously. In the United Kingdom, as in much of Western Europe, the term *Gypsy* is an ethnic name for groups of people who throughout central and eastern Europe are often described as the Roma. UK Gypsies are distinct from Irish Travellers, who do not share the same ethnic background but do share some lifestyle characteristics, including a historic attachment to a degree of nomadic movement. One consequence of these dual usages is a blurring of meaning that often disguises racist or derogatory uses of these terms. In this chapter the term *Gypsy* is used to refer generically to UK groups and *Roma* to European groups who may describe themselves or be described by others as Gypsies, Roma or Travellers. However, it should be noted that beyond a generic discussion of similar groups of people, self-ascription is a more appropriate means of identifying accept-able nomenclature. So in the United Kingdom, individuals might refer to themselves as Scottish Travellers or English Romanies and in Europe as Sinti or Lovari, and such self-ascription should be respected.

The scale of concern about Gypsy education throughout the United Kingdom was underlined in the most recent literature review of the Department for Children, Schools and Families (DCSF); it suggests that

> the school attendance and achievement of Gypsy Traveller pupils remain well below expected levels. Discriminatory school policies and practices, low expectations of Gypsy Traveller pupils, negative attitudes and stereotyping, racism, bullying, lack of curriculum relevance, lack of understanding of Traveller culture, as well as social and economic disadvantage, have all been identified in the literature as factors adversely affecting [outcomes for Gypsy and Traveller children]. (Wilkin et al., 2009, 11)

Between publication of the Plowden Report and the most recent DCSF research, the field is littered with academic research and policy initiatives all of which identify the same patterns of disaffection between educational institutions shaped around the lives of a sedentary population and the realities of Gypsy life in Britain (e.g., Swann Report, 1985; Liégeois, 1998; Bhopal et al., 2000). If at first sight the Plowden Report appears to have delivered very little, with Gypsy children remaining consistently at the bottom of measures of achievement and attendance, this is not the whole picture. Significant changes include dramatically increased numbers of children attending school (in 1967 fewer than 5% of Gypsy children attended school, today that figure is probably more like 60% or 70%); the emergence of the Traveller Education Services (TES) and the Scottish Traveller Education Programme (STEP) to work actively on behalf of Gypsy families; and a changing perception for many Gypsy families of the value of a school education often driven by new economic realities.

The problem with schools

Gypsies arrived in Britain in the fifteenth and sixteenth centuries following a diasporic movement from India of people who travelled through the Middle East before settling across Europe and further afield (Okely, 1983; Clark and Greenfields, 2006). In Britain, Gypsies have been understood by the native population in a hugely stereotyped fashion; they are generally portrayed as a dirty, idle population with tendencies towards criminal behaviour, sometimes tempered by a secondary romanticized stereotype that celebrates the alfresco, close-to-nature life-style of a wild, independent group of people (Mayall, 2004; Saul and Tebbut, 2004). Throughout Europe similar discriminatory perceptions of Gypsies are commonplace, often materializing in violent state action; for example, the dismantling of campsites and deportation of thousands of Roma from France in 2010, extreme discrimination such as the fingerprinting of all Italian Roma including 80,000 children and also in Italy the burning of Roma camps by vigilante groups.

Following a visit to the United Kingdom, the Council of Europe's Commissioner for Human Rights noted,

> to judge by the levels of invective that can regularly be read in the national press, Gypsies would appear to be the last ethnic minority in respect of which openly racist views can still be acceptably expressed. I was truly amazed by some of the headlines, articles and editorials that were shown to me. Such reporting would appear to be symptomatic of a widespread and seemingly growing distrust of Gypsies resulting in their discrimination in a broad range of areas. (Gil-Robles, 2005, 43)

Ironically the Commissioner's report preceded an escalation in vitriolic media attacks aimed at Gypsies during the 2005 general election. A campaign run by the *Sun* newspaper under the headline 'Stamp on the Camps' was used by Michael Howard, the Conservative leader at that time, to exemplify his views on 'fairness'. He suggested Gypsies unfairly manipulated planning law by playing on human rights legislation, a viewpoint subsequently echoed by many newspapers. Conflating stereotypes about Gypsy antisocial behaviour within the context of European political correctness gone mad played on well-understood prejudices in which Gypsies were seen to behave against the interests of the wider population and to be protected by European liberal 'rights'-based policies. Michael Howard's intervention within right-wing politics might seem predictable, but it is worth noting the willingness of politicians from across the political spectrum to play upon Gypsy stereotypes, as the Labour Home Secretary Jack Straw had previously described Gypsies as likely to

> Go burgling, thieving, breaking into vehicles, causing all kinds of trouble, including defecating in the doorways of firms. (Straw, 1999)

For Gypsy families the problem with sending their children to school is that it is a situation in which their lives and those of non-Gypsies most markedly intersect. While Gypsy lives intersect in other areas, work and employment in particular, in many other respects – accommodation and social gatherings for example – Gypsies maintain their distance. Schools are also distinguished by parental separation, so when students are exposed to populist racist stereotypes, such as those promoted by politicians and the media, they do so without immediate family support. Stereotypes about Gypsies that are commonplace in the wider world are endemic within schools both among other students and staff. Much race-equality guidance notes that Gypsy culture is misunderstood and calls on schools to reassess their assumptions about Gypsies in order to tackle racism. Although a positive step forward, such guidance underestimates how entrenched racist attitudes to Gypsies really are. Stereotypes that were commonplace in the fifteenth century are being repeated today by politicians and the media, teachers and students. Something more than a simple recognition of the problems faced in the classroom is necessary to ensure Gypsies are valued and given similar opportunities to those given their non-Gypsy peers.

Two main areas of concern for Gypsies emerge out of these problems. The first centres on fears for their children's safety, and the second on fears of cultural erosion associated with school attendance. These concerns peak around or just after the transition period from often smaller primary to bigger secondary schools and with the onset of adolescence.

Gypsies and schools: Racism and safety

The greatest fear for most Gypsy parents is that their children will be subjected to racist name-calling and bullying when they attend school. This often reflects parents' and other family members' own past experience of schools. More depressingly, parents regularly report that their concerns about racism are either ignored by schools or are treated differently to those of other non-white families who experience racism. The constant use of derogatory names such as 'dirty gyppo' and 'pikey' is regularly cited as a major reason children are withdrawn from school.

Parents often describe how schools fail to take such name-calling seriously and do not consider such incidents to have racist motivations (Myers et al., 2010).

Recent education policy has attempted to address racism towards Gypsies through the inclusion of ethnic categories within PLASC data and also through the Race Relations (Amendment) Act (2000). Since the passing of the Equality Act (2010) harmonizing much anti-discrimination legislation, there has been a great deal of guidance issued by the DCSF and local authorities that explicitly notes potential situations in which Gypsy children and their families are discriminated. So far, so good; unfortunately, however, when discussing the impact of such legislation with families whose children are attending school, what emerges is a distinctly mixed bag. Some schools, usually those with large, long-standing Gypsy populations in their locality and led by sympathetic heads or senior teaching staff, have adopted almost model approaches of 'good practise' to Gypsy families (Bhopal and Myers, 2009) which might include

- senior staff building relationships with families;
- recognition of different cultural heritage;
- treating different family practices (e.g., employment) as being respectable;
- recognizing that fears of bullying and racism are often well founded.

In other words they adopt a relatively simple set of behaviours that might be considered routine in dealings with many diverse communities. Unfortunately such approaches appear in very few schools. So while one school may have a reputation for understanding Gypsy families, most other schools within the same local authority will probably be regarded as failing to be sympathetic towards Gypsy families.

In schools that do not engage well with Gypsy families, some very typical patterns emerge which generally work to hinder the educational opportunities of Gypsy children. Where bullying and racist name-calling are not tackled by teaching staff, this almost inevitably leads either to students being withdrawn from school by their parents or to Gypsy students retaliating to their aggressors. In the latter circumstances Gypsies tend to be more readily excluded than do non-Gypsy students. Such schools fail to recognize Gypsy culture within the curriculum and fail to address the specific educational needs of Gypsy students. Many parents complain that their children are placed in special-needs classes as a means of grouping all the Gypsy students together, outside their year classes.

Talking to Traveller Education Service (TES) team members about such practices will reveal a feeling that Gypsy students are often classified by schools as disruptive because they answer teachers back and argue their case. Within many schools the expectation is that students should adopt a subservient role to their teachers mirroring child–adult relationships in the majority sedentary population. However, by early adolescence most Gypsies would be shown the same status indicators as other adults within their family and communities; for example, in terms of property ownership or income generation. In the classroom many teachers are unable to adapt to Gypsy students who have made a transition from childhood into adulthood. The onus to adjust to this different sort of relationship lies with the school, which is tasked within British and European legislation to meet the needs of the student and not for the student to adjust to a sedentary lifestyle (DfES, 2004; HMSO, 1998).

Loss of identity: The fear of cultural erosion

Fears about the pernicious influence of 'gaujo' culture means many families are unwilling to allow their children to attend school. *Gaujo* (pronounced 'gor-ger') is the Anglo-Romany term for 'non-Gypsy', covering a broad range of related meanings. Individuals, objects and institutions can all be understood to fall within understandings of, for example, gaujo people, gaujo goods or gaujo schools. In this very wide sense it would not be uncommon to hear parental concerns about a process of gaujofication of their children caused by school attendance. That is the sense of losing a child because he or she was subsumed into an alien, non-Gypsy culture. For many Gypsy parents non-Gypsy adolescent culture is typified by its immorality, by the early sexual relations of adolescents, by excessive drinking and alcohol abuse. Such behaviour is seen to fit within wider understandings of non-Gypsy lives that are insecure, are isolated and lack cohesion and are lived without close connections to family or neighbours.

Secondary schools are sites in which Gypsy families encounter the greatest anxiety. As their children make the transition towards adolescence they are simultaneously subjected to gaujo peer pressure. Secondary schools are also characterized as being more dangerous places than primary schools; they are generally bigger institutions, perhaps in towns rather than village locations, with less obvious security and less supervision. There is a consistent pattern of children either not making the move to secondary school or, alternatively, dropping out early. There is an overwhelming fear that teenaged Gypsy girls will be subjected to the immoral codes of behaviour regarded as the norm among their non-Gypsy peers. At worst their safety is threatened; at best they are torn between two very different worlds. For boys the same pressures are allied to expectations around the early onset of adulthood that they should go to work, often with their father, to learn the skills that will ensure their future economic security.

The pressures of this transitional time are made all the more difficult because of rapidly changing economic opportunities and the prospect that in the future many traditional means of generating an income will become less viable. Many families recognize specific benefits and skills that can be derived from formal education, but at the same time such an engagement is freighted with fears of gaujofication. In the balance is the making of decisions that might benefit their children's future economic security but might also damage the community. Research throughout the 1980s and 1990s often highlighted families whose sole interest in schooling was the attainment of basic literacy and numeracy skills, typically within primary education. In many families, children attending school at this time were the first to attain basic literacy skills. Levinson (2007) describes this as a 'pragmatic adaptation' to changing economic circumstances which saw the erosion of employment routes that did not require some degree of literacy. It is fair to say that pragmatic adaptation has won the day (Myers et al., 2010) – and this should not come as a surprise, as the history of Gypsies and Roma throughout Europe and the world is marked by adaptation to changing circumstances (Hancock, 1987). Today families often want their children to gain more than just basic literacy and numeracy skills. Today parents note that their children require qualifications to make them eligible for low-skilled jobs; they recognize the importance of IT skills, and they expect schools to provide opportunities for more practical vocational training.

Conclusions

In the past there was a much greater imbalance between what might be seen to be gained from education compared to what was lost through cultural erosion allied with the pain inflicted by racism. Today that balance has shifted. Economically, parents see greater benefits from school education, and at the same time in some schools the advocacy role played by Traveller Education Services and the marginal, though increasing awareness of Gypsy ethnic rights have made formal education more likely for some Gypsies.

Thomas Acton stresses that the continued improvement in education provision for Gypsy students is 'absolutely dependent on the multicultural respect which welcomes Roma/Gypsy/Traveller children as who they are with a culture that is also valid content for the education of other children' (Acton, 2004, 10). He is half right: schools *do* need to recognize and openly welcome Gypsy and Roma families and their cultural backgrounds. It would be unthinkable for a school to teach students about World War II without mentioning the genocide of the Jews in the Nazi Holocaust, just as it would be unthinkable for a school to fail to address the slavery of black people when discussing the history of American trade routes. The great cornerstones of Gypsy and Roma culture – such as its diasporic origins, their enslavement throughout Europe and the genocide of Gypsies and the Roma by the Nazis – are, however, not widely understood and rarely given much space in the curriculum. Even less likely would be an acknowledgement in the curriculum of everyday aspects of Gypsy lives in the United Kingdom today, such as the importance of self-employment and strong community values.

In addition to demonstrating such multicultural respect, schools need to recognize that Gypsy parents are actively trying to access school education for their children. In many ways the failure of some schools to take seriously the desire of Gypsies for educational resources is one of the most damning criticisms of the failure of education in Britain. And yet many Gypsy families will find that their requests for an education that respects their values and way of life will not only not be met, but will be aggressively countered by local authorities who feel that parts of the Gypsy community are uneducable. And this is the adjunct to Thomas Acton's comments regarding the multicultural respect that welcomes children: there is also a great need to honour the obligation for educational provision. Marshall (1950), in his famous account of citizenship, very clearly notes that education is not a right to be demanded, but an obligation to be provided to ensure that individuals are able to contribute to their communities. The failures to meet this obligation represent the very worst engrained racist attitudes in society. Even after 600 years, Gypsies are positioned on the outside of our society and not seen as deserving very basic human rights.

Suggested questions

- Do British schools contribute to the marginalization of outsider groups?
- Is it possible to legislate effectively for inclusive education?
- Should Gypsy families have the right to choose their children's education?

Further reading

- Bhopal, K., and Myers, M. (2008), *Insiders, Outsiders and Others: Gypsies and Identity*. Hertfordshire: UHP.
- Clark, C., and Greenfields, M. (2006), *Here to Stay: The Gypsies and Travellers of Britain*. Hatfield: University of Hertfordshire Press.

References

Acton, T. (2004), 'The Past, Present and Future of Traveller Education', unpublished paper presented at Conference on Working Together: Raising the Educational Achievement of Gypsy and Traveller Children and Young People.

Bhopal, K., with Gundara, J., Jones, C., and Owen, C. (2000), *Working Towards Inclusive Education: Aspects of Good Practice for Gypsy Traveller Pupils, Department for Education and Employment Research Report RR238*. London: HMSO.

Bhopal, K., and Myers, M. (2009), 'Gypsy, Roma and Traveller Pupils in Schools in the UK: Inclusion and "good practice"', *International Journal of Inclusive Education*, 13 (3), 219–314.

Clark, C., and Greenfields, M. (2006), *Here to Stay: The Gypsies and Travellers of Britain*. Hatfield: University of Hertfordshire Press.

DCSF (2008), *The Inclusion of Gypsy, Roma and Traveller Children and Young People (The Inclusion of Gypsy, Roma and Traveller Pupils: Strategies for Building Confidence in Voluntary Self-declared Ethnicity Ascription)*. London: DCSF.

DfES (2004), *Every Child Matters: Change for Children*. London: Department for Education and Schools.

Equality Act (2010), London: The Stationery Office.

Gil-Robles, A. (2005), *Report by Mr. Alvaro Gil-Robles, Commissioner for Human Rights, on His Visit to the United Kingdom CommDH(2005)6*. Strasbourg: Council of Europe.

Hancock, I. (1987), *The Pariah Syndrome*. Ann Arbor, MI: Karoma.

HMSO (1998), *Human Rights Act*. London: The Stationery Office.

Levinson, M. P. (2007), 'Literacy in Gypsy Communities: A cultural capital manifested as negative assets', *American Educational Research Journal*, 44 (1), 5–39.

Liégeois, J.-P. (1998), *School Provision for Ethnic Minorities: The Gypsy Paradigm*. Hatfield: University of Hertfordshire Press.

Marshall, T. H. (1950), *Citizenship and Social Class*. Cambridge: Cambridge University Press. Reprinted in Marshall and Bottomore (eds) (1992), *Citizenship and Social Class*. London: Pluto Press.

Mayall, D. (2004), *Gypsy Identities 1500–2000: From Egipcyans and Moon-men to the Ethnic Romany*. London: Routledge.

Myers, M., and Bhopal, K. (2009), 'Gypsy, Roma and Traveller Children in Schools: Understandings of community and safety', *British Journal of Educational Studies*, 57 (4), 417–34.

Myers M., McGhee, D., and Bhopal, K. (2010), 'At the Crossroads: Gypsy and Traveller parents' perceptions of education, protection and social change', *Race, Ethnicity and Education*, 13 (4), 533–48.

Okely, J. (1983), *The Traveller Gypsies*. Cambridge: Cambridge University Press.

Plowden Report (1967), *Children and Their Primary Schools*. London: HMSO.

Race Relations (Amendment) Act (2000), London: The Stationery Office.

Saul, N., and Tebbut, S. (eds) (2004), *The Role of the Romanies*. Liverpool: University of Liverpool Press.

Straw, J. (1999, 22 July), BBC Radio West Midlands.

Swann Report, (1985), *Education for All: The Report of the Committee of Enquiry into the Education of Children from Ethnic Minority Groups*. London: HMSO.

Wilkin, A., Derrington, K., and Foster, B. (2009), 'Improving the Outcomes for Gypsy, Roma and Traveller Pupils', *Literature Review*, DCSF Research Report DCSF –RR077.

Migration 19

Jill Rutter

In the United Kingdom, immigration is one of the most controversial current issues. Many of the discourses articulated by adult voters and in the media are reproduced by young people in playgrounds across the United Kingdom. In the less restrained world of the school, there is a rather slim borderline between children's anti-immigration sentiments and the bullying of migrant and minority children. From the mid-1990s until the early years of this century *asylum seeker* was a term of abuse in many of our schools. Rutter (2006) describes children being taunted with this term, or others such as *Afghan*. Today many newly arrived migrant children still report being bullied, particularly those who speak little English or who are seen as being different from the dominant peer group (de Abreu and Lambert 2003, 127–33; Rutter, 2006). Yet schools have a duty to prevent children from being bullied, and exploring diversity is part of citizenship education.

Despite these obligations, this chapter argues that school-based interventions that aim to promote a more mature understanding of migration, are largely ineffective. Schools rarely take children's own perceptions about migration as a starting point. In many secondary schools, students are denied the opportunity to talk about migration as teachers fear that such discussions may prove difficult to control. Where children are taught about diversity, well-meaning programmes of study can entrench perceived differences between migrant children and those who see themselves as 'English' or 'British'.

This chapter presents an alternative vision. It starts with a brief outline of migration flows to and from the United Kingdom and public perceptions about this issue. Drawing on primary research, the chapter looks at how schools approach their teaching about migration. The chapter argues that if we are to equip children with a mature understanding of migration, we need to give them space to talk about their perceptions. The school curriculum and its teaching resources need to move beyond static notions of diversity and towards a cosmopolitan approach that stresses universal humanity and global citizenship.

Historical context

The history of migration to and from the United Kingdom is as old as British history itself.

Those who sees themselves as English or British could well have ancestors who were pre-Celtic migrants or belonged to groups collectively described as Celtic. Their ancestors may also include Angles, Saxons, Jutes, Danes, Normans, Flemish, Plantagenets from Anjou and so on – all of them migrants. Skipping to more recent times, there was by the early eighteenth century a significant Jewish community, re-established again through migration, a community which was expelled in 1290, as well as large numbers of Huguenots who fled from religious persecution in France (Gwynn, 2000). The seventeenth and eighteenth centuries also saw a substantial German migration comprising both prosperous business owners and the 'poor Palatines' who had fled the famine and warfare consuming the Rhineland. Winder's history of immigration to the United Kingdom (2004) also documents Italians, Greek Christians, Armenians and black Africans in eighteenth-century Britain, all of whom inter-married with longer-established communities.

Census records from Victorian England present an accurate picture of immigration into the United Kingdom in all its complexity. The 1901 census showed 136,092 persons born in British colonies and India and a further 339,436 persons born overseas; outside the colonies and dependences, the largest populations came from Russia, Russian Poland, Germany, France and Italy. At the same time, the United Kingdom lost population through emigration – either overseas-born persons re-migrating or UK-born people emigrating.

In the early part of the twentieth century, the United Kingdom gave sanctuary to waves of refugees, including Belgians and Basques and those escaping Nazi-occupied Europe (Kushner and Knox, 1999). The period 1948–1962, characterized by labour shortages and growing prosperity, saw large-scale post-war labour migration, primarily from Britain's colonies but also from Ireland and Poland. In the 1960s, economic contraction along with restrictive immigration legislation, led to decreased primary immigration into the United Kingdom. Indeed, throughout much of the 1960s and up to the early 1990s, the United Kingdom saw a net loss of population through migration, with more people leaving the United Kingdom every year than arriving (see Figure 19.1).

As Figure 19.1 shows, the United Kingdom has seen net immigration since the early 1990s, caused by growing numbers of asylum arrivals in the 1990s, student migration, sustained work visa flows and the large-scale migration of people from the new member states of the European Union after 2004. The impact of rising immigration has been to increase the proportion of the population born overseas from 4.2 per cent of the UK population in 1951 to 11.3 per cent by the end of 2009[1]. These

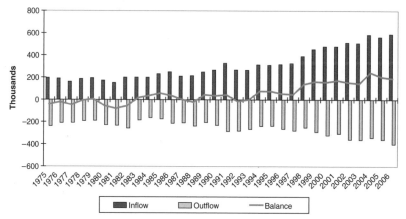

Figure 19.1 UK Immigration 1975–2006

migrants come from many different nations, with the largest refugee groups being people born in India (1), Poland (2), Pakistan (3), Ireland (4), Germany (5) and South Africa (6).[2]

Alongside this increase in immigration, there has been a similar increase in emigration – of both UK and non-UK nationals. By 2008 some 5.4 million UK nationals lived abroad (Rutter and Latorre, 2009). But despite extensive immigration and emigration going back thousands of years, migration is not part of the British national story. In this respect United Kingdom differs from nations such as Canada and the United States. As a consequence of this omission from our collective memory, more recent arrivals are seen as usurpers, particularly those whose ethnicity makes them visible. Our sense of entitlement to a public service such as social housing can derive, not from formal citizenship, but from notions about the length of time a particular group has lived in these islands.

Understanding public attitudes to migration

There have been a significant number of studies that have attempted to map and understand public attitudes to immigration and asylum. These studies suggest that concerns about immigration are rather fluid and reflect both dominant national media debates and local issues. During peak immigration from Poland, for example, the belief that immigration drove down wages was a dominant concern in some areas. During the 2010 general election campaign, concerns about uncontrolled immigration flows and the Labour government's lack of success in managing migration dominated national debates (Ford et al., 2010). While immigration was, and remains, a major concern, much but not all research suggests that it has not determined eventual voter choice.

Polling data also suggest that the overall population is least concerned about white immigrants and those whose language and culture is seen as closest to their own (Ford, 2009). Other factors influencing attitudes to immigration include

- level of contact with migrant and minorities, with more contact resulting in less prejudice;

- age, with older people more hostile to immigration, but younger more likely to commit racially aggravated assaults;
- qualifications and occupation – those with few or no qualifications and unskilled and manual workers are more likely to be hostile to migrants.

There has been no polling on attitudes to immigration among school students, although ethnographic studies highlight the fluidity of concerns held by children and that they usually mirror attitudes held in the locality of the school (Rutter, 2006).

Educational interventions

Just as there has been a long history of hostility to migrants, there has been a long history of educational interventions that have aimed to build better inter-ethnic relations. The multicultural education movement of the late 1970s and early 1980s aimed to prepare white 'British' children for life in an increasingly multi-ethnic society. At this time schools began to celebrate festivals other than those that were Christian. School textbooks were also reviewed for their portrayal of minority cultures.

But by the mid-1980s, multicultural education began to attract criticism for homogenizing and exoticizing the cultural forms of minority groups, as well as failing to challenge the deep-rooted inequalities within British society. 'Multicultural' approaches to education were also criticized for creating notions of difference rather than stressing the common humanity of all UK residents. A growing antiracist movement in the 1980s led school projects that explicitly examined ethnic inequalities in the United Kingdom, as well as school policies that aimed to confront racism (Klein, 1993). Many diversity initiatives have their roots in this period, for example, Black History Month.

But there was some criticism of antiracist initiatives. Academics challenged dominant constructions of race and antiracism for failing to acknowledge the range of different types of racisms in the United Kingdom and the experiences of groups such as Cypriots, Irish, Polish and Gypsy Roma (Anthias and Yuval-Davis, 1992; Rattansi, 1992). By the 1990s implementing wider educational reforms made demands on teachers' time and energy, and in such a climate educational initiatives that examined diversity or ethnic inequality were given less priority. But this lull was only temporary. Increased refugee migration during the 1990s and the demonization of this group in the media led a number of refugee NGOs to produce teaching resources and organize educational programmes as a means of getting their message across to a youth audience (Rutter, 1996; Save the Children, 2004). And since the September 11 atrocities and the Oldham and Bradford disturbances of 2001, the central government has encouraged schools to act to promote social cohesion. In England in 2004, the central government imposed a duty on schools to promote social cohesion. It later initiated a review of the school citizenship curriculum, with the aim of using this subject to bring diverse communities together and create a common British identity. This review led to a redrafting of the English secondary citizenship curriculum, with the obligation that schools teach children to explore

> the diverse national, regional, ethnic and religious cultures, groups and communities in the United Kingdom and the connections between them . . .
>
> the interconnections between the United Kingdom and the rest of Europe and the wider world . . .
>
> community cohesion and the different forces that bring about change in communities over time. (Qualifications and Curriculum Authority, 2007)

School level interventions

But what is happening in practice at school level? Drawing from research undertaken in six schools in 2005 and 2009, it can be argued that most schools spend very little time examining migration (Rutter, 2006). Research undertaken in 2005 examined the citizenship curriculum in four schools, focusing on teaching about migration. The school that spent most time examining migration undertook a six-week unit on diversity in the United Kingdom, of which one lesson was about refugees, supplemented by a speaker visit from a refugee organization. The school used commercially produced citizenship textbooks, plus a history of the *Empire Windrush*[3] and photocopies of older material written in the 1970s and 1980s that looked at the black and Asian presence in London. Children were also directed to the Moving Here website, for homework research. The same school also held assemblies for Refugee Week and Black History Month, when it also held an 'international evening' where children, parents and staff cooked and sold food from the cuisines of migrant communities. There was no representation of 'British' food, an omission that has the potential to exclude white British students or any deconstruction of the global origins of 'national' cuisines.

In another school, the only coverage of migration occurred in assemblies during Refugee Week and Black History Month, despite considerable tensions on the school that eventually ended up in a gang fight. Indeed, in none of the four schools did teachers attempt to deal with conflicts and tensions associated with migration, or address the rather fluid and often localized concerns. Euphemisms were used when talking about inter-ethnic tensions and controversial issues associated with migration. Students were rarely encouraged to articulate their views on migration, usually because teachers feared the vehemence of their views. Students were thus unable to reflect on their opinions, nor were they given the opportunity to discuss the benefits and disadvantages of migration. Teachers did not pose questions that asked about justice and whether the local or national treatment of groups such as asylum seekers was right or wrong. Most teaching about diversity and migration emphasized the importance of being 'nice to each other'. There was a mismatch between school and the 'nasty' outside world. Suppressing debate about this issue conveyed to students from the majority and non-migrant groups that their opinions were not valued, as no one was interested in listening to them. One recommendation is that teachers should not fear controversy, that they need to engage in more dialogue about migration.

Managing a dialogue about migration requires skills, although there are a great many resources to help teachers do this (e.g., Andreotti and Warwick, 2007; Crombie and Rowe, 2009; Oxfam, 2010). The table below draws from these resources, summarizing good practice in relation to debating controversial issues. A small number of schools have also used 'forum theatre' to support an open dialogue about migration. This is a type of theatre created by Augusto Boal, where actors or members of the audience can stop a performance and suggest different actions in order to change dramatized outcomes (Boal, 2000). Examples are Cardboard Citizens, a London-based theatre company, that has used forum theatre to explore the treatment of asylum seekers. The Complete Works, another London-based group, worked with a group of young people in south London to explore community relations in an area experiencing population change.

Preparation Before embarking upon lessons or workshops, it is essential to meet with the students to learn what their perceptions about migration are. This enables the teacher or group leader to understand students' concerns, knowledge gaps and value bases and to personalize and negotiate the topics for subsequent workshops.

Step 1 Creating a safe space for debate

Using fun icebreaking activities, this step focuses on creating the open space in which students feel safe to debate. The teacher focuses on establishing the trusting conditions that are conducive to a community of enquiry being formed. Facilitators cannot create this space on their own; they need the help of all participants to ensure that no one is left out and that each person feels able to share his or her own point of view. It is useful to highlight challenges in creating the right atmosphere such as listening attentively to each other, working as a team, staying focused and thinking hard.

Step 2 Engagement with different perspectives – presenting the stimulus

Participants are introduced to different and 'logical' perspectives about migration. The perspectives should present different angles of the issue, can be taken from a variety of sources and can be presented in different formats such as newspaper articles, cartoons, stories, pictures and online videos.

Step 3 First thoughts – clarifying and sharing points of view

Participants work in pairs to consider and respond to the sources of information about migration (identifying mainstream and non-mainstream perspectives). Participants can be provided with a number of reflective questions that help participants to consider their personal responses to the stimulus. Handouts can also be used to invite participants to individually draw or write down thoughts about the stimulus material.

Step 4 The group dialogue

Questions that critically explore migration (generated by the students or the facilitator) are explored by the whole group. During this group dialogue the facilitator's role is to try and encourage the participants to explore different angles and points of view on the topic and allow students to make their own considered judgements.

Step 5 Enquiry activity (optional)

Commonly the group dialogue generates new questions that the participants wish to research and enquire further about. This can lead to an independent research project or to student generated perspectives which can serve as stimuli for another workshop. Alternatively a problem-solving task can be devised which gives participants an opportunity to apply the skills and knowledge gained in the dialogue process to a real-life or simulated situation of responsible decision making.

Step 6 Last words – closing the open space

Participants are invited to reflect on their participation and learning and provide some feedback, either written or verbal, concerning what they have learned about migration, about themselves, about others and about the learning process.

Adapted from Andreotti and Warwick (2007)

Figure 19.2 Dialogue-based procedure for engaging with controversial issues

Meeting the 'aliens'

Providing safe spaces to meet new migrants, talk to them and break down barriers is also important where controversy about migration has developed into real frictions. Some parts of the United Kingdom have seen tensions rise when significant numbers of new migrants have arrived in a specific area. For example, tensions rose in Dover in the late 1990s after the arrival of eastern European Roma and Kosovar refugees. Notions of 'us' and 'alien other' soon developed in this area. In one school in Dover the police and the local authority organized a number of arts and sports workshops for new migrants as well as longer-settled residents. Migrant and non-migrant children met at the weekend and after school and participated in activities such as silk-screen printing and felt making. While participation in the activities was voluntary, there was a high uptake among the year group selected for the project. The degree of cooperation needed in activities such as football and felt making appeared to break down barriers between 'them' and 'us'.

Education Action, Refugee Action and the Refugee Council are among a number of organizations that provide refugee speakers to visit schools. More intimate question-and-answer sessions, rather than assembly talks, seem most successful in changing attitudes and getting children to think about asylum, human rights and migration.

Beyond diversity and towards cosmopolitanism

Teachers also need to consider how schools interpret *diversity* – a concept that forms part of the citizenship curriculum. An acknowledgement that the United Kingdom is a diverse nation has moved schools forward, encouraging them to teach about the multi-ethnic character of all parts of the United Kingdom. But such a strategy has limitations. Unless handled very well, schools, through their teaching, can promote a static and mosaic interpretation of diversity, where society is seen as being composed of a number of discrete, exclusive communities (Stevens, 2009). Moreover, an emphasis on diversity risks establishing new hierarchies, as schools decide which communities to include in their teaching and which to leave out. In restricting teaching to representing the Asian and

African-Caribbean presence in the United Kingdom, schools may have replaced a single dominant story with a series of dominant stories that are static and fail to connect. In an age of super-diversity, where many different peoples live side by side, the story is much more complex.

Rather than migration being seen as an aspect of cultural diversity, cultural diversity should instead be seen as a subset of a much more far-reaching national migration story. Situating contemporary diversity in the context of the long history of population movement in and out of the United Kingdom makes it harder to maintain existing assumptions about majority and minority communities and puts greater emphasis on commonality than on differences between people. This places teaching about migration firmly within a cosmopolitan tradition. Cosmopolitanism is a philosophical theory and social movement that stresses that all ethnic groups belong to a single community based on shared moral values (see Chapter 7, 87–8). Drawing from the work of Kant and Derrida, recent writing on cosmopolitanism advances the notion of a global citizen and universal set of rights (Appiah, 2006). As such, cosmopolitanism has become an increasingly influential strand within the citizenship education movement. Osler and Starkey (2005) outline a vision of Global Citizenship Education based on universal values, a vision that does not involve erasing local and national identities but enables children to understand their connection with the wider world and express solidarity with others, both in the United Kingdom and abroad.

How can schools challenge hostility and misinformation?

The research for this chapter indicates that most students hold many misconceptions about migration. One of the key questions of my research was to look at how teachers might challenge both hostility and misconceptions about migration. From this respect an open rebuttal of inaccuracies – pitting students 'facts' against teachers' 'facts' – is extremely unproductive. The most effective way to challenge hostility and misconceptions is to start with the personal experiences of migrants and use these to develop understandings of migration. This mirrors approaches taken in Holocaust education, where personal experiences also start much teaching.

My research highlighted the following issues:

1. Arts education – creative writing, poetry, testimony and the visual arts – appeared to be successful in developing empathy and notions of common humanity. Creative writing appeared to promote personal reflection and discussion about migration, within a safe environment.
2. The allocation of time resources appears to be a key factor in determining if a curricular initiative about migration is successful or not. Given the pressures of delivering a packed curriculum, it is thus essential that teachers work in cross-curricular teams if they are to teach about migration in a way that challenges racism and develops students' moral reasoning.
3. Curricular initiatives are not successful where teachers do not have consensual authority, or have a very authoritarian teaching style. Informed debate cannot take place where a teacher struggles to control a class. Empathy towards new migrants cannot develop where there is poor classroom behaviour.
4. Students need to be given the opportunity to express their opinions and feel that they are being heard. At the same time, a lesson should not become a platform for racism, and a too easily formed consensus on immigration needs to be challenged.

So how should schools approach teaching about migration?

Global Citizenship Education should help students understand their long-standing human connections to the wider world and encourage them to learn about the development of international human rights, as well as reflect on universality and our moral obligations to others (see Chapter 5, 49–50). To achieve this in the migration context, teachers need to encourage their students to research contemporary migration in the United Kingdom, so that they clearly understand who is coming and going, why people migrate and how government and local communities treat migrants. Students should be helped to be critical of information sources in this context and should also be encouraged to reflect on 'Britishness' and citizenship itself and that national citizenship, with its rights and responsibilities, is increasingly mediated by membership of other collectives: political, social, ethnic, local, regional and transnational. Approaches should include debates, discussions and the use of personal testimony from visiting speakers, written texts, DVDs and online sources. Finally, those students who wish, should be given the opportunity to express solidarity with migrants, whether in local communities or overseas, through volunteering, fund-raising, campaigning or merely trying to promote a more informed and mature debate on this controversial issue among their peers.

Suggested questions

- What newly arrived migrant groups are represented in your local community?
- How do children talk about immigration in your school?
- How is your school presently covering 'diversity' in its curricular and extra-curricular activities?
- How can children be given more space to talk maturely about migration?

Further reading

- Spencer, S. (2011), *The Migration Debate: Policy and Politics in the Twenty-First Century*. Bristol: Policy Press.
- Winder, R. (2004) *Bloody Foreigners: A History of Immigration to Britain*. London: Little, Brown.

References

Andreotti, V., and Warwick, P. (2007), *Engaging Pupils in Controversial Issues Through Dialogue*. www.citized.info/?strand=3&r_menu=res.

Anthais, F., and Yuval-Davis, N. (1992), *Racialized Boundaries: Race, Nation, Gender, Colour and Class and the Anti-racist Struggle*. London: Routledge.

Appiah, K. A. (2006), *Cosmopolitanism: Ethics in a World of Strangers*. New York: Norton.

Boal, A. (2000), *Theatre of the Oppressed*. London: Pluto Press.

Crombie, B., and Rowe, D. (2009), *Dealing with the British National Party and Other Radical Groups*. London: Citizenship Foundation and Association for Citizenship Teaching.

de Abreu, G., and Lambert, H. (2003), *The Education of Portuguese Students in Channel Island Schools*. Luton: University of Luton.

Ford, R. (2008), 'Coming to Terms with Diversity: British Attitudes to Ethnic Minorities and Immigrants', unpublished presentation, www.ccsr.ac.uk/staff/rf/Britain%20coming%20to%20terms%20with%20diversity%20-%20Kent%20March%202008.ppt#256,1.

Ford, R., Flynn, D., and Somerville, W. (2010), 'Immigration and the Election', *Renewal*, www.renewal.org.uk/articles/immigration-and-the-election/.

Gwynn, R. (2000), *Huguenot Heritage: The History and Contribution of Huguenots in Britain* (2nd edn). Brighton: Sussex Academic Press.

Klein, G. (1993), *Education Towards Race Equality*. London: Cassell.

Kushner, T., and Knox, C. (1999), *Refugees in the Age of Genocide*. London: Frank Cass.

Osler, A., and Starkey, H. (2005), *Changing Citizenship: Democracy and Inclusion in Education*. Buckingham: Open University Press.

Oxfam (2007), *Teaching Controversial Issues.* Oxford: Oxfam.

Qualifications and Curriculum Authority (QCA) (2007), *Citizenship: The National Curriculum Programme of Study at Key Stage 3.* London: QCA.

Rattansi, A. (1992), 'Changing the Subject? Racism, culture and education', in J. Donald and A. Rattansi (eds), *Race, Culture, Difference.* London: Sage, pp. 11–49.

Rutter, J. (2003), *Refugees: We Left Because We Had To* (3rd edn). London: Refugee Council.

—(2006), *Refugee Children in the UK.* Buckingham: Open University Press.

Rutter, J., and Latorre, M. (2009), *Making the Most of the British Diaspora: How the UK Government Should Respond to British Citizens Who Live Abroad.* London: Institute for Public Policy Research.

Stevens, M. (2009), *Stories Old and New: Migration and Identity in the UK Heritage Sector.* London: Institute for Public Policy Research www.ippr.org/publicationsandreports/publication.asp?id=682.

Winder, R. (2004), *Bloody Foreigners: A History of Immigration to Britain.* London: Little, Brown.

Notes

1 Estimate taken from the Labour Force Survey, Quarter Four, 2009.

2 Data about country of birth groups is from the Labour Force Survey, Quarter Four, 2009.

3 The *Empire Windrush* arrived in Tibury on 22 June 1948 carrying 492 passengers from the Caribbean. Although mostly of African-Caribbean origin, the *Empire Windrush's* passengers also included non-immigrants and 60 Polish women who had been moved to the Caribbean during World War II.

Conclusion and Policy Implications

Henry Maitles and Paula Cowan

We said in our preface that we expected to raise as many questions as definitive answers, as discussions around controversial issues are complex. Nonetheless, there are a number of general conclusions coming from the varied contributions.

Promoting positive values

First, a key message coming from the contributors to this book is that the learning and discussion of controversial issues have a positive impact on the values and attitudes of young people and that teachers can make a real difference. This is reassuring given that many educators join the teaching profession because they want, whether it be naively or indeed passionately, to make a difference to the lives of young people. Many of the topics discussed in this book are not mandatory and schools can be forgiven for adopting a reactive approach to their teaching, rather than being proactive. However, many young students have relatives who are in the armed forces in Iraq, Afghanistan or other conflict areas, and derogatory jibes of 'gay', 'Paki', 'gyppo' and 'Jew' can be heard in the play-grounds of primary and secondary schools. This justifies the discussion of controversial issues in primary classrooms and supports a proactive approach, as young students may have negative attitudes towards specific groups of people before their first walk through the school gate.

With the exception of Holocaust education, which *is* mandatory in several countries around the world, including England, France and Germany, teachers can easily maintain their professionalism and effectiveness and climb the promotional ladder with little or no consideration to any of the topics in this book. The original meaning of educating, 'rearing, bringing up children' (Williams, 1983), raises relevant questions for all educators. What exactly do we mean by 'education' today, and what are responsible citizens? Perhaps this can be summed up by the iconic comment from a head teacher who was a Holocaust survivor:

> I am a survivor of a concentration camp. My eyes saw what no man should witness. Gas chambers built by learned engineers. Children poisoned by educated physicians. Infants killed by trained nurses. Women and babies shot and burned by high school and college graduates. So, I am suspicious of education. My request is: help your students become more human. Your efforts must never produce learned monsters, skilled psychopaths, educated Eichmanns. Reading, writing, arithmetic are important only if they serve to make our children more humane. (Ginott, 1972)

Citizenship and better learning

Secondly, the development of discussion around controversial issues is firmly in the orbit of citizenship, yet we must keep in mind that tackling controversial issues as a part of education for citizenship as a formal policy of government is still relatively in its infancy across the world and, indeed, the debate as to its direction and effectiveness even younger. Even when teachers are convinced of its value, the perceived needs of the curriculum, the constant flux of reform, the lack of time available and a worry on the part of some teachers as to subject knowledge can conspire to ensure that it is not well done and the students get more cynical about democracy, citizenship education and the motives of educators. In the words of one of Chamberlin's (2003) student interviewees,

'. . . education for citizenship? Only if you haven't got a life!'. Although many of the ideas and practices described in the chapters in this book flow from long-established good practice in schools, it is also true that the political literacy part of education for citizenship is boringly, routinely introduced so as to appease audit forms and inspectors. This is a shame as students can discuss issues with their school peers that seem relevant to their understanding of the outside world within the safe environment of the school and classroom. In particular, contributors to this book highlight active learning, interdisciplinary approaches and contributions from external agencies and eye witnesses as being central pedagogical tools. This can lead to better relationships, better behaviour, less bullying and ultimately better learning.

This can be seen clearly in learning around the Holocaust and genocide and is brought out in many of the chapters. Teaching in the classroom, particularly in the secondary school, where interdisciplinary work is more difficult to organize, suggests that there can be issues around learning about genocide and the Holocaust as history topics (where general lessons may not be drawn) or as a moral issue (where the historical contexts of areas such as anti-Semitism, discrimination towards Gypsies and Roma families and human rights are not developed). In either case, students may not understand both the lessons *about* and *from* the Holocaust. Yet, where developed well – and particularly with interdisciplinarity at its core – the research outlined in the book suggests that there can be significant and meaningful learning experiences. In Scotland, for example, the introduction of the Curriculum for Excellence (Scottish Executive, 2004) has encouraged teachers in both primary and secondary schools to plan lessons and topic areas in such a way as to encourage both active learning and interdisciplinary learning. There is some very early evidence that where a strong lead from one particular teacher or senior management is forthcoming and where time is made available for planning, there can be a positive impact on student understanding and values and attitudes across the age and level stages (Maitles, 2010; Maitles and McAlpine, 2011). Discussion around controversial issues can develop students' awareness and enable the skills of decision-making, reasoned argument and critical approaches to evidence. By so doing, students may emerge not only with a fuller understanding of democracy, but also with an ability to live democratically in adult life and appreciate and value it. Hahn (1998) found that where there was the opportunity to explore controversial public policy issues in an atmosphere where several sides of an argument can be aired and where points of view are encouraged even where they differ from the teacher's and other students', there is a greater likelihood of the development of the kinds of skills needed for democratic life. Hahn concludes that groups where this is encouraged showed comparatively higher levels of political efficacy, interest, trust and confidence than their peers without such experiences. Further, these students were more likely to develop attitudes that have the potential to foster civic participation. Thus, the full realization of developing informed student skills and attitudes towards the controversies involved in democratic life will require both shorter-term and longer-term strategies on behalf of all members of a school community.

Winning hearts and minds

Thirdly, whether there is a subject on the curriculum called Citizenship or whether there is a model of permeation throughout the school and subject areas, initial teacher education and the continuing professional development of existing teachers need to concentrate on winning hearts and minds to education for citizenship and consequent discussion around controversial issues. Research into the attitudes of student teachers suggests that education for citizenship needs to permeate the curriculum in faculties of education. Wilkins (2001) found disturbing attitudes towards race in his survey of student teachers in England's two largest teacher education institutions (TEIs). He found that a large majority of his sample of 418 tended to reject the notion of institutional racism in favour of a personal prejudice view, although it must be taken into account that the research was undertaken before the MacPherson Report, which exposed police and institutional racism. Further, approximately 10 per cent of the sample agreed with statements linking black people with unemployment and crime. Finally, 37 per cent felt that positive discrimination in favour of ethnic minorities had 'gone too far' and there was a generalized backlash against political correctness, which Wilkins attributes to a culture shift of the Thatcher years, continued by New Labour. Clearly, if significant numbers of new teachers hold these kinds of views, attempts to challenge racism need significant discussion/ debate in the TEIs. While there has been some attempts to introduce these issues into the core of teacher education programmes, there is still much work to be done.

As regards global citizenship, Robbins et al. (2003) concluded that while there was a willingness and even a desire among their sample of 187 student teachers at the end of their course to teach and develop this area in schools (with 67% of secondary and 59% of primary trainees agreeing that it should have a high priority), only 35 per cent felt confident enough to contribute to a whole-school approach. Further, they noted that those students with geography and design and technology as their major areas were the most positive, while those with mathematics and PE were the least. Nonetheless, Maitles and Cowan (2010) found in their study of 20 newly qualified teachers in their induction year that there were many positive things in the general field of citizenship education in their schools, with a particular emphasis on ecology and human rights issues. However, there was less positivity about student voice in the school and the teaching of controversial issues.

In terms of both tackling challenging issues and developing active learning approaches, Wilkins (1999) found negative attitudes among his sample. They themselves were cynical towards politics (not a problem per se) but they tended to see discipline and traditional teaching as being the important issues in education. All this was reinforced by their teaching placements, where they reported widely varying degrees of attention given to citizenship education and little explicit guidance as to how it should be delivered.

This research thus has implications for our initial teacher education institutions and indeed for initial standards frameworks. While education for citizenship is now a part of this, there is no evidence that discussing controversial issues plays more than just a relatively cursory part, with many students able to avoid deep discussion or thought on the subject. It needs to permeate the curriculum of initial teacher education and be developed enthusiastically by university lecturers and tutors, particularly as student teachers and those in the probationary year are exposed to some very cynical views, particularly in the subject departments in secondary schools, where they spend most of their time.

If student teachers are the future, the evidence from experienced classroom teachers suggests that there is a need for significant CPD in the area. Ruddock and Flutter (2004) maintain that teachers lack confidence about handling aspects of citizenship education, and particular controversial content is likely to be excluded, especially if teachers lack confidence in their own mastery of that content. This means that there is a need for continued professional development which builds on primary and secondary teachers' content knowledge and pedagogy and shares good practice. Whether this will be feasible in a climate of general cuts in education may itself prove problematic and is a political discussion that needs to be had with authorities in charge of education spending.

The implementation and impact of initiatives around teaching controversial issues depends on whether one sees the glass as half full or half empty. This book has suggested that there is excellent work going on to develop young people's interest, knowledge, skills and dispositions in the broad areas of citizenship, human rights and democracy; yet it is very limited, indeed rare, to find examples of genuine democracy based on children's human rights. No amount of hectoring and/or government instructions can counter this; as Bernard Crick who chaired the Advisory Group on Education for Citizenship and Democracy in England and Wales, put it, 'teachers need to have a sense of mission . . . to grasp the fullness of its moral and social aims' (Crick, 2000). Research now needs to concentrate on the impact of education for citizenship type initiatives and look towards highlighting instances of good and effective practice.

Attitudes towards religious, ethnic, cultural and sexual diversity are everchanging and can vary from different degrees of tolerance to total acceptance and celebration. Irrespective of the subject they teach, teachers should be mindful of this and ensure that their classroom ethos is conducive to good citizenship practice. It is also important to remember that many individuals from minority groups are from our schools – they are not from the outside looking in but are part of the school community. Societal norms can influence the classroom environment but we would argue that addressing controversial issues in the classroom can also influence the wider environment and is worth investment.

References

Chamberlin, R. (2003), 'Citizenship? Only If You Haven't Got a Life: Secondary school pupils' views of citizenship education', *Westminster Studies in Education*, 26 (2), 87–98.

Crick, B. (2000), 'A Subject at Last', *Tomorrow's Citizen*, Summer, 2.

Ginott, H. (1972), *Teacher and Child: A Book for Parents and Teachers*. New York: Macmillan.

Hahn, C. (1998), *Becoming Political*. Albany: State University of New York Press.

Maitles, H. (2010), 'Citizenship Initiatives and Pupil Values: A case study of one Scottish school's experience', *Educational Review*, 62 (4), 391–406.

Maitles, H., and McAlpine, C. (2011), '"I've Adopted a Tiger": Enhancing teaching and learning with infants through an active and integrated approach', *Education 3–13*, 39 (3), pp. 1–17.

Robbins, M., Francis, L., and Elliott, E. (2003), 'Attitudes Towards Education for Global Citizenship Among Trainee Teachers', *Research in Education*, 69, 93–8.

Rudduck, J., and Flutter, J. (2004), *How To Improve Your School*. London: Continuum.

Scottish Executive (2004) *A Curriculum for Excellence*. Edinburgh: Scottish Executive/Learning and Teaching Scotland.

Wilkins, C. (1999), 'Making "Good Citizens": The social and political attitudes of PGCE students', *Oxford Review of Education*, 25 (1/2), 217–30.

—(2001), 'Student Teachers and Attitudes Towards "Race": The role of citizenship education in addressing racism through the curriculum', *Westminster Studies in Education*, 24 (1), 7–21.

Williams. R. (1983) *Keywords*. London: Flamingo.

Index